MANAGING
DIPLOMACY

MANAGING DIPLOMACY

The United States and Japan

Harrison M. Holland

Foreword by John K. Emmerson

Hoover Institution Press
Stanford University, Stanford, California

Hoover Press Publication 300
First printing, 1984
Manufactured in the United States of America
88 87 86 85 84   9 8 7 6 5 4 3 2 1

Library of Congress Cataloging in Publication Data

Holland, Harrison M., 1921–
  Managing Diplomacy

  Bibliography: p.
  Includes index.
  1. United States—Diplomatic and consular service. 2. Japan—Diplomatic and consular service. 3. United States—Foreign relations—Japan. 4. Japan—Foreign relations—United States. I. Title.
JX1706.A4 1984   351'.892   84-12989
ISBN 0-8179-8001-6

Design by P. Kelley Baker

To the Memory of
John K. Emmerson

CONTENTS

List of Tables and Figures   ix

Foreword by John K. Emmerson   xi

Acknowledgments   xv

Introduction   xvii

Chapters

①   The Setting   1

②   The Human Factor in Diplomacy   18

③   Organization and Management   39

④   Personnel Systems in Operation   71

⑤   Decision-Making   112

⑥   Problems in Diplomatic Management: Japan   136

⑦   Problems in Diplomatic Management: United States   172

⑧   The Image Problem   188

⑨   Conclusion   197

Appendixes

Ⓐ   Japanese and U.S. Interviewees,
August 1980–January 1982   203

Ⓑ   The Foreign Service Act of 1980   207

Ⓒ   E change of Documents on Visit of
Nuclear-Powered Submarine *Sea Dragon*   216

Ⓓ   Bureaus and Departments of the
Japanese Foreign Ministry   222

Notes   231

Glossary of Japanese Terms   241

Selected Bibliography   243

Index   245

TABLES AND FIGURES

Tables

1. Number of State Department Employees, 1781–1980   45

2. Number of U.S. Diplomatic and Consular Posts, 1790–1980   46

3. Changes in Personnel Categories Effected by the Foreign Service Act of 1980   58

4. State Department Annual Recruitment Estimates, FY 1982–FY 1986   81

5. Candidates Passing U.S. FSO Written and Oral Examinations, 1975–1978   82

6. U.S. Ambassadorial Appointments, 1961–1981   90

7. State Department Projected Generalist Promotions, 1981–1986   104

8. State Department Retirement Projections, 1981–1985   110

9. State Department Bureau of East Asian and Pacific Affairs: Budget and Personnel   122

10. Annual Increase in Japanese Foreign Ministry Personnel, 1974–1980   139

11. Personnel Recruitment Outside the Japanese Foreign Ministry, 1975–1980   169

Figures

1a. Organization of the Japanese Foreign Ministry   40
1b. Foreign Ministry Bureaus   41
2. Organization of a Typical Japanese Bureau   43
3. Organization of a Typical Japanese Embassy   44
4. Organization of the State Department, May 1, 1978   48
5. State Department Budget Request, FY 1980   54
6. Changes in State Department Personnel Structure
Effected by the Foreign Service Act of 1980   56
7. Office of the Japanese Foreign Ministry Vice-Minister   62
8. State Department Bureau of Personnel   67
9. Japanese Foreign Ministry Line of Authority, 1981   114
10. State Department Bureau of East Asian
and Pacific Affairs   120
11. Japanese Foreign Ministry Manpower Capacity:
Tokyo and Overseas   140
12. Size Comparison of Foreign Offices in Seven Major
Countries   141
13. Staff Complement at Japanese Overseas Posts   142
14. Increase in Japanese Manpower and Work Load,
1969–1979   143
15. Organization of First North American Division,
North American Affairs Bureau of Japanese Foreign Ministry   146

FOREWORD

M ODERN DIPLOMACY, ORIGINATING WITH THE ESTABLISHMENT OF PROMI-
nent diplomatic missions in the states of Italy in the fifteenth century,
has been defined both as the "art of conducting international negotiations"
and as the "science of external relations." Whether an art or a science, the
practice of diplomacy has evolved with the rapidly changing and increasingly complex nature of relations among governments. To some of us
who began our Foreign Service careers by poring over the thick book of
regulations with its heavy binding and insertable pages and passing an
examination on its contents, the art in international relations seems now to
have overshadowed the science. Especially in the U.S. Foreign Service,
senior officials, drawn frequently from political life, bring a personal touch
to the practice of diplomacy, for they are less circumscribed than the classic
diplomats of another age whose punctilious behavior and predilection to "go
by the book" were so noteworthy.

The expansion of diplomatic establishments around the world is but a
symbol of the enormous extension of the nature of our international affairs.
Before World War II, a typical U.S. embassy consisted of an ambassador, a
deputy chief of mission, and four sections: political, economic, consular,
and administrative. Occasionally officers of some other agencies, such as
the Department of Agriculture, would be sent from Washington to join the
embassy staff. But these instances were rare. Today almost every agency of
government that has any responsibility with regard to foreign affairs has a
representative in a major embassy. This proliferation has occurred in the

overseas establishments of most major nations, but the United States must be among the leaders in numbers of personnel.

The study of the Japanese and U.S. Foreign Services that Dr. Harrison Holland has undertaken is unique in that it is an examination of two establishments that represent nations having fundamentally different cultures and languages and a history of successive friendship, war, partnership, and alliance. Because of the importance of the Japanese-U.S. relationship in the 1980s, called "second to none" by Ambassador to Japan Mike Mansfield, an analysis of the way these two countries carry out their respective foreign policies — something that has never been done before — is more pertinent than a similar study of any other two countries. The prewar Japanese Foreign Office (*Gaimushō*) earned a reputation for having outstanding diplomats. Some of them joined with the military in carrying out wholeheartedly Japan's policy of expansion in Asia in the 1930s; others, idealistic, believed firmly in a Japanese "civilizing mission" to carry to less fortunate undeveloped nations some of the beneficial modernization that Japan had acquired in the late nineteenth century, during the experience of the Meiji period. Some Japanese diplomats showed great courage in the final days of the Pacific war, exerting audacious efforts to stop a struggle with the United States that they knew could only come to a tragic end.

After the war ended, the Gaimushō had to totally reconstruct its organization and personnel. Fortunately, many of the younger diplomats who had joined the service shortly before the war were ready to step into positions of responsibility. The United States, as part of the Occupation policy, brought a number of these junior officers to Washington to offer them a chance to observe the State Department in action. Many became good friends of the United States.

The experience of the Occupation and the inevitable tutelage of the United States that the Japanese diplomatic organization experienced resulted in a foreign policy that coincided almost entirely with that of the United States. It has taken Japan a long time to escape from this dependence; only since the mid-1970s can Japan be said to have developed a foreign policy of its own. This independence was encouraged by the United States; differences over trade and defense have injected controversy into the alliance, although it remains as solid as ever.

Distinctions in the implementation of diplomacy by the two Foreign Offices are brought out clearly in Dr. Holland's book. The career principle is observed far more strictly in Japan than in the United States. The bureaucracy is a strong element in the Japanese body politic; it prevails throughout the government service and exerts an enormous influence on policy. "Bureaucrat" in English is often a pejorative term; its equivalent in Japanese is defined as an honored person. When a Japanese bureaucrat retires to take a position in business, his transition is called *amakudari* or "descent from heaven."

A Japanese ambassador who has not risen through the ranks of the Foreign Service is indeed rare, whereas appointments of individuals from outside the U.S. Foreign Service, at least to the large and more prestigious posts, are often the rule rather than the exception. The young Japanese recruit can look forward with reasonable assurance to the reward of an ambassadorship at the end of his career. The young U.S. Foreign Service officer is far less certain that he will reach the coveted rank of chief of mission. The Japanese service is approximately one-fourth as large as that of the United States. This is a problem, as Dr. Holland points out, in view of Japan's tremendous economic growth and its ever-expanding worldwide responsibilities.

Dr. Holland was a Foreign Service officer for more than 25 years, 12 years of which were spent in Japan. He is therefore peculiarly qualified to discuss the workings of the Gaimushō, with whose officials he made many associations and carried on negotiations, and of the State Department, where he served with distinction in many capacities. Much has been written by academics and former ambassadors about the making and the results of foreign policy. However, the practitioner — the officer who must deal with the day-to-day problems and controversies, small and large, that affect relations between two countries and the resolution of which is an important aspect of the making of foreign policy — has spoken little of his eye view of the diplomatic trade. It is of special interest and significance that Dr. Holland includes a vivid description of how two foreign offices, and their embassies and consulates, work and relate to each other; of the problems of organization, perception, and cultural differences; and, above all, of the human factor, so often belittled and neglected by those who watch from the outside.

This is a book that should find wide readership among those who value our primary Pacific partnership and wonder just how these two nations conduct diplomacy.

JOHN K. EMMERSON

Nikko, Japan
August 8, 1982

ACKNOWLEDGMENTS

I WISH TO EXPRESS MY GRATITUDE TO THE MANY INDIVIDUALS IN JAPAN AND the United States who helped me prepare this manuscript — specifically, the Japanese and U.S. diplomats and other government officials, academicians, newspapermen, politicians, bankers, and businessmen who consented to be interviewed. Most of them requested anonymity and their wish has been honored. Interviews were conducted in Tokyo from September 1980 to July 1981, when I was a visiting professor at Keio University. A list of those Japanese interviewees and Americans interviewed in January 1982 is included as Appendix A.

Much of the research conducted during my residence in Japan was made possible by a grant from the Kajima Foundation, Tokyo. President Tadao Ishikawa and his staff at Keio University were most hospitable and supportive. I owe a special debt to Miss Kumie Kushizaki, who translated many of the Japanese documents used in writing the book. She toiled long and tirelessly.

My friends and colleagues in the U.S. Foreign Service gave generously of their time. I am particularly indebted to John Emmerson, senior research fellow at the Hoover Institution on War, Revolution and Peace, Stanford University, without whose support, counsel, and sensitive criticisms the task of completing the study would have been infinitely more difficult. Equally helpful was Claude Buss, emeritus professor of history, Stanford University, who spent many hours with me reviewing the drafts and suggesting changes that have strengthened the presentation. Mr. Yoshinori

Tsujimoto, an official of the Japanese Ministry of Foreign Affairs, devoted much time to arranging interviews with ministry officials and helped me immeasurably to understand the organization of the foreign ministry.

To the other individuals who read the early drafts and gave me the benefit of their wisdom — Professor Chalmers Johnson of the University of California, Berkeley; Dr. Howard Levy, former director of the U.S. Embassy Japanese Language School in Tokyo/Yokohama; and Mr. Yoshio Uchida, an official of the Japanese Ministry of International Trade and Industry — I am also most grateful.

Research for the sections on the U.S. Foreign Service and the final preparation of the manuscript were made possible by a grant from the Hoover Institution. The excellent East Asian collection at that institution and the valuable library facilities at Stanford University greatly facilitated my research. I, alone, am responsible for any errors of omission or commission that may remain.

INTRODUCTION

Relations between the United States and Japan have been marked by periods of harmony and cooperation as well as trial and tribulation since Commodore Perry's "black ships" opened Japan to the world in 1853. The competitive spirit has left its imprint. From Perry to Reagan, the two countries have known periods of calm and friction, war and threat of war, intense economic rivalry, immigration tensions, and above all, an uncertainty bred of ignorance and lack of mutual understanding.

The roller coaster relationship started with Perry threatening the Tokugawa shogunate with naval bombardment to open Japan to world commerce, and has come full circle with officials of the Reagan administration and some members of Congress threatening Japan with protectionist legislation because of the "closed Japanese market." It is the story of two intensely energetic and patriotic peoples—one homogeneous, the other heterogeneous; the civilization of one grounded in the religions and customs of the East, that of the other based on Christianity; both countries having highly strategic geographic positions and such diversity in culture, mores, and language that communication has been difficult at best.

Because of its importance to the entire world, the relationship hungers today for better understanding but there is uncertainty about how to proceed. More trials and frustrations and more economic, political, and security conflicts lie ahead; the professional diplomat will undoubtedly have an increasingly important role to play in the solution of those conflicts.

My 25 years of experience as a Foreign Service officer (FSO), most of which were spent in Japan, have led me to believe that many misunderstandings between Japan and the United States are rooted in the role of diplomacy in their modern state systems, the public attitudes toward the professional diplomat, and the management styles in the practice of diplomacy. I am convinced that an appreciation of these differences can lead each side to a better understanding of the points of view of the other and begin a trend away from the current confrontation toward cooperation.

I believe that greater knowledge of the Japanese foreign ministry and its career Foreign Service on the part of Americans will add an important dimension to an understanding of Japanese foreign policy and of the society that sanctions that policy. Similarly, a Japanese public that is more informed about the Department of State and the role of the U.S. Foreign Service officer in the conduct of that nation's foreign policy will better understand the problems and practices of U.S. diplomacy. Greater mutual understanding is desperately needed. Without it, the inexorable drift toward confrontation on trade and defense issues will continue and will further disturb not only economic and security relations but political relations as well. We can ill afford such an eventuality. The diplomats see this clearly; the public does not.

This study will concentrate on the differences in the Japanese and U.S. Foreign Service systems and is intended as a contribution to greater understanding on the part of the public, in both Japan and the United States. It focuses on diplomatic management as an avenue of improvement in United States–Japan relations and is based on the assumption that potential conflicts will be softened and cooperation will be promoted if deeper insights are gained into the types of persons entrusted with the management of diplomacy: their professionalism, their career expectations and frustrations, their roles as negotiators and decision-makers, their place in the bureaucracy of the national government, and the image they project to the public they serve.

The search for understanding should begin with a clear perception of the political systems that have had such a profound impact on the organization and prestige of the foreign ministry in Japan and the Department of State in the United States. Japan's modern parliamentary system of government has fostered a strong, career-oriented bureaucracy that is relatively free of undue political influence. Traditionally, government bureaucrats have played a key role in policymaking and have had the respect, if not the affection, of the Japanese people. The Japanese diplomat is a part of this tradition.

In the United States, the formulation of foreign policy is the responsibility of the president and his senior advisers with input from the Congress.

The accountability of elected leaders to their various constituencies is adjudged to be essential to the democratic process. Therefore, the Foreign Service has been subject in varying degrees to political manipulation. Despite civil service reform and the ostensible elimination of the spoils system, the State Department bureaucracy has come under the strong influence of Congress and some members of the White House staff. With each change of administration, there is a new influx of political appointees at executive levels in the State Department and at ambassadorial posts. This has created instability, or at least the appearance of instability, in the system and has caused some anguish among the Japanese officials who must educate these new U.S. policymakers.

Pressures have been building for structural and manpower reforms. In Japan, the demand for change has become more insistent; in the United States, the Foreign Service Act of 1980 was an effort to channel continuous change to maximize its effectiveness.

This study begins with an analysis of the setting in Japan and the United States, including some of the important traditions that have influenced the organization of the Japanese foreign ministry and that affect the behavior of its diplomats, and some of the historical factors that have shaped the development of management systems in the Department of State. The human factor in diplomatic management is addressed in Chapter 2; Chapter 3 is devoted to an examination of the organization and management of the Ministry of Foreign Affairs and the Department of State. Chapter 4 focuses on the personnel systems in operation. Both systems are analyzed in terms of recruitment and examination, assignment procedures, performance evaluation and promotion, and training — all of which have a profound effect on the career development of Foreign Service officers, for they determine career progression and the pace of career development.

After assessing the role of the professional diplomat in the decision-making process, I explain the limitations that bureaucratic organizaton and formalized procedures place upon the Foreign Service officer, whether on duty at home or in an overseas post. An account of my own experiences while serving in the U.S. Embassy in Tokyo — negotiating with the Japanese government to obtain its agreement to the visit of the first nuclear-powered submarine, *Sea Dragon*, as well as to the consular convention between the United States and Japan, and carrying out my responsibilities for coordination of security matters — illustrates the difficulties inherent in the decison-making process.

Subsequent chapters address the manpower dilemma faced by Japan and the United States in seeking optimum allocation of their personnel resources. Because of serious staffing problems, both in the foreign ministry and at its overseas posts, management practices in Japan are constrained by the heavy hand of tradition. The Department of State, however, is more concerned with modernization and reform than with tradition. Its major problems center around equities in promotion and assignment and operaton of the diplomatic establishment in accordance with accepted management principles.

A final problem to be solved by the foreign ministry and the Department of State, if they are to make an optimum contribution to greater understanding between the two nations, is their public image. Neither finds it easy to communicate with the public or to gain acceptance of its policies and programs. The task will not be easy, especially for the foreign ministry, but there is a growing recognition by ministry officials that greater efforts must be made to gain public confidence and understanding.

THE SETTING

MANAGING DIPLOMACY IN JAPAN AND THE UNITED STATES CAN BEST BE understood by considering the different settings of the two nations since World War II, as well as the traditions and practices that have influenced the two diplomatic establishments and specifically the behavior of career Foreign Service officers.

Japan

The Historical Setting

Immediately following the war, Japan's foreign policy was deeply influenced by a pervasive public antipathy to war and militarism and by a single-minded dedication to economic revival and expansion. The major pattern of diplomatic activity was passive and/or reactive, with promotion of Japanese economic interests abroad the main focus of the foreign ministry's efforts. Article 9 of the Constitution, in which Japan renounced war as an instrument of national policy, set the foreign policy pattern. The *amae*, or dependency, on the United States gave that nation a sort of surrogate role in Japanese foreign affairs that was a source of some frustration and unhappiness to the ministry and its career officers.

Fortunately for both countries, a stronger sense of national esteem and consciousness gradually emerged in Japan, permitting the ministry to administer a foreign policy that was determined more by Japanese interests.

Pride returned to the career Foreign Service, and there was evidence of an upbeat mood in the ministry. However, problems remained. Even in 1976 a distinguished Japanese diplomatic historian wrote that "today's Foreign Office lacks the daring and initiative necessary for policy making... It becomes passive, presenting data and taking only the slightest initiative in its work. This passivity apparently stems from an instinct for self-preservation, a desire to avoid as many risks as possible. Generally speaking, this play-it-safe attitude is the main reason for the decay of the Foreign Office."[1]

This critical appraisal of the foreign ministry reflects a continuing uncertainty on the part of many Japanese about the direction Japanese foreign policy should take in a nuclear age. The memories of defeat in World War II still persist, and the predominance of the politician in postwar Japan has had the effect of causing the ministry to shy away from taking a leading role in foreign policy. The initiatives concerning rapprochement with China and the solution of the Okinawa problem, for example, were taken by politicians, not diplomats. The continued presence of U.S. military forces on Japanese soil was also a psychological reminder of Japan's dependence on the United States. These factors have tended to inhibit initiative and to heighten caution and sensitivity to changes in policy direction.

Nevertheless, the ministry is continuing to gain confidence. It is adjusting to an environment in which Japanese military power no longer dominates East Asia. It is attempting to devise a foreign policy that will protect Japanese vital interests without recourse to military force. It is attempting to gain greater expertise in the solution of complex economic, political, and security problems in order to regain its leadership role in the making of foreign policy. It is attempting to reawaken the pride and patriotism of its career personnel, to make them more proficient diplomats. Finally, it is trying to reassert a leadership role for Japan that will not be subordinate to but rather will complement the foreign policy initiatives of the United States and other Western nations.

Time will be required to accomplish these things; constant reassessment and re-evaluation of Japan's foreign policy options can be expected. China, the Soviet Union, oil, Korea, raw materials, trade surpluses, the security treaty with the United States, nuclear weapons, geographic vulnerability in a nuclear age—these and other issues will consume the time and energies of the foreign ministry and the career Foreign Service.

Thus the postwar Foreign Service, strongly influenced by the past and under increasing pressure to deal more effectively with growing foreign policy problems, has developed a modus operandi according to which major problems have often had to be handled on a case-by-case basis. The Japanese Foreign Service has no legislative charter comparable to the State Department's Rogers Act of 1924 or the Foreign Service Acts of 1946 and

1980 to guide administrative practices. It is a career service that has stubbornly refused to give an active decision-making role to the noncareer specialist on the lame excuse that he has not been properly educated or trained to undertake such responsibilities. It has been in a form of hibernation since the 1950s, content to live with a two-tiered personnel system and only gradually recognizing the need for changes in that system.

Tradition: Challenge to Progress

The inertia that has worked against change in the organization and personnel policies of the Ministry of Foreign Affairs is rooted in tradition. Honoring and adhering to the cultural and behavioral patterns of the past have exerted powerful influences on the conduct of foreign policy since the Meiji period. The impact of tradition on the daily lives of career officers and the substantive activities of the foreign ministry is probably greater than in any other ministry of the Japanese government.

Other ministries have their own constituencies (farm, industry, finance, fisheries, labor), but the foreign ministry has traditionally represented all of Japan—that mix of special-interest groups that profess no particular affection for nor interest in the work of the ministry. This lack of constituency has affected the ministry's status in the Japanese bureaucracy and has shaped not only the attitudes of its diplomats but their careers as well. It has created a special set of traditions and has reinforced those general bureaucratic principles that distinguish Japanese government employees from their counterparts in other lands. Such noteworthy traditions as seniority, heirarchy, class identification, harmony, elitism, and conformity have become the hallmarks of the Japanese Foreign Service and flourish in a system conscious of its worth to Japan yet troubled over the intrusion of modern ideas that threaten to bend some of these time-honored ways of doing things to the demands and challenges of a new era.

Seniority. Seniority (*nenkō joretsu*) has deep roots in Japanese society. It is a universal doctrine that, in one sense, is the adhesive binding the system together. Thus it has long been a stabilizing element in employer/employee relations. It has given direction and congruity to personnel management and has been an article of faith for the government worker, the basis for career development. This tradition is not peculiar to the foreign ministry but is recognized throughout the Japanese government bureaucracy. In the ministry, seniority plays its customary role—regulating assignments and promotions so that juniors will not pass seniors on the career ladder, and seniors will not replace juniors in the assignment process.

Most career officers with whom I talked favored keeping the seniority system. One senior official said that it gave him a comfortable feeling to work for a man senior to himself; another described it as part of the Japanese way of life. Although there is considerable support, especially from retired senior officials, for increased application of the seniority principle in the assignment process, change is coming slowly. Some believe that to obtain a higher quality of personnel at senior levels (vice-minister, director general, or ambassador to an important post), appointments should not be made solely by virtue of seniority but that competition and merit are also important considerations.

Seniority continues to predominate at operating levels of the ministry, but it is perhaps more subject to abuse at senior levels where merit and competition are important determinants in the assignment process. The Personnel Division, the principal guardian of the tradition of seniority, applies it daily in making appointments to the positions of division chief, deputy director general, director general, and counselor or minister of embassy. Officers themselves rely on it to assure their place in the career hierarchy; it is also a standard of measurement for the assignment of officers from other ministries and agencies to the foreign ministry or to overseas posts.

There is competition, however disguised, among senior officers for choice assignments. If, for example, two officers in the same class are being considered for an important ambassadorship or for the position of director general of a bureau, the individual believed to be more able will be chosen regardless of age. If the two officers being considered are from different classes, the choice becomes more difficult, and the more senior official will probably be chosen. But more and more exceptions are being made to assure that the best officers obtain the best assignments.

Hierarchy.   Hierarchy (*jō-ge kankei*) is closely related to seniority in the Japanese social structure and bureaucratic process. It holds a pre-eminent position in Japanese society and government and is rooted in feudalism, a social device to establish stability and order. Hierarchy can be defined as position stratification in which each level carries its own responsibilities and privileges.

Hierarchy establishes the framework of rank order in an organization and seniority establishes the ground rules for administering assignments and making promotions within that framework; however, in the daily operation of the bureaucracy the two traditions are often indistinguishable. In the foreign ministry, the occupant of each rank or position must fulfill certain requirements, but he is generally in that particular position because of the influence of seniority.

Some officials criticize hierarchy in diplomatic management for not allowing flexibility in the promotion and assignment processes. One former vice-minister told me that hierarchy hinders mobility in the personnel system and sometimes prevents the best officers from reaching the top of the service. Combined with seniority, the tradition of hierarchy places a heavy hand on the system and precludes it from responding to needed change. Such accusations are seldom heard in a public forum, for the most part because these traditions provide a kind of security, a sense of professional satisfaction, and a stability indispensable to the average bureaucrat.

Just as the tradition of seniority is increasingly subject to question, so is the tradition of hierarchy. There are those in the senior ranks who argue that the foreign ministry has a special role to play in the Japanese government and that strict application of this principle may be appropriate for ministries dealing with domestic affairs, but it weakens the ability of the ministry to respond to new challenges in an ever-changing international environment.

Such cogent arguments for change do not have much overall impact. Hierarchy is deeply ingrained in the fabric of Japanese society, and it seems to have general acceptance in the career service. Even the career officers who belong to the younger generation, which one might expect to be in the vanguard of movements for change, accept hierarchy as a system they know and understand. In a sense, this response is understandable. Because they were educated in a society that recognizes rank as fundamental, they entered the ministry understanding the part rank would play in their own career development. They bear witness to its influence, for they have accepted its constraints on their aspirations and have followed the rules it imposes; they also fully expect the rewards it promises.

Rank carries privileges and rewards, along with the injunction to comply with its precepts for order. It allows certain people to enter at certain levels only after these officials have complied with the requirements for entrance. Those with the proper credentials are encouraged; the unqualified are not. Although it is not a caste system or a hierarchical system reminiscent of the Tokugawa period, the system of rank nevertheless has numerous and influential adherents in Japanese society and operates vigorously in the foreign ministry.

Rank is especially important in the foreign ministry's working relationships with other ministries. It is necessary for a deputy division chief in the foreign ministry to have the same rank and title as his counterpart in another ministry if workable relations are to be established. The absence of such equality in rank creates many difficulties for interagency communication. To facilitate the work of the foreign ministry in its dealings with other departments, a new bureau rank was established in the 1970s—that of senior deputy director general, or *shingikan*. Previously, there had been only one rank—junior deputy director general, or *sanjikan*; however, it was found to be inadequate for the development of effective working relations, especially with officers in the Ministry of Finance and the Ministry of International Trade and Industry (MITI).

As one personnel officer put it, Japanese career officers feel demeaned if they have to deal with an officer in their own or another ministry who is inferior to them in rank. It offends their sense of elitism and lowers their morale. The managers of the system have this very much in mind when designating members of delegations to international conferences or to interministerial discussions.

Hierarchy nurtures pride in rank, feeds the ego, causes bureaucratic logjams where rank problems exist, and stifles initiative and ambition when they threaten to exceed the parameters of rank established by hierarchy. It nevertheless has powerful champions, and there is very little evidence that its influence is waning.[2]

Class Identification.   Class identification (*dōki ishiki*) is a tradition that requires that a new appointee entering the foreign ministry identify with his class until retirement. His career progress will be influenced by the reputation of his class, and his career aspirations will often be subordinated to the general good of his class. He will not be promoted ahead of his colleagues in the class; rather, all will receive their promotions automatically, and simultaneously. In accord with traditional Japanese practice, he will be assured of lifetime employment, and he will thus attain a sense of personal security that he will share with other members of his class. Senior officers in the foreign ministry begin to evaluate members of a particular class early, and the class begins to assume a reputation that members take great pride in and work hard to enhance. Class reputations are often made or lost as a result of the circulation of rumors.[3]

It is natural for a member of a class to identify with his group. As a youth, he learned to identify his interests with those of his family. As an adult, he tends to repress his individualistic tendencies. The goal is to conform to one's group or class, not to indulge in self-assertion or self-fulfillment—to achieve organizational order and peace.

In Japan, a domineering person is socially handicapped, because that personality quality is likely to work against his own interests. Submissiveness, on the other hand, is not necessarily an undesirable quality. The young career officer in the ministry does not totally bury his own interests to promote those of the group; he identifies his interests with those of the class to which he belongs.[4]

The following passage clearly describes how Japanese society molds the personality of a youth and prepares him for adulthood:

As the years grow in number, a network of constraints begins to be woven around the divine tyrant [the young child]. As the child grows into a youth and then into a young man, the demands of society strengthen their hold on him, slowly and with increasing severity. When the student graduates from his university, he is like a tree enclosed within a hard and colorless bark. A mask has been growing on him, made out of discipline, tradition, self-restraint and diffidence. Within this crust, a thin sap of individual life is still mounting and falling, but this flow, too, seems to be regulated by the tides of the season and of the national destiny; the formation of the mask is complete.[5]

The author goes on to explain that

the pressure exercised by a "common will" on each [group member] is not resented as an intrusion by the group into the life of the individual; for the group is conceived of as the individual's better self. More correctly, he does not live outside his group with which he has come to feel identified, and to whose decisions and movements he contributes in such a way that he can scarcely distinguish his own contributions from that of his fellows. . . . The unconditional surrender of the adult Japanese to the rhythm of fate, his apparent . . . contentment in being buffeted by the great forces beyond his control, his horror of isolation and his satisfaction in yielding to circumstances appear to be molded on the traces left in his unconsciousness by those securely fettered and lovingly balanced states of early childhood.[6]

The young career Foreign Service officer, molded by his society into a group-oriented individual, becomes a totally committed member of his class, and his fate is inextricably bound to that of his class. Even when he reaches the senior ranks and there is rivalry for the desired posts of ambassador and bureau director general, tradition does not permit overt expression of competitive hostility. Instead, he calmly awaits the decision of his seniors after having done his best, within the parameters of tradition, to prepare himself for such assignments.

Harmony.   Harmony, or *wa*, is a tradition in the foreign ministry that impacts importantly on employee careers. Those who cooperate in the fulfillment of this goal gain a sense of well-being and satisfaction; those who do not often find their careers in jeopardy. Promotion of office harmony is an important factor in the evaluation of an officer's performance. The following paragraph is a superb description of harmony:

Harmony is to be valued, and an avoidance of wanton opposition to be honoured. All persons are influenced by class-feeling, and there are few

who are intelligent. Hence there are some who disobey their lords and
fathers or who maintain feuds with the neighboring villages. But when
those above are harmonious and those below are friendly, there is concord
in the discussion of business, right views of things spontaneously gain
acceptance. Then what is there that cannot be accomplished.[7]

These teachings have been incorporated into everyday life in Japan and
seem to have acquired the force of biological instinct, serving the ends of a
human society that aspires to rival in cohesive power the societies of bees
and ants.[8] "To make the stream of human intercourse flow gently is the
supreme goal here. Nobody is allowed to stand on his own right, much less
fight for it. Conflicts must be submitted for mediation and are solved by
compromise. Justice is praised, but its pursuit is deemed inappropriate if
the peace of the community is thereby threatened. To avoid friction seems to
be more important than to eradicate evil."[9]

Harmony is the goal in the diplomatic bureaucracy as in other groups
because it is a social imperative, a rule by which the Japanese live. I
observed it on countless occasions when negotiating on behalf of the U.S.
Embassy in Tokyo with Japanese counterparts on security and consular
matters. During these sessions, there was no lack of effort or determination
on the part of the Japanese to defend their interests; nor was there any
intention to confront the United States with ultimatums or any attempt to
indulge in sharp rejoinders or comments, to embarrass, or to challenge.
Discussions were carried on seriously, impartially, and without histrionics;
there was an obvious intention of reaching agreement in a spirit of good
feeling. For the Japanese, harmony is the oil that lubricates the bureaucratic
machine.

Elitism.   Elitism is the sense of being a member of a select corps in the
Japanese bureaucracy. Elitism has its genesis in a diplomatic officer's early
education and becomes more pronounced when he enters a top university in
Japan, usually Tokyo University. Here he is trained to think of himself as a
very special person and as a member of an elite educational group. It is a
relatively short step from this feeling to a sense of superiority as a career
diplomat. The diplomatic officer believes that the destiny of Japan rests on
his shoulders and on those of his colleagues.

Pride in the foreign ministry, pride in class, and a subdued and often
camouflaged pride in self are the natural by-products of this elitism. They
are often manifested in curious and not always attractive ways. The oft-
described discrimination by career officers against noncareer officers derives in some measure from this elitist attitude. The image of the typical
Japanese diplomat as a haughty and unapproachable individual can also be

traced to this preoccupation with elitism. The self-imposed isolation of the career officer from the public and specifically from the business, academic, and political communities is another expression of elitism, or what the late Unitarian minister A. Powell Davies (a noted U.S. clergyman) once described as "egotoxicity." This trait is not consciously flouted before colleagues and the public, but it is so ingrained in the psyche of the career officer that it is hard to conceal.

Many career officers think of the foreign ministry as a corps bound together by common interests, whose members come from the best schools and the upper levels of society and that must remain small and exclusive in order to remain elitist. This attitude works against the efforts of those who recognize the need to expand the career service to meet Japan's growing responsibilities in the world.

There is some indication of a slow yet perceptible change in the thinking of career officers who wish to preserve the image of a small, exclusive career corps. Even though they remain in the majority, they complain about the heavy work load and admit to a need for more career officers to meet future demands.

A poignant example of the influence of elitism on the thinking of the public and on the media in Japan was the assignment of a noncareer officer in the Ministry of Finance, S. Ishii, to be director general of the printing bureau on July 19, 1981, a position normally slated for a senior career officer.[10]

Conformity. Conformity is a tradition somewhat similar to harmony but has more negative than positive aspects; a conformist attitude often prevails in the foreign ministry. A former deputy vice-minister has said that conformity is a characteristic of the career officer class and has its roots in the nature of diplomacy itself—respect for continuity, respect for international law, and respect for policy already initiated and carried out.

Powerful conformist pressures exist within the career service. Because the basic instinct of the career officer is self-preservation, there is a desire to avoid risks[11]—to express opinions thought acceptable to senior officials and to show oneself to be a team player, not a maverick. The chronic dissenter, the persistent critic, and the outspoken iconoclast have no place in the Japanese Foreign Service. An officer knows that the direction his career takes, be it vertically to top ministry positions or horizontally to an overseas post, is influenced by the personal relations he develops with his seniors and his ability to play by "bureaucratic rules." He knows that he is always on display. Not unlike his colleagues in the U.S. Foreign Service, he perhaps unwittingly accepts the sage advice for career success voiced by veteran

U.S. politician Sam Rayburn, the late Speaker of the House of Representatives: "To get along you have to go along."

Bold strokes in Japanese diplomacy are seldom made by ministry bureaucrats. Initiatives on the reopening of relations with China, the reversion of Okinawa, and the re-establishment of diplomatic relations with the Soviet Union were originated by leaders of the Liberal Democratic Party (LDP). Once the policy was decided upon, the ministry "conformed" and carried out the general intent set forth by the politicians. Several career officers told me that since political leaders are elected by the people to carry out their wishes, bureaucrats must be the politicians' servants and carry out policies initiated by them.

This is an interesting viewpoint, considering that career officers believe themselves to constitute an elitist group and generally disparage politicians in their private commiserations. But it nevertheless reflects a growing realization on their part that politicians are increasingly involved in foreign affairs and usually take the lead on important policy questions. Few Foreign Service officers would admit that this development reflects their inability or disinclination to take policy initiative, but in effect they do not take the initiative because of the instinct to conform. The power vacuum thus created has allowed the enterprising and ambitious politician to step in and provide the impetus for change. However, the system compels even politicians to follow the rules and not to depart too far from the ordinary norms of conformity.

Despite the growing influence of the Liberal Democratic Party and the Diet in foreign affairs, the bureaucrats in the foreign ministry, as well as in other ministries, still wield considerably more influence over domestic and foreign policy, are trusted more and shown greater respect, than their counterparts in the United States.

The tendency to conform often reveals itself when the ministry is searching for new policy initiatives or when the Diet must defend past policy actions. An example of the latter is the effort of the government in May–June 1981 to defend the policy that prior consultation with the United States was required for introduction of nuclear weapons into Japan. Former U.S. Ambassador Edwin Reischauer set the stage for the debate in the Diet and the media when he said that the United States had allowed naval vessels with nuclear weapons aboard to enter Japanese ports without informing Japanese authorities through the prior consultation process. The Japanese government responded to opposition attacks in the Diet by arguing that there was an understanding with the U.S. government concerning prior consultation and that no U.S. vessel with nuclear weapons had entered Japanese ports because there had been no prior consultation. "We trust the U.S. government to keep its word," said the chief Cabinet secretary.[12]

The Japanese government, never waivering from its previous policy pronouncements, brought a phalanx of foreign ministry officials from the Treaties Bureau and the North American Affairs Bureau to the Diet to explain the policy of prior consultation and its history—in effect, to confirm past policy. "To have admitted that Ambassador Reischauer was right," said one high ministry official, "would have caused serious political problems."

The tradition of conformity establishes the parameters within which modern diplomacy must be conducted. Although Japanese diplomats are relied upon by their own people to defend past policies and to chart new policy courses, they are not expected to depart too far from the restraints placed upon them by their own traditions and social precedents.

The United States

The Historical Setting

The responsibilities of the United States as a world leader have increased steadily since World War II, and it has had to shoulder them with a diplomatic establishment administratively ill prepared for the task. Since 1946, the Department of State and the Foreign Service have developed a set of administrative policies and practices and have implemented a series of bureaucratic reorganizations, reforms, and personnel expansion programs that have allowed them to fulfill their growing diplomatic responsibilities. Their efforts have been unfettered by the kinds of societal proscriptions and cultural mandates that have affected and continue to affect the Japanese foreign ministry and its career diplomats.

We have seen that Japan's foreign policy since World War II has been managed by a career service that has largely controlled the administration and operation of the foreign ministry; the career officer and the traditions that have influenced his conduct, attitudes, and role in the decision-making process have been placed at the center of diplomatic management. In the United States, foreign affairs have been more a function of government departments and agencies. Under the direction of the president and with strong congressional input, these departments, especially the Department of State, have played more of a role in diplomatic management than the career Foreign Service.

The role of U.S. Foreign Service officers has nevertheless been significant. They have sought and have been granted anonymity in performance of their daily tasks, and they have developed the diplomatic expertise essential to participation in the decision-making process. In the United States, as in Japan, tradition has placed its stamp on the Foreign Service, but in a modified form. Seniority, hierarchy, class identification, and harmony are less important to the U.S. Foreign Service officer; the urge for change is more compelling. Being highly competitive and intensely individualistic, and performing in an organization whose credo is "up or out," the U.S. Foreign Service officer has learned to adjust his career sights to the realities of his competitive environment. He has also had to be aware of the major tenets of U.S. foreign policy, the historical background of certain policies, and the forces, both in the United States and in other nations, that have influenced the evolution of U.S. diplomacy.

From the beginning, the central purpose of the Department of State has been to interpret, defend, articulate, manage, and ensure the continuity of U.S. foreign policy and to assist the president in formulating that policy. To carry out this basic function, the department has constantly had to adjust to changes in the national and international enviroment—from the war for national independence to the war in Vietnam. The department's power to manage U.S. foreign policy has been in direct proportion to the strength and ability of the incumbent secretary of state and the closeness of his relationship to the president. The increase in the number of personnel and in the size of the budget necessary to keep in step with the growth of U.S. influence abroad has meant that the department has continually had to ask Congress for adequate funds to fulfill the nation's increased international responsibilities mainly because of public indifference and the department's narrow constituency. Yet these struggles ironically have produced a group of career Foreign Service officers with a dedication to public service and to defense of the national interest—a career corps that through the years has maintained a high quality of performance. It is a remarkable story of a government agency relatively lacking in public and congressional support, yet sustained by a sense of mission, functioning with integrity and often with distinction at the center of government policy in times of both war and peace.

During the first 50 years of the twentieth century, the number of State Department employees grew from about 1,220 to over 16,000. The budget grew in proportion. In 1900, the department's budget amounted to a little over $3 million, but by 1950 it had grown to over $350 million. As a result of its involvement in economic, scientific, cultural, trade, and military assistance programs, the department gradually assumed new operational responsibilities in addition to its more traditional tasks of political reporting and negotiation. The number of diplomatic and consular posts increased from 2 diplomatic and 10 consular posts in 1790 to 133 diplomatic and 100 consular posts in 1980.[13]

Pressures also began to build within and outside the State Department during this period to introduce greater professionalism into the Foreign

Service—to establish a corps of diplomats that would serve the nation regardless of the political leadership. Reorganization of the Foreign Service was proposed in numerous bills between 1919 and 1924. Finally on May 24, 1924, with passage of the Rogers Act, a permanent, unified, career Foreign Service was established, with merit alone the basis for appointment and promotion.

Further efforts at personnel reform were undertaken in 1946 and resulted in passage of the Foreign Service Act the same year. The Foreign Service Act of 1980 consolidated many of the features of the two previous acts.

The Postwar Department of State

The United States emerged from World War II as a global power (a superpower to some observers), with widespread international interests. It was at that time of transition that the department asserted its primacy in the area of policy planning by providing the content of and direction for foreign policy deliberations over East-West relations (U.S. relations with the Soviet Union and East European countries). The department's leadership found expression in the policy of containment of Ambassador George Kennan, a career Foreign Service officer, which was vigorously supported by two strong secretaries of state, George Marshall and Dean Acheson. The State Department was able to take the lead in policy decisions on containment, the Marshall Plan, and the North Atlantic Treaty Organization largely because of the close working relationship between Secretaries of State Marshall and Acheson and President Harry Truman.

Complicating the role of the department was the enactment of the National Security Act in 1947. The act established a National Security Council (NSC) with a national security adviser who reported directly to the president. An adversary situation was often created between the adviser and the secretary of state for dominance in foreign policy formulation that sometimes inhibited effective articulation of U.S. foreign policy to friends and foes. This dual power structure continues to plague the management of U.S. foreign policy. After Marshall, Acheson, and Truman had left center stage, the department's influence began to decline. It did not resurge significantly under John Foster Dulles (1953–1959) because of his style of conducting foreign affairs and managing the department. He tended to isolate himself from the career Foreign Service and did not share power with senior department officers, depending instead on a small coterie of highly trusted associates who themselves began to take on the secretive characteristics of their boss. It was a time of frustration and low morale for the Foreign Service. A succession of secretaries of state since Dulles have grappled with these multiple problems. Each has had his own style in asserting the prerogatives of the department in foreign policy.

Even with these negative developments, the department's operational responsibilities continued to expand from the 1950s onward, as U.S. interests continued to expand. Its new tasks included promotion of U.S. exports, concessional sales of agricultural commodities, narcotics control, allocation of military and developmental aid, inspection and licensing of airline routes, cooperation in the peaceful application of atomic energy, conduct of scientific and technological exchange programs and cultural and educational activities, and coordination of international monetary policy.

In 1981, the United States maintained relations with 144 nations and was participating in approximately 46 international organizations. In 1946 there were 4,285 Foreign Service officers and staff members; in 1981 there were over 9,000. The United States is conducting foreign relations in the 1980s with almost the same number of Foreign Service personnel as it had in 1959, when it maintained relations with only 85 nations.[14]

David Trask, director of the department's Office of the Historian, notes some of the problems that continue to reduce departmental effectiveness:

> The turmoil of recent years, comparable to prior experiences during periods of basic change in the international setting, poses certain challenges for the immediate future, all of which have materialized in different forms in the past:
>
> The Department still lacks a domestic constituency comparable to those that support most Cabinet-level agencies, and it does not seem likely that one will emerge in the foreseeable future. . . .
>
> The Department is still without an effective means of insuring an appropriate role in policy-making. . . .
>
> The administrative cumbersomeness of the Department sometimes prevents it from providing cogent and timely advice, one of the reasons why a number of Presidents have turned elsewhere for counsel on important policy matters.[15]

The department will continue to be scrutinized by Congress and the public regarding the degree of its effectiveness in managing U.S. foreign policy. The challenges to that policy are substantial; the burdens of responsibility of the career Foreign Service to meet those challenges are heavy; the ability of the senior managers to efficiently manage a department still subject to political influence, especially at the policymaking level, is uncertain. What is certain is that tensions and antagonisms are built into the bureaucratic process in Washington and often become manifest in the quest for influence over U.S. foreign policy.

The growing complexity of international affairs and U.S. leadership of the Western Alliance have added fuel to the contest between the department and the NSC and its competition with the Pentagon, the Treasury Department, and the Commerce Department, as well as other government departments for the ear of the president on crucial foreign policy questions. There has been contentiousness before, especially in times of crisis, and it will undoubtedly continue. But for the Department of State, the challenge and the desire to play the primary role in the management of U.S. foreign policy are ever present, the challengers ever more powerful. The department cannot be complacent, even though it has a highly trained and experienced corps of career officers upon whom to rely for counsel, for policy recommendations, and for effective management. When the career service teams up with a strong secretary of state who has a close working relationship with the president, the department can produce the kinds of results that will have a major, positive effect on U.S. foreign policy. Without such an effective working combination, the department's leadership role in the foreign policy process will be eroded, resulting in low morale and some confusion among U.S. allies. As one prominent Japanese diplomat put it, "Until the State Department can free itself from undue political influence and become a truly career department with career officers in policy-making positions, the problems that have troubled the Department over the years in the management of foreign policy will continue to exist."[16]

The Postwar Foreign Service Officer

Despite the uncertain role of the State Department in managing U.S. diplomacy, there does appear to be a new mood in the corridors—an upbeat spirit that one senses upon returning to Foggy Bottom. A greater propensity for litigious behavior is evident, and due process is a solidly entrenched principle. The American Foreign Service Association (AFSA), the labor union representing the Foreign Service, had its mandate for collective bargaining regularized in law through the Foreign Service Act of 1980 and is maturing as a bargaining unit. Wives of Foreign Service officers are demanding and getting greater recognition for their role in the system and are seeking to supplement the family budget by part-time or full-time employment at posts where their husbands are stationed. (The United States has recently concluded agreements with several countries allowing reciprocal employment opportunities for wives of diplomats.) There is a general tightening of regulations for time in class (TIC), which always sends nervous tremors throughout the service.[17]

But despite these innovations, constancy is a characteristic of the U.S. Foreign Service, a service that sometimes seems immune to change by law or regulation. The system continues to be based on the merit principle. Competition for promotion is still the heartbeat of the Foreign Service. Young officers, especially, have high expectations, and they demand and are getting ambassadorial assignments and office director and country director positions. Like his Japanese counterpart, today's Foreign Service officer considers himself part of an elite, possessed of those special qualifications that set him apart from his fellow bureaucrats in other government departments. He still believes he will have the best chance of getting the choice assignment and moving up the career ladder if he politicks intensely with his friends in the powerful geographic bureaus. He still emphasizes the concept of service, but perhaps a little less so than his predecessors. He is playing the bureaucratic game very much as his older colleagues did in the 1970s, but he is armed with a grievance procedure that guarantees due process when he feels injured by an "unfair" efficiency report.

Tradition and Change

Tradition may be less strong in the United States than in Japan, but it helps the U.S. diplomat to preserve his ties with the past. The secretary of state and his senior advisers still occupy the same suite of offices on the seventh floor of the State Department building as they have since the 1960s, and the regional bureau assistant secretaries and the senior managers of the personnel system are still within easy reach on the floor below. The department continues to provide a home for the Agency for International Development (AID) and the U.S. Arms Control and Disarmament Agency (a separate agency whose director reports directly to the secretary of state and serves as principal adviser on arms control and disarmament to the secretary and the president). Changes in administration still bring predictable confusion to the executive levels of the department; with newly arrived political leaders often harboring suspicions about the loyalty of the Foreign Service to the new administration.

On revisiting the State Department after a long absence, one senses that stability and constancy, the bureaucrat's two most cherished principles, remain firmly entrenched in the system. But there is also a restlessness, a desire for change, influenced in part by social and economic permutations. Inflation has made living in many posts difficult and costly, and terrorism has created new conditions of service that test the courage and fortitude of the Foreign Service officer and his family. (The murder of a U.S. military officer of midlevel rank in Paris in 1980 suggests that terrorists may be targeting in on less senior people.) The continued relatively small number of women and minorities in the ranks of the career service rankles those affected and has brought remonstrances from AFSA to accelerate recruitment of women and minorities. Finally, the younger Foreign Service officers seem to be less deferential to authority, more insistent on management accountability for personnel actions, and less reluctant to resort to litigation in seeking redress for a perceived injustice.

Much of the demand for change that led to enactment of the Foreign Service Act of 1980 (see Appendix B) was triggered by the shifting mood of Foreign Service officers toward the service and their role in it. A combination of circumstances moved the FSOs, the department, and Congress to press for a new Foreign Service act to replace the act of 1946, which was losing its effectiveness. On June 21, 1979, in his opening testimony before the joint meeting of the House Subcommittee on International Operations of the Committee on Foreign Affairs and the Subcommittee on the Post Office and Civil Service, Secretary of State Cyrus Vance explained that the 1946 act could no longer meet the changed circumstances of the Foreign Service.[18]

Equipped with a charter for managing diplomacy, charged with a determination to fend off competition for primacy in foreign affairs, and assured of a continual flow of top-rate candidates into the Foreign Service, the department is facing the challenges of the future.

2

THE HUMAN FACTOR IN DIPLOMACY

THE TYPICAL FOREIGN SERVICE OFFICER IN JAPAN AND THE UNITED STATES joined the diplomatic service for generally the same reasons—some idealistic, others pragmatic; moved up the career ladder from junior through midlevel to senior status but with different ground rules governing the ascent; and was exposed to many of the joys and frustrations that accompany the choice of a bureaucratic career. Diplomats in both countries may differ in their attitudes toward the service, their diplomatic styles, and their working conditions, but they share a dedication to their profession and to the goal of diplomacy: a peaceful world for all.

Choosing a Diplomatic Career in Japan

In Japan, some aspiring young diplomats have been influenced in their choice of career by families and friends; others are excited by the prospect of living abroad and experiencing new cultures. Some desire the prestige and glamour of being a diplomat, others want to work for peace, and still others want specifically to serve Japan. Different motivations and emotions are involved in making the ultimate choice.

One young career officer, whose father was a former Japanese ambassador and whose two brothers had chosen the private sector, told me that his objective in joining the Foreign Service was to be in the public service and to work for peace. A less important but still prominent consideration in his mind was the desire to become an ambassador like his father.

When I met with nineteen young Foreign Service officers (including two women) undergoing training at the ministry's Foreign Service Training Institute in June 1982, I specifically asked them why they had chosen a diplomatic career. One young man said he had always been interested in foreign affairs and wished to pursue his interests through a career in the Foreign Service; another said that he had always wanted to travel and to experience the challenge of new cultures and languages and that the ministry provided this opportunity; a third replied rather acidly that he had chosen a public service career as the best way of putting distance between himself and the business sector; he was completely disenchanted with the emphasis on materialism and the growing commercialism of Japanese society. One of the women said that public service would free her from the discrimination against women that often exists in private business and would give her an opportunity to engage in cultural exchanges with representatives of other countries. A rather intense young man said he wanted to be involved in the policymaking process, to make a contribution to Japanese foreign policy at a time when that policy was undergoing change. He was unsure exactly how he could make this contribution but wanted to prepare himself for such responsibility nevertheless. Another young man said his sole reason for joining the ministry was that he detested the policy of apartheid and had decided that the only way he could do anything about it was to become a diplomat. When I suggested that such a single-minded crusade might limit his career or create difficulties for the ministry, he seemed surprised.

One young man replied rather diffidently that he joined because he had been under some pressure from family and friends to enter the legal profession but had no desire to do so. Besides, he said, lawyers are not as important as diplomats in Japanese society. The last young officer to comment said he chose the ministry because he had friends in the Foreign Service, and they had persuaded him to take the examination. He was glad that he had.

I received interesting answers and impressions when I asked, "What do you hope to achieve in your career?" As the group was composed of twelve career and seven noncareer officers, the answers tended to reflect the differences in status of the two groups. For example, all career officers said that they expected to become ambassadors. Noncareer officers were rather vague on this point and emphasized developing a specialty. The majority of both groups said they were indifferent to promotions at this early stage in their careers; they just wanted to do the best they could. When I pointed out to the two female officers that the overwhelming majority of officers were men and that there was only one woman ambassador in the service, they did not appear to be impressed and reiterated their determination to compete

on an equal footing with men.[1] Career officers wanted to be generalists and
noncareer officers wanted to be specialists, though both groups seemed a
little unsure about the meaning of generalist and specialist. Most officers,
whether career or noncareer, wanted an early assignment in a geographic
bureau, believing that these bureaus provided the best opportunity for
substantive work.

These young men and women appeared to be dedicated and determined. Although they had joined for different reasons and had different
career aspirations, all seemed united in the belief that the diplomatic service
was a respected profession and that they would be serving in an area that
could profoundly influence the course of Japanese society.

Most young career officers who had been in the service for four or five
years had similar hopes for the future. They still spoke of the nobility of
public service, of the importance of foreign policy to Japan's future, and of
their own role in the process. Older officers (those who had been in the
service for over five years), who had begun to understand the realities of
bureaucratic life, spoke of the need to plan careers carefully in order to
qualify for appointment to the coveted posts of ambassador or director
general of a bureau; they were more pragmatic in looking at themselves and
their careers. Yet these men, too, had a deep sense of the importance of
public service and of the excitement and challenge of participating in the
policymaking process.

Sons of Foreign Service officers tend to follow in the career paths of their
fathers, for a number of reasons. These men generally have a good command of foreign languages because much of their young lives has been spent
in foreign countries, going to foreign schools, and experiencing foreign
cultures. They have grown accustomed to diplomatic life—its perquisites,
its excitement, its challenges, and its prestige. They have noted the important role their fathers have played in supporting and furthering Japanese
foreign policy interests, and many have received guidance from their
fathers concerning a career in the diplomatic service. Thus they have
gradually come to accept the notion of a Foreign Service career for themselves. About a third of career officers have relatives who have been or are in
the Foreign Service.

For youths desiring careers in the Foreign Service, the most formidable
obstacle is the entrance examination. Those attending the universities of
Tokyo, Kyoto, Keio, Waseda, or Hitotsubashi seem to be more successful in
passing this examination than their contemporaries in other universities.

Regardless of the university attended, preparation for the examination
requires long hours of study, with little opportunity for recreation. The
result, according to one newspaper reporter, is that young men entering the
foreign ministry are not physically vigorous because they have had so little

time for sports. This reporter believes a strong body is as important as a strong mind, because living and working abroad, especially in hardship posts, put a strain on the endurance of career officers. He advocates that the entrance examination carry a section testing the physical condition of a candidate.

The U.S. Foreign Service Officer

The motivations of young Americans for choosing a career in the Foreign Service are complex and highly personal, and they are almost the same as those of young Japanese—travel, the opportunity to work for peace and to influence U.S. foreign policy, the excitement and challenge of new cultures, the security of government employment, the prestige of being a diplomat (although this may be a questionable benefit inasmuch as many Americans rate their diplomats about midway on the career "prestige" scale), and a chance to enrich one's professional life through advanced training and assignments to state and local government institutions and to corporations and professional organizations.

To a lesser extent than in Japan, there is the influence of family and friends. A father who wants his son or daughter to be an engineer, chemist, or concert pianist will very likely discourage any ambition toward a diplomatic career; the young business major at a university such as Yale or Columbia might be persuaded by his or her roommate to join a computer company rather than take the Foreign Service Entrance Examination.

Social science majors, particularly, may lean toward a career in the State Department, especially if they have a faculty for and/or an interest in such subjects as political science, history, and international relations and an aptitude for foreign languages. The condition of the economy and the "popularity" of a career also determine the career choices of young men and women.

Individuals who have experienced wars—in Korea and Vietnam, especially—and have become convinced of the futility of military conflict may choose the Foreign Service out of a conviction that the best way to settle disputes between nations is through diplomacy. Even though living and working conditions abroad are difficult and sometimes hazardous, the number of young Americans applying to take the Foreign Service Entrance Examination continues to grow.

According to a senior State Department official with whom I spoke on January 25, 1982, of the candidates for the Foreign Service in 1981, 98 percent had bachelor's degrees, 48 percent had master's degrees, 10 percent had doctor of philosophy degrees, and 10 percent had law degrees; 30

percent were women and 25 percent were members of minority groups. Many had worked at the professional level for about three years before taking the examination. The average age of these candidates was 29. However, there is no age limit for candidates for the Foreign Service. For example, a 42-year-old retired U.S. Air Force colonel took and passed the Foreign Service Entrance Examination and was given a probationary appointment at grade 5, which is one grade above the most junior entry level. (Junior officers are generally tenured at age 33 and enter the senior ranks at ages 45–50.)

Most successful candidates have graduated from a four-year college or university, and most have degrees in the social sciences. Their study program probably included courses in U.S. history, government, literature, economics, and the arts, as well as international relations and international law. Work experience, especially abroad, is also helpful. Knowledge of a foreign language is not a prerequisite to initial appointment as an untenured junior officer, but an individual must meet the language requirements before tenure is given. The ability to speak and write effectively is also essential for a successful Foreign Service career. A large part of diplomacy involves communication—enunciating the position of the United States on current issues to foreign governments and peoples, reporting to Washington on significant developments in other countries, and preparing policy or program papers. Therefore, drafting skills, sound organization of ideas, and persuasive presentation of recommendations are essential.

Individuals are entering the Foreign Service from a variety of backgrounds. Fewer have military experience than previously, and some are entering later in life. Most are more assertive than their older colleagues and less inclined to hide their ambitions; they are more open about their desire to become ambassadors at age 35 and deputy assistant secretaries at age 40. They are also more determined to hold management accountable for its actions, and less deferential to authority.

The FSO of the 1980s is more confident of career success, more determined to achieve success as early as possible, more ready to take career risks, and more concerned about getting ahead and "working the system" to his advantage than his older colleagues. Intense competition often gives rise to aggressiveness, manifesting an intense desire to move ahead at whatever cost. But this is a fact of life in the Foreign Service (as well as in corporate and professional life), and sooner or later it is recognized as such by young FSOs. Most older FSOs feel that younger officers are less service oriented today—that they are more prone to put self ahead of service and to give rights greater weight than responsibilities such as personal sacrifice and duty to country. Such a tendency is perhaps symptomatic of the society that nurtured and educated them, and therefore this may appear too harsh an indictment, but in some respects, today's FSO has given credibility to this assessment.

All FSOs recognize that a good efficiency report is crucial to career advancement and that they will not get a good report if they are mavericks or insensitive to their supervisor's responsibilities. They also know that they generally will not get assigned to the position of country director in an important geographic bureau unless they are well and favorably known to the assistant secretary or the deputy assistant secretary of that bureau. Such a reputation is not built upon acts that reflect irreverence for authority or indifference to one's superiors.

The FSO who has lived most of his life abroad has much to learn when he is cast back into the role of a Washington bureaucrat and must compete with non–Foreign Service types who have spent most of their lives in the Washington bureaucracy and know how to survive and at times even to win. The bright, mature, and pugnacious FSOs exhibit some durability in meeting Washington's challenges, but others, less suited for the contest, soon begin to make plans to return to the sanctuary of an overseas post.

The young officer must complete a probationary period of up to 48 months and must pass a junior officer threshold examination before gaining permanent status. Most junior officers succeed after the second try, and over 90 percent of them gain tenure.

After gaining tenure, the FSO is generally assured of promotion until he reaches class 1, when he must again pass a threshold examination to enter the Senior Foreign Service. This system is intended to give the FSO some measure of employment security during the early and midcareer periods of service. Rapid promotions are still allowed for the more able and slower promotions are given to the less able; job security is ensured from junior threshold to senior threshold, making possible a 20- to 25-year career. Few will be selected out because of marginal performance, and TIC is a real concern only for those in the Senior Foreign Service. Officers who retire at class 1 (roughly the equivalent of colonel in the U.S. Army or captain in the U.S. Navy) are assured of an annuity under the Foreign Service Retirement and Disability System.

The new FSO will wonder about the rewards of remaining a generalist, of the new and uncertain challenges to be met on becoming a specialist, whether to accept a mediocre efficiency report or to present a grievance, how to succeed at "office politics," and, most importantly, how to leave an imprint on U.S. foreign policy. Periods of uncertainty, frustration, doubt, exhilaration, satisfaction, and depression are inevitable as the career picks up momentum. Each young FSO will at least have the comfort of knowing that his peers are experiencing the same moods.

Settled by midcareer, the FSO will be thinking more of his assignment patterns, their relationship to his promotions, and the substantive nature of his work. (Conal affiliation will largely determine the substantive nature of his work, the promotion track he will be on, and his chances of being assigned to executive positions in the State Department or to ambassadorships. The four cones, or functional groups, are political, economic, consular, and administrative.) He will also give some thought to the education of his children and the family budget (one does not get rich in the Foreign Service), and whether he should take the senior threshold examination or retire at class 1 and begin a new career. This latter decision will probably be one of the most difficult he will have to make.

If he passes the senior officer threshold examination and enters the Senior Foreign Service, he will take on increasingly heavy responsibilities, will be driven by the desire to cap his career with an appointment as ambassador, assistant secretary, or deputy assistant secretary, and will feel the heat of competition more intensely than at any other time in his career. At age 65 he will have to retire; he will have mixed feelings about leaving but if he is still reasonably healthy, he will be looking for new challenges in the private sector. Two exceptions to retirement at age 65 should be noted: (1) if the officer is in a position appointed by the president with advice and consent of the Senate, that officer may continue to serve until that appointment is terminated, and (2) if the Secretary of State determines it to be in the public interest, the officer required to retire at age 65 can be retained on active duty for a period not to exceed five years.

For officers who have experienced these realities, that is, who have known the highs and lows of gained and lost promotions, who have completed key bureau assignments or tour of duty assignments to the White House, who have filled visa officer slots in Latin America or have been posted to a branch office of the Office of Security, Patrick Linehan's description of the service strikes a responsive chord.[2] Flexibility, common sense, rational expectations, honesty with self—these are some of the qualities that increase the likelihood of survival and promise career fulfillment.

Career Progression in Japan and the United States

A Japanese Foreign Service officer's career progression, like that of his U.S. counterpart, is three-phased: entry as a junior officer, transition to midcareer status, and retirement as a senior diplomat.

The young Japanese officer begins his career at about age 23 and at salary grade 7, and his first assignment is to spend four months at the Foreign Service Training Institute, where he learns about the Foreign

Service, the foreign ministry, diplomatic etiquette, and related matters. He also spends considerable time improving his foreign language capability.

He then moves to the foreign ministry, where he is generally assigned to on-the-job training in a functional or geographic bureau. As a career officer, he will work in the general affairs section of a division, learning how to deal with substantive issues. His superiors are very conscious of their responsibility to see that he begins to build the experience that will forever mark him as a career generalist.

Upon completion of ten months of such duty, he is sent abroad for more training, at the conclusion of which he may be assigned to the embassy located in the country of his study, or he may be returned to the ministry for work in the division with responsibility for the country where he trained. If assigned to an embassy, he may work as an ambassador's assistant or as an economic or political officer concerned with general affairs, or he may work in the protocol section of the embassy. He will normally be in such a position for eighteen months to two years and will then be transferred to the foreign ministry.

Grades 7 and 6 are considered to be junior officer grades. During his approximately seven years of service in these grades, he will very likely get married and begin his family, and will deepen his commitment to the ministry and his diplomatic career as he becomes more immersed in his daily work. His self-confidence will grow as he takes on more responsibility; he will develop his diplomatic skills and will become wiser in the ways of the bureaucracy as he observes with growing attention the art of "getting things done" in the traditional way. He will begin to think about and plan his career, aiming always for the important positions of division chief or director general, or a prestigious ambassadorial post. He will also become ever more conscious of his position as a member of his class, and his career moves will be planned and carried out not as individual initiatives but as cooperative efforts with other members of his class to enhance the reputation and stature of the class. He will be observant of tradition and custom— deferential when necessary and conscious of the importance of harmony in an office. He will be cautious in carrying out his responsibilities and patient despite early career frustrations. Upon graduation to midcareer status, he will be ready for new challenges and responsibilities.

The U.S. Foreign Service officer enters the service in a probationary status. At the outset, and on the basis of the officer's education and prior experience, he is assigned a tentative primary skill code indicating a cone placement. The tentative designation may be changed to a permanent skill code in the same cone after the officer is tenured. If an officer wishes to change his cone and skill code, he must apply to his career development officer, who then refers the request to a cone panel for decision. Once the skill code and cone have been determined, the young probationary officer begins to work toward and train for the day he must pass the junior officer threshold test. His probationary appointment can last a maximum of 48 months; if he does not pass the test and receive tenure by the forty-fourth month, his appointment expires and he must leave the service. When the junior officer career candidate who does pass the junior officer threshold test receives tenure, he is at grade 4 and usually in his early thirties.[3]

The average probationary FSO spends eight months in training at the Foreign Service Institute in Rosslyn, Virginia, before being assigned abroad. The initial overseas tour includes not only a consular assignment but a minimum one-year assignment in the officer's own cone. The latter assignment is an important step in his effort to gain tenure. Another requirement for achieving tenure is to pass an S-3, R-3 (S=speaking, R=reading; maximum proficiency =5) test in a "world" language (French, Spanish, German), or an S-2, R-2 test in a "hard" (difficult) language, such as Japanese, Chinese, or Arabic. Probationary officers without these language capabilities must take a 20-week course in a world language or a 25-week course in a hard language and be tested before assignment to their first post abroad. Wives of probationary officers are given 12 weeks of language study, and those with small children are provided funds for baby-sitters so they may attend language classes.

The initial training/assignment model for the junior officer career candidate includes FSO orientation for six and a half weeks; area studies for two weeks; study of antiterrorism tactics for two days; and functional training (administration core, tools of analytic reporting), language training, and bureau orientation for up to six months—all in the State Department. If time permits, there is a department assignment within the eighteen-month maximum period.

In determining the young officer's first overseas assignment, the Bureau of Personnel takes into account the work history, interests, and educational background of the candidate and, to the extent possible, proposes a limited number of placements based on the officer's existing area and/or functional knowledge. The assignment finally selected will be to a position in a large post where the candidate can profit from the tutelage of an experienced Foreign Service supervisor who is an expert in the candidate's functional area.

A junior officer career candidate is not expected to possess complete familiarity with the U.S. Foreign Service and therefore, whenever possible, is assigned to a position that will provide the most immediate and in-depth exposure to the full range of its work.

There are also differences in the midcareer phase of the Japanese and U.S. Foreign Service officer. When the Japanese FSO is promoted to grade 5 at about age 30, he will have completed his apprenticeship and will be ready to take on heavier responsibilities. He will spend the next seven years as a midcareer officer (grades 5, 4, and 3) working as a senior member of his division's general affairs section and eventually as deputy director of the division. If serving overseas, he may be assigned the position of first secretary specializing in political or economic affairs. During this stage of his career, he will come to understand more clearly the career system, his role in it, and what he needs to do to advance his career. After ten years in the service, he now has a sense of where he is going. He knows he is not competing for promotions but for assignments to prestigious posts. Such assignments indicate that he is being groomed to be chief of an important division or ambassador to an influential post and remind him to be careful, to work harder, and to strive for positions in divisions, bureaus, and embassies where there are influential division chiefs, directors general, and ambassadors. He has studied the successful careers of former and present ministry leaders and understands why these individuals have been successful. He recognizes the importance of a knowledge of the West.

In this phase, the FSO on an overseas assignment may begin to place family ahead of career (the attitude of *my home shugi*). Several senior officers described this attitude as detrimental to an officer's career and to ministry goals. It is, said one officer in the Minister's Secretariat, an unfortunate outgrowth of Japan's prosperity. A former career officer who had left the service in midcareer said that some career officers are more interested in material comforts than in dedicated service, and as a result, my home shugi is becoming a more pervasive influence. Of special importance to a midcareer officer are the approbation and support of important senior officials in the ministry. In *Mirror, Sword, and Jewel*, Kurt Singer describes the importance of the patron-client (*oyabun-kobun*) relationship in the Japanese social structure. He observes that the typical Japanese is acutely sensitive to differences in rank and power and will often put his services at the disposal of a potential patron. Singer points out that one can often determine a man's capability by who his patron is and on what clients the patron can rely.[4]

Merely having a strong patron is not enough to assure a successful career. The ambitious career officer must demonstrate his ability on the job (for example, by performing well as chief of an important division) before he can expect either the overt or covert support of a strong and influential benefactor. According to a former high official in the Japanese United Nations delegation, relationships established by career officers in their early assignments (such as that between a *kachō*, or division chief, and a subordinate) often determine future assignments and thus an officer's career.

Another important consideration for the aspiring division chief is who his supervisors were in the earlier stages of his career when impressions of his ability were first registered. If these impressions were favorable, the young officer can feel confident that he is building a good reputation and probably has a cadre of supporters who will help him advance to the top of the career ladder. If they were unfavorable, he may be in some career difficulty.[5]

Those promoted to kachō positions, especially in major geographic bureaus such as North American Affairs, Asian Affairs, or European and Oceanic Affairs, can reasonably expect to move on after four to six years to either deputy director general in a major bureau or minister or deputy chief of mission in a large embassy. If a division chief is especially able, he may be retained in his position for several tours of duty. But eventually he will move on, secure in the knowledge that he is on the right track for appointment to a major ambassadorship in the area of his language and area expertise or to the position of director general of an important bureau.

The midcareer officer in the tenth or eleventh year of his career can judge his prospects for advancement to senior positions with more clarity and precision. He knows that the career service is a relatively small, compact service with each officer privy to some information about the other; he also is able to judge the quality of his competition by the assignments his peers receive, by the degree of supportiveness of the patron, by the social prominence of his wife, and by the "corridor reputations" of his colleagues. At times he worries that he will not get to the top; he wonders whether an assignment to Africa or Latin America, for example, is a signal by the system that he has reached the summit of his career. But he is careful to keep these anxieties to himself lest the members of his class think him a self-promoter rather than a supporter of the class. Finally, after deciding for himself whether he has done all he can to advance his career—by evaluating his performance record, his loyalty to his class, his personality and the strength of his marriage, and whether he has former supervisors who support his career objectives as well as a sympathetic and influential patron who is his advocate in dealing with management—he waits for the decision of management.

In the midcareer phase of his career, the U.S. Foreign Service officer can look forward to ten or fifteen years' service in the middle grades (4 through 1) and some four to six different assignments. During this period he is expected to develop solid expertise in his functional field (cone) and have at least two assignments in his primary field. In addition, he will have at least one assignment outside his cone and will gain some experience in policy development and management of people and resources as well as a specific language and area expertise.

He will seek a bureau identification or assignment to a country director-ate or to the political or economic section of an embassy in his geographic area of specialization. His observation that officers of his grade and age are becoming ambassadors at various posts will spur him to attempt to obtain the right assignment and the right sponsor in management so that he can secure an ambassadorship for himself an an early age.

One sure way of gaining the desired ambassadorial post is to become indispensable to his ambassador and to catch the eye of the assistant secretary or deputy assistant secretary of his bureau. But he must be careful because his supervisor, the country director, also desires an ambassadorship and does not wish to be upstaged by his subordinate. It is a delicate game for the midcareer officer to play, a game in which the rewards can be considerable (such as a senior policymaking position in the State Department), but the career punishment severe if there is a misstep along the way. If he is bright, ambitious, circumspect, ready to seize responsibility and opportunity when presented, alert to the shifts in the relative power positions of the senior officers in the bureau—and lucky—he has a reasonably good chance of moving up the career ladder at a fast pace. He knows the value of language and area expertise in a geographic sector important to U.S. foreign policy (such as the Soviet Union, Japan, or the Middle East), of developing a corridor reputation as a "comer" in the service: a hard worker, a good drafter, a good analyst of political trends, and a team player who is (outwardly, at least) indifferent to career advancement.

Officers with these demonstrated abilities generally reach the senior threshold in their early forties. They represent the top 10 percent of the midcareer officer group and are quicky recognized as such by the Selection Board, which evaluates all officers annually for promotion. They seldom, if ever, discuss their careers with a career development officer, but instead rely on their bureaus to ensure that they move ahead at a faster-than-average pace. They are sought after, and some cannot resist being rather smug about it. On the other hand, they do not spare themselves, often putting in long hours when on an assignment in Washington, and perhaps even longer hours when posted abroad. By applying their knowledge, they make substantial contributions to foreign policy. Their greatest moments of frustration are when their advice is ignored by their seniors. They experience personal triumph when they see their recommendations incorporated into a policy paper going to the White House or when they find that a particular outstanding report or evaluation they have written has been sent to the president for his evening reading. This is how corridor reputations are built; this is how the service rewards its top performers.

For the majority of midcareer officers, the political and economic cones are still considered the best avenues to advancement. Officers in the consular and administrative cones develop an attitude of resignation when they realize that they will not move as fast or as far as their colleagues. Some of them feel that it is enough to be an FSO—to have opportunities to serve in interesting posts, to absorb new cultures, and to gain new insights. For others, this realization causes career frustration, and they resolve to leave the service when they qualify for an annuity, to seek a career in the private sector.

Promotions do, of course, come along for midcareer officers in the four cones, with political officers receiving the largest share because they are in the majority. The pace of promotions depends on performance. Submarginal officers must be identified by Selection Boards, but several appeal avenues are available to them before they are involuntarily retired. The consensus of most personnel officers is that few officers will be selected out under the 1980 Foreign Service Act.

Midcareer officers are mainly concerned about promotions, assignments, and future career prospects. Why was I not promoted by the Selection Board? Why did another FSO get that job as no. 2 in the political section at the embassy when I was led to believe that I was the top choice? Is my career on track, and is it too late for redirection? What should I do about the efficiency report that alluded to my lack of decisiveness? Why was I low-ranked? What is a promotable assignment? Should I invest two years to learn a hard language? How can I remain competitive with officers in substantive assignments when I am in training? Should I change cones?

Their apprehensions are probably no different than the uncertainties felt by midlevel executives in the corporate world. When in their forties, many individuals experience self-analysis and self-doubt, and many FSOs become uncertain about their career advancement. For most midcareer officers, this period passes, and they settle into working hard at the job of diplomacy. When the promotion to class 1 finally comes, they are in a position to evaluate their chances of promotion to the Senior Foreign Service.[6]

Remarkable differences between Japan and the United States are also evident in the third phase of the diplomat's career. At age 37, after about seven years as a midcareer officer, the Japanese FSO and the other members of his class are promoted to grade (class) 2. For him this promotion has special significance because it means that he has also been assigned as a division chief in a geographic bureau. He has passed the critical test; he is now reasonably certain of obtaining an important ambassadorship, or an appointment to a post in a major consulate general prior to such an ambassadorship, or an assignment as a director general. He is now considered a senior officer, albeit a junior one, and since he will face growing competition for the limited number of top positions, he must strive ever harder to achieve his career goals. His performance as a division chief will be a determinant of his success.

The senior officer group comprises classes 2 and 1 and the special Designated Class (the highest class a career officer can reach in the service). Officers can remain in the senior category until retirement at ages 61–63. Time in grade from class 2 to class 1 is usually six years, and from class 1 to the Designated Class, four years. After reaching the Designated Class, officers can remain for another approximately fifteen years, moving between the ministry and overseas posts.

In 1981, a class 2 officer could contemplate being assigned to one of the following positions: ambassador (totaling 108), consul general (48), division chief (63), director general (10), senior deputy director general, or shingikan (14), and junior deputy director general, or sanjikan (11).

Officers fluent in English, French, German, or Spanish generally have a better chance of obtaining choice assignments abroad and important positions in the major geographic bureaus. At this point in his career the officer, after having served two successful tours as an important kachō, will have established the professional credentials necessary to carry him further up the career ladder. The pattern is discernible: from kachō to deputy director general of an important bureau, and then either to a senior position in a major embassy (deputy chief of mission or minister) or to the position of consul general in a country of major importance to Japan. Then he may return to Tokyo as director general of a major bureau or as an assistant deputy vice-minister, or he may fill one of several senior positions in the Minister's Secretariat. A return to Tokyo at this stage in his career is especially welcome because it allows him to provide a Japanese education for his children; he can be with family and friends and can live a reasonably comfortable life with the perquisites accorded his rank.

The senior officer with less ability can generally expect to receive an ambassadorship to a small country or an appointment as consul general in a medium-sized post. In status-conscious Japan, such assignments are a deep disappointment and are often an embarrassment to the officer concerned, because they are a signal to him as well as to his class and colleagues that his career has peaked and that he must be satisfied with less important positions. He has two choices. He can stay the course, accepting mediocre assignments at home and overseas, or he can contemplate early retirement. The latter option is not always as attractive as it may seem. Even the more successful senior officers find that good retirement positions are often difficult to obtain, so the officer contemplating early retirement whose career is not judged to have been entirely successful according to the tough standards of the Japanese bureaucracy may ultimately decide to remain with the ministry for reasons of financial security.

For those so-called junior senior officers, the long years of working, developing skills, and building a performance record culminate in a series of assignments that indicate either further career advancement or a leveling off. Because the career corps is relatively small and because an officer's reputation often precedes him as he moves up the career ladder, a consensus begins to build within the system early in his career concerning his ability as a diplomat. If his record is outstanding, he becomes one of the front-runners for the coveted ambassadorships to the United States or Great Britain or for the position of deputy vice-minister or vice-minister.

The U.S. Foreign Service officer enters the Senior Foreign Service by passing the senior officer threshold examination. He has won promotion and now holds the rank of counselor (before the 1980 act, known as FSO-2). Because his TIC period has been shortened, he must either be promoted again within six years, be granted a limited career extension, or leave the service. He must compete strenuously for the promotable assignments. If he is a political officer, he must be assigned as a deputy chief of mission, a consul general, or an ambassador to have a good chance of surviving as a senior officer.

If he is in the top 10 percent of his class, he has little to worry about. If he is anywhere in the middle, he must rely on the recommendation of friends and of his parent bureau and especially the record he has compiled during his midcareer years to help him obtain promotable assignments. The officer worries that stretch assignments (senior positions occupied by select mid-career officers) will reduce his chances of obtaining promotable assignments. He is at times resentful that the personnel counselors did not fight hard enough to secure the necessary assignments for him, but he probably realizes, upon reflection, that it would not have been in his best career interest to be "forced" on an embassy or bureau.

The senior officer will spend considerable time with his senior career counselor in order to determine the right assignment. When I visited the State Department in January 1982 to observe the operation of the new system, I noted that it was business as usual for the senior personnel counselors, who were trying to arrange the right assignment for one FSO who had been without a job for three months; trying to persuade the bureau to support the assignment of another FSO to a particular embassy as deputy chief of mission; cajoling a reluctant FSO to be an administrative officer in a medium-sized African post; and explaining to a disappointed senior consular officer why the ambassador in a certain country wanted another officer as consul general. More personal attention must be given to senior officers, because fewer positions are available at the senior levels. Discussion, negotiation, persuasion, and arm-twisting are often necessary in working out assignments. Frustration and complaint are more prevalent in the senior ranks and are caused, no doubt, by more intense competition and by a shorter TIC period. A persistent complaint of many senior officers, especially those who believe themselves qualified for appointment as ambassadors, is that too many such appointments are going to political appointees.

Records of the American Foreign Service Association indicate that in the first two years of the Reagan administration, 100 people were appointed ambassadors at U.S. embassies. Of these, 48 were political appointees and 52 were career Foreign Service officers.

Whether they are appointed ambassadors or not, career FSOs are confronted with more stringent TIC regulations as a result of the 1980 act. The TIC limit for counselor-rank FSOs, as noted earlier, is six years, for minister counselors five years, and for career ministers four years. Upon expiration of TIC, members of the Senior Foreign Service can be considered by Selection Boards for limited career extensions of three years each. (Selection Boards meet annually and also evaluate Senior Foreign Service personnel for promotion or for selection out for substandard performance, and determine allocation of performance pay.) Management determines the number of extensions to be granted on the basis of State Department needs. Those not granted extensions must leave the service and are given an immediate annuity.

It remains to be seen how the senior officer system will work in terms of promotions, assignments, and limited career extensions. For senior officers, assignments still appear to be managed as before, but with perhaps more personal attention given to postings critical to an officer's TIC.

Different Requirements for Career Success in Japan and the United States

In both Japan and the United States, the Foreign Service places a high premium on service, loyalty to country, and dedication to hard work for the national polity; however, the different traditions in the two countries have resulted in establishment of different career patterns and imperatives for success.

In the Japanese Foreign Service, for example, the personnel system and the thinking of career officers focus more on the class than on the individual. Official records indicate the year of an officer's class, and statements (in the media and elsewhere) concerning his activities inevitably mention the class to which he belongs.

The officer, as a result of his education, training, and exposure to the influence of family and social custom, is conditioned to accept a subordinate role in relation to the group, although there are some signs, especially among today's youth, that the strength of dōki ishiki is beginning to wane.

The transition from family to school, to university, and to a professional career has an inevitability about it that transcends any notion of personal advancement at the expense of the group. The more senior an officer becomes, the more the game is played with an emphasis on ego constraint and harmony. The self-promoter, the overtly ambitious officer who denigrates competitors and embarrasses his class has no place in this system. Such behavior is simply not countenanced, and an officer so tempted soon feels heavy pressures to conform. If he accepts the edicts of custom, career damage will be minimal; if he does not, his career will be in jeopardy.

As an example of the unity and esprit de corps of a class, a senior officer said that if managers were to decide that 30 percent of the career officers in a particular class would probably not be promoted to the position of division chief or to an ambassadorship (a senior official in the Personnel Division said this could happen if, in the next decade, career officer recruitment were to increase from 25–27 to 30 or 35 individuals annually), class members would feel a deep sense of disappointment but would begin at once to maneuver to forestall such a development. To have nearly a third of the class fail to reach the position of kachō would be deeply embarrassing and would adversely affect the class reputation. This in turn would reflect unfavorably on each member of the class and could have unfortunate career consequences. To preserve the honor and stability of the class, members would work hard to ensure that every one would become a kachō.

The officer explained that promotion from one salary grade to another is less important to a careerist than the knowledge that his class was considered by senior managers to be the one that would produce the best deputy directors general and directors general of important bureaus. The deep satisfaction gained from such recognition is a clear indication of the allegiance to class.

During my interviews, I was often reminded of the importance of dōki ishiki for understanding the career thinking of a Japanese Foreign Service officer. It is an entirely different attitude from that prevailing in the State Department, one senior personnel officer said. Of course, Japanese officers are concerned about their careers and are ambitious to succeed, but this ambition is tempered by the knowledge that there is a right way and a wrong way to be ambitious. In the foreign ministry, one must disguise ambition, sublimate it to the higher motive of class identification. Only in this way will the officer move ahead in his career in accordance with the prescriptions of the system.

When the discussion turned to the impact on the system of vigorous competition for the positions of division chief and ambassador, one official appeared to hedge on the inviolability of dōki ishiki. He opined that the effect of heightened competition on an officer's loyalty to his class would depend to a considerable extent on whether he accepted such competition as an equitable way of choosing senior officers. There might be some erosion of the dedication some officers feel toward their class, but it would likely stop short of the alienation or "trench warfare" that often characterizes the competitiveness of the U.S. Foreign Service. He ventured that career officers are beginning to think more about their own careers and less about the reputation of their class, but it is difficult to estimate the strength of this trend.

It is my impression that dōki ishiki continues to be a dominant force, mainly because it is a manifestation of a societal tradition—that the group's interests transcend individual concerns. Contemporary Japanese society is becoming more atomized, and this eventually will change some of the ground rules for personal behavior, but today, despite perceptible social change, most Japanese tend to think of their society as oriented toward the group rather than the individual. The career corps in the ministry dutifully follows this tradition. Class identification is pervasive. Its motive force may diminish as a result of the growing competition for key posts, but it will do so gradually. Dōki ishiki is an institution, said one high official, that provides career officers with security, satisfaction, and a sense of belonging. It will continue to play a role in career development, though whether the allegiance of younger career officers will continue to be as strong is difficult to predict.

We have noted that prescriptions for success in the Japanese Foreign Service underscore the importance of a cooperative attitude to achieve harmony (wa). The kachō and his deputy set an example for the office staff. Careerists and noncareerists alike, despite the gulf separating them, tend to submerge personal anxieties and frustrations and work together for the good of the division. This is not always easy to do, especially for the noncareer officers, who sense their inferior status vis-à-vis career officers. Several noncareer officers I spoke to in a number of important divisions indicated with some resignation that there were few alternatives to cooperating to achieve harmony in order to further one's career. Both career and noncareer officers, they said, are prisoners of a system that requires observance of wa as an imperative for good office management. It is the Japanese way of doing things, accepted both in the government and in the private sector.

Most career officers have been thoroughly conditioned during adolescence and early adulthood to respect the tradition of wa in their family and university relationships. Hence these officers begin their professional lives with a regard for wa as a true and tested element of Japanese behavior.

During my years of observing the ministry and its personnel system, I found little evidence that the average career officer was willing to jeopardize his career by ignoring wa. Whatever their private feelings about the present state of their careers, most career officers showed a disposition to maintain good relations with colleagues. Their behavior toward noncareer employees often revealed an air of superiority, which I am sure privately grated on the nerves of noncareerists from time to time, but surface relations appeared to be harmonious.

It is usually difficult to detect strain in an office when you are an infrequent visitor. However, from comments offered by noncareer officers and by some unusually forthright and insightful careerists, I am certain that tensions exist, especially if the kachō leadership tends to be prejudiced against noncareer personnel. Such instances do not detract from the importance or relevance of wa but rather reinforce its essentiality.

An officer's feeling about his career success is increasingly being influenced by the attitude of my home shugi, and the two are not always compatible. This feeling that career is secondary is not limited to the ministry but is gaining currency throughout Japan, especially among younger workers. It is a reflection of the slow social change induced in part by the impact of modern industrial technology on Japanese society. A senior official in the Personnel Division told me that some career officers prefer not to take overseas assignments because they wish their families to enjoy the material comforts of Japan. He said that some young Japanese diplomats have indicated, rather subtly, that they are more concerned with success in their personal lives than with establishing a record of public service. A *Tokyo Shimbun* reporter also said that more young officers are opting to stay in Tokyo rather than go abroad, especially to less developed countries. When I asked him why these young men entered the ministry if they did not want to serve abroad, he shrugged and said that after they enter, they gain a clearer idea of living conditions abroad, and it is at this point that their attitude of my home shugi becomes evident.

That such an attitude could adversely affect an officer's career was made quite clear to me by a senior official in the Minister's Secretariat. While acknowledging that my home shugi was gaining more attention from the media and was becoming more prevalent among young Japanese, he said he believed that those holding such a view were in the minority. It is obvious, he said, that a career Foreign Service cannot be effective if officers will not serve abroad. Those officers refusing to accept overseas assignments would find their careers in jeopardy, for such behavior is completely inconsistent with the mission of the ministry. He believed that any such movement in the ministry would be effectively contained by the force of tradition and peer pressure.

In my discussions with young career officers, I received no intimations that they took my home shugi seriously. One officer said it was perhaps natural for a "modern Japanese husband" (his words) to think seriously about the welfare of his wife and children, but this did not necessarily mean he would fail to carry out his responsibilities as a Foreign Service officer. The title, he said, meant "foreign service," and when he and his colleagues entered the ministry they knew what they were doing and what their responsibilties were. Although they enjoy the comforts of Japan and want security and health for their families, they believe in public service and are willing to sacrifice to serve.

Statistics on officer refusal to serve abroad were unavailable. However, it is my impression, after talking with numerous officials, that the number of officers refusing—for any reason—is small. Usually some physical ailment is given as the explanation, and this has to be verified by a doctor. As one official put it, the aim of career officers is to serve their country; it is not in their nature to refuse to serve. Most with proclivities for my home shugi were screened out before appointment as Foreign Service officers.

On the way to the top, the U.S. Foreign Service officer is not concerned about class identification, subordinating himself to the group to which he belongs, or promoting office harmony to advance his career. Nor is he ready to restrain his drive for rapid promotion, to achieve career success at as early a stage as possible. He is a highly competitive person, grounded in his own individuality, flexible when flexibility is required, and generally unconcerned about his peers except to the extent that they represent competition for choice assignments. Although his Japanese counterpart is probably just as ambitious, both are playing by different ground rules that reflect differing cultures and mores.

In the United States, achieving career success is a stressful business. Manuals, monographs, and manuscripts are available in bookstores and libraries on such topics as how to succeed as a businessman and how to develop a winning personality. These do-it-yourself handbooks generally end up on the bookshelf at home or in the office after being given an initial and perhaps disappointing perusal. A very senior and wise FSO once told me that there are no panaceas for an ailing career; career success requires hard work, reasonable expectations, and a little luck. A young FSO might be somewhat impatient with such advice, preferring to trust the computer and his union, but the fact remains that the successful Foreign Service officer has had to work hard, plan his career carefully, be endowed with a good mind, some intellectual curiosity, and a sense of humor, and have a supportive family. Being in the right place at the right time also helps; many successful FSOs owe their rise in the service to such an enviable circumstance. But mastering the core diplomatic skills, having good friends in the right places, being a team player, serving on Selection Boards and various departmental and interdepartmental committees, speaking on U.S. foreign policy before citizens' groups, participating in extracurricular activities at the overseas post—these are the remedies for a career that seems on dead center.

In career development, increasing attention is being given to the family —to the wife who wishes to work (possibly as an FSO) at the post to which her husband is assigned, to the requirements of children's education, and to the more basic consideration of the family budget. And there are additional rewards to encourage the able and ambitious FSO: higher executive positions in the State Department and in overseas posts for younger officers, higher performance pay, and tighter TIC requirements. Implicit in the Foreign Service Act of 1980 and in the several hearings before Congress on the act was an emphasis on performance and ability as the determinants of success in the service. I sensed this also in talking with senior personnel officials charged with implementing the act and with AFSA members that greater weight will also be given to merit in developing the careers of FSOs. In a sense, this has always been so, as is clear from an analysis of the careers of former and present FSOs who have succeeded.

3

ORGANIZATION AND MANAGEMENT

M UCH HAS BEEN WRITTEN ABOUT THE SKILL AND IMAGINATION OF JAP-
anese managers and the application of management techniques to
corporate organization in Japan. Little is known about the organization and
management of the foreign ministry. The collective decision-making process, with heavy emphasis on achieving consensus, is still the principal
method of handling foreign policy issues. Strict adherence to seniority in the
promotion and assignment of officers remains unchanged. The system
rewards career and noncareer officers with automatic promotions to ambassadorships; merit plays only a marginal role, except in assignments to the
more prestigious posts. A strict demarcation has been imposed between
career and noncareer personnel. The discrimination against noncareer
personnel that has always existed (it takes a noncareer officer nearly twice as
long to be promoted as a career officer) is allowed to continue because to
impose change would be to break with tradition. The score on the entrance
examination determines the career path of officers for their entire professional lives.

The Ministry of Foreign Affairs is very proud of its past, of the elitism of
its career personnel, and of its role as the protector of Japanese foreign
policy interests—and rightfully so. It is remarkable that a relatively small
group of career officers (about 690 in 1980) has been able to steer Japan
clear of most of its foreign policy pitfalls. But the job is becoming too big for
the existing organization, and pressures are mounting for a change in
personnel policies.

At the Department of State, however, many important changes are taking place in personnel and management operations. Unlike the Japanese system, no distinction is made between career and noncareer personnel, decision-making does not have to achieve consensus and is sometimes more arbitrary, promotions are not automatic, and Foreign Service officers do not have as complete control over their destinies as do Japanese FSOs. Tradition is also less important. Allowing for these differences, however, there is much that is similar in the organization of the two foreign policy establishments. Both have bureau structures whose jurisdictions are defined geographically; both are concerned with achieving a proper balance in economic and political reporting from overseas posts, which are organized to reflect these priorities; and both are coming under increasing pressure to allocate resources in a more efficient manner.

Figure 1a
Organization of the Japanese Foreign Ministry

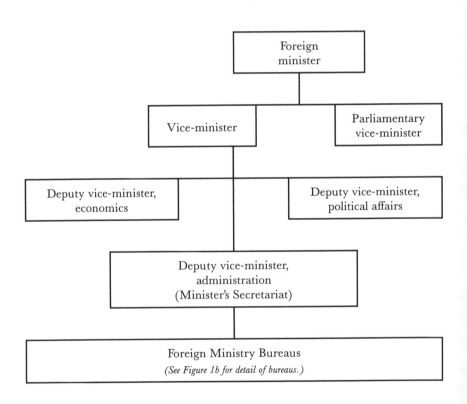

Figure 1b
Foreign Ministry Bureaus

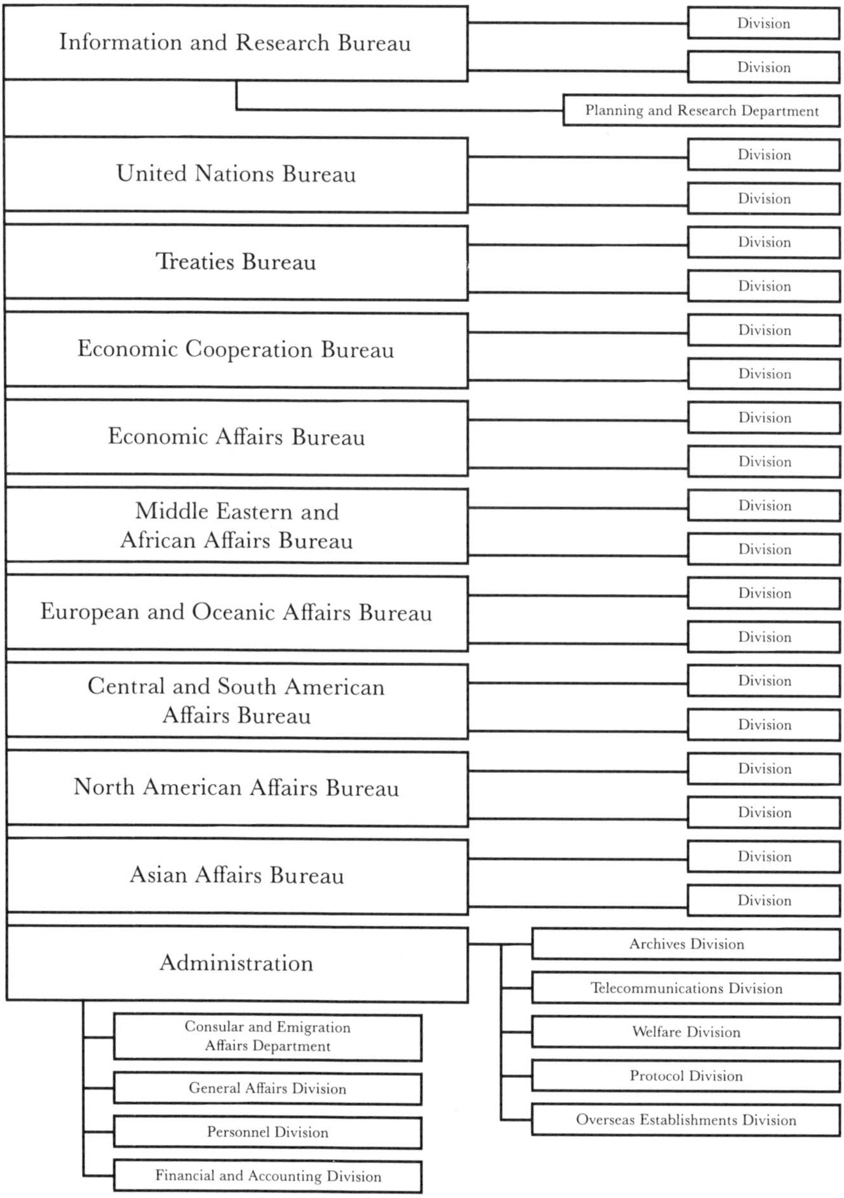

Bureau/Department	Divisions
Information and Research Bureau	Division / Division
Planning and Research Department	
United Nations Bureau	Division / Division
Treaties Bureau	Division / Division
Economic Cooperation Bureau	Division / Division
Economic Affairs Bureau	Division / Division
Middle Eastern and African Affairs Bureau	Division / Division
European and Oceanic Affairs Bureau	Division / Division
Central and South American Affairs Bureau	Division / Division
North American Affairs Bureau	Division / Division
Asian Affairs Bureau	Division / Division
Administration	Archives Division / Telecommunications Division / Welfare Division / Protocol Division / Overseas Establishments Division

Administration:
- Consular and Emigration Affairs Department
- General Affairs Division
- Personnel Division
- Financial and Accounting Division
- Archives Division
- Telecommunications Division
- Welfare Division
- Protocol Division
- Overseas Establishments Division

The challenge to change the existing organizational structure is a pressing problem for both systems and is reflected in the call for more personnel in the Japanese foreign ministry and for the redistribution of authority and functions in the State Department as mandated by the Foreign Service Act of 1980.

Organization of the Foreign Ministry

The Japanese foreign ministry is organized along career lines, patterned after the French and British Foreign Offices. It is staffed by a small but highly competent group of professional diplomats, ranging from the vice-minister at the top to the most junior officer at the division level. The work of the ministry is divided along both geographic and functional lines. The five geographic bureaus (Asian Affairs, North American Affairs, Central and South American Affairs, European and Oceanic Affairs, and Middle Eastern and African Affairs) handle substantive policy matters, and the five functional bureaus have jurisdiction over treaties and legal arrangements, economic affairs, economic cooperation, the United Nations, and public information and research affairs. In total, the ministry has one secretariat, ten bureaus, two departments, and 63 divisions. The large administrative unit includes the departments of general affairs, personnel, archives, telecommunications, financial affairs, overseas establishments, protocol, and welfare. In addition, there are two departments, research and planning and consular and immigration, the former under the jurisdiction of the Information and Research Bureau and the latter under the deputy vice-minister for administration.

The geographic bureaus generally handle bilateral problems involving countries under their jurisdiction, whereas the functional bureaus deal more with multilateral affairs. The largest geographic bureau is Asian Affairs, with six divisions; the smallest is Central and South American Affairs, with two divisions. The latter bureau was established by the Foreign Ministry Establishment Law Revision Bill of 1979, which stipulated that jurisdiction over Central and South American affairs was to be removed from the American Affairs Bureau and given to a separate bureau. The American Affairs Bureau then became the North American Affairs Bureau, with jurisdiction over relations with the United States and Canada.

A director general heads each of the ten geographic and functional bureaus, supervising several deputies (depending on the size of the bureau) and division chiefs. Figure 1 shows the broad organization of the ministry; for a detailed breakdown of the various bureaus and departments and a brief description of each unit's responsibilities, see Appendix D.

The director general of a bureau (*kyokuchō*) is a senior official of the ministry and belongs to the Designated Class.[1] The deputy director general, the director general's principal assistant, can be either a senior deputy (shingikan) or a junior deputy (sanjikan).

A large bureau like Asian Affairs generally has two deputy directors general, senior and junior; the former is a member of the Designated Class and the latter is a lower grade 1 officer. Both are "staff" positions—that is, these deputies are supportive of the director general but have no stated policymaking responsibilties. They advise the director general, preside over special meetings in the bureau, and occasionally sit in for the director

Figure 2
Organization of a Typical Japanese Bureau

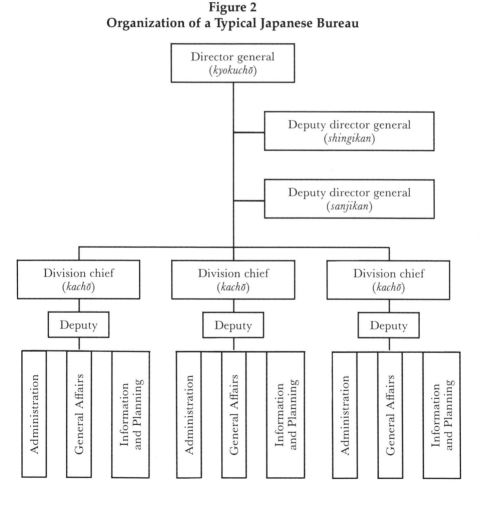

Figure 3
Organization of a Typical Japanese Embassy

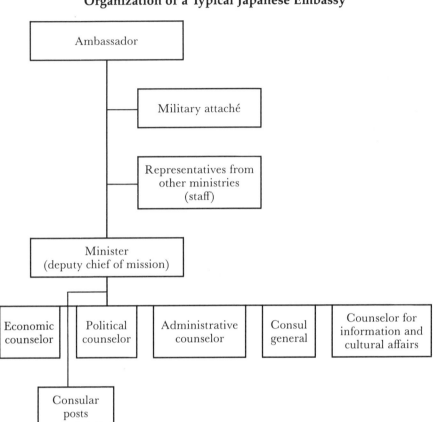

general at important interbureau conferences. They have no "line" (deci-sion-making) responsibilities. The line generally runs from the director general to the division chief or kachō, a "line" position. (Figure 2 shows the organization of a typical bureau.)

In 1980, there were 108 embassies, 48 consulates general, 6 consulates, and 5 delegations to international organizations. Posts abroad are divided into three classes. Class 1 posts (the most important) are located in countries having permanent membership in the U.N. Security Council: the United States, the Soviet Union, Great Britain, China, and France. Diplomatic titles held by embassy staff members include ambassador; minister; coun-selor; first, second, and third secretary; consul; and attaché. Overseas posts normally deal with such matters as political and economic reporting;

Table 1
Number of State Department Employees, 1781–1980

Year	Domestic	Overseas	Total
1781	4	10	14
1790	8	20	28
1800	10	62	72
1810	9	56	65
1820	16	95	111
1830	23	153	176
1840	38	170	208
1850	22	218	240
1860	42	281	323
1870	65	804	869
1880	80	977	1,057
1890	76	1,105	1,181
1900	91	1,137	1,228
1910	234	1,043	1,277
1920	708	514	1,222
1930	714	577	1,291
1940	1,128	762	1,890
1950	8,609	7,710	16,319
1960	7,117	6,178	13,295
1970	6,983	5,865	12,848
1980	8,433	5,529	13,962

SOURCE: *Department of State Newsletter,* January 1981.

consular affairs (passport, visa, and protection and welfare); information gathering and analysis; assisting visiting Japanese dignitaries; promoting Japanese commercial, cultural, and political interests; and providing policy recommendations as required. Figure 3 shows the organization of a typical Japanese Embassy.

Organization of the State Department

Whereas the Japanese foreign ministry is organized along conventional lines and has experienced difficulty in mustering a sufficient number of personnel to carry out fully and efficiently the many and varied tasks associated with the management of diplomacy, the State Department has had a different kind of problem. In 1980 the Department of State had over 3,700 career Foreign Service officers (compared with Japan's 690). This disparity has a profound effect on the structure and operation of the two agencies. Table 1 gives the number of State Department employees from 1781 to 1980; Table 2 shows the number of U.S. diplomatic and consular posts from 1790 to 1980. The general increase in the number of domestic employees from 1940 onward reflects the added responsibilities of the State Department in the foreign aid and communication fields; additional employees have been needed, especially in the Washington area, to provide policy and administrative backup to State Department employees overseas. Domestic or non–Foreign Service personnel also provide "home office" support for overseas posts and staff such domestic operations as passport offices, State Department security field offices, and reception centers located in various sections of the United States.

The Department of State, unlike the Ministry of Foreign Affairs, suffers from a surplus of personnel reflected in a layering of officialdom that, if not inefficient, is certainly puzzling and frustrating to the White House and to many government departments. This is a bureaucratic ailment that afflicts

Table 2

Number of U.S. Diplomatic and Consular Posts, 1790–1980

Year	Diplomatic	Consular
1790	2	10
1800	6	52
1810	4	60
1820	7	83
1830	15	141
1840	20	152
1850	27	197
1860	33	279
1870	36	318
1880	35	303
1890	40	323
1900	41	318
1910	48	324
1920	45	368
1930	57	299
1940	58	264
1950	74	179
1960	99	166
1970	117	122
1980	133	100

SOURCE: *Department of State Newsletter*, January 1981.

government departments throughout the world, but it poses a particular danger for foreign offices.

In the Department of State there are ten levels of officialdom:

Level 1	secretary of state
Level 2	deputy secretary of state
Level 3	under secretaries of state
Level 4	assistant secretaries of state
Level 5	deputy assistant secretaries of state
Level 6	office or country directors
Level 7	deputy officer or country directors
Level 8	division chiefs
Level 9	branch chiefs
Level 10	section chiefs

The greater percentage of officers occupying the positions from level 3 downward are Foreign Service officers, and they have a career stake in the inflation of the importance of their positions. Figure 4 does not reveal the true dynamics of the personnel structure. The department is a top-heavy organization with a plethora of assistant secretaries, deputy assistant secretaries, senior advisers, and not-so-senior advisers. The abundance of positions at the upper levels tends to reduce the effectiveness of communication with other areas of the department and to reduce efficiency. The congregation of top officials and their assistants, a sort of satellite suborganization, near the secretary of state's suite is based on the questionable premise that the degree of importance of a particular function or official is in direct proportion to the physical proximity to the secretary's office.

Given the inflated opinion most Foreign Service officers have of the importance of their work, and given the limited space on the seventh (secretary's) floor, it soon becomes apparent that some realignment of structure is necessary to improve efficiency and coordination in carrying out the mission of the department. Important work must be performed at all levels of the organization, and recommendations must flow upward, through major decision-makers at the top to the secretary.

The logic of the aforementioned premise is made evident by the State Department's attempts to appease various interest groups. For example, if the department wishes to acknowledge the importance of labor affairs in foreign policy while currying favor with the AFL-CIO, it will invite labor to nominate a special assistant to the secretary for international labor affairs, even though such an official will rarely, if ever, report directly to the secretary on international labor problems. The secretary of state obviously cannot personally supervise every activity regarded as important. (There

Figure 4

Organization of the State Department, May 1, 1978

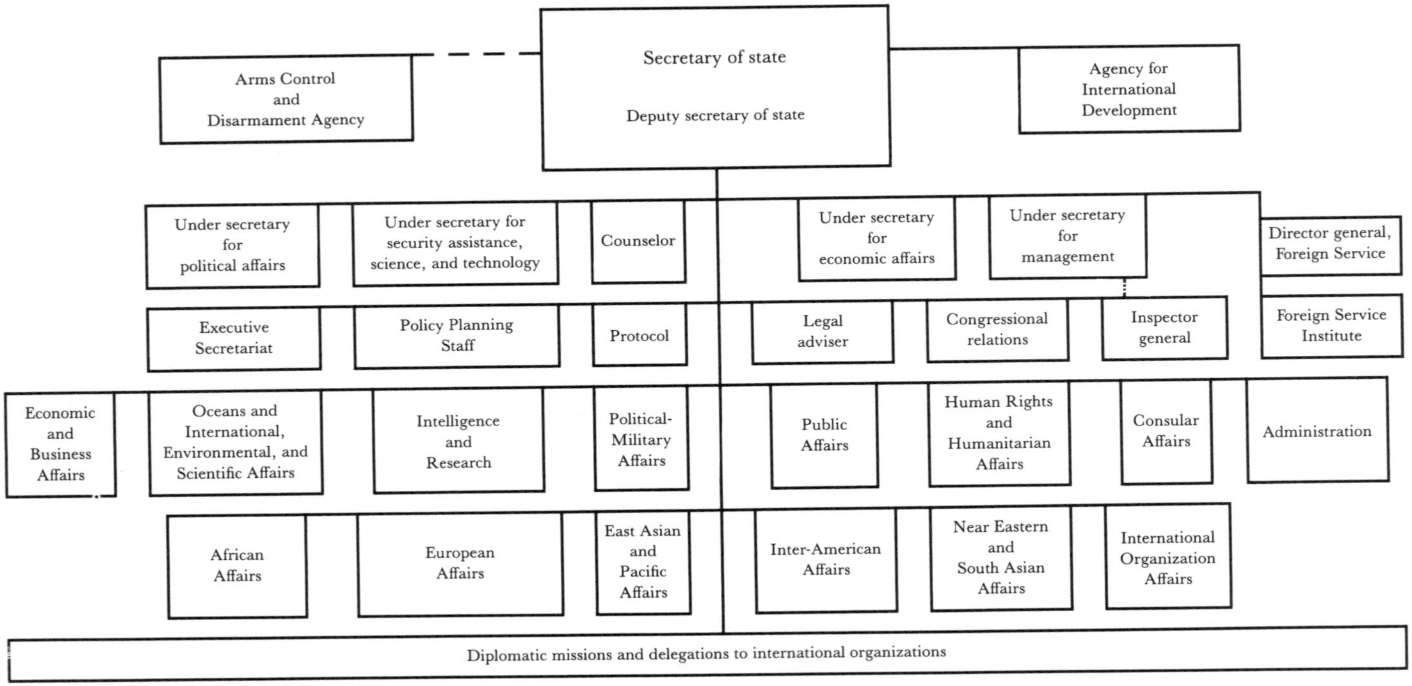

are other examples: special assistant to the secretary for population affairs, special assistant for Panama Treaty matters, special adviser to the secretary on the Soviet Union, senior adviser on narcotics control, and several ambassadors-at-large who presumably report to the secretary on such matters as the Law of the Sea Conference, Middle East affairs, and arms control.)

As long as the premise continues to have important believers and as long as power continues to be concentrated on the seventh floor, there will continue to be a proliferation of top-level positions. And there will also continue to be bottlenecks in the decision-making process that will foster an image of the State Department as an organization that is often unable to provide guidance and support to the president.

Much time and energy have been given to finding a solution to the layering problem by outside consultants and inside task forces, but to little avail. There are no quick solutions. A Management Center was established in the late 1970s to streamline the organization of the State Department—specifically, to bring together top officials, staffs, and facilities to coordinate the resources used in the formulation of foreign policy. The senior management team, which is the core of the Management Center, is composed of the under secretary, the under secretary for political affairs, the under secretary for economic affairs, the under secretary for management, the counselor of the department, the executive secretary, and the planning and coordination staff. A problem originating in an operating bureau is assigned to the member of the management team who is most familiar with the subject. His responsibility is to see that appropriate action is taken.

Although it is organizationally attractive, this approach to problem management overlooks the special relationships that sometimes develop between the secretary and his aides over time in dealing with crisis situations. The secretary often relies on an assistant secretary of an important geographic bureau, for example, when an issue arises in the area of the assistant secretary's responsibility that bears importantly on U.S. security interests. If a special relationship develops because of the secretary's confidence in the judgment of the particular officer concerned, the management team could be bypassed. If enough incidents of this kind occur, the effectiveness of the management team as an efficient administrative tool could be diminished. It should be remembered that diplomacy is an art that depends for its success as much on the personal relationships that develop among the practitioners (confidence, trust, loyalty, substantive skill and knowledge, a common understanding of the fundamentals of a particular issue, and congeniality of personality and interests) as on an organizational structure that defines responsibilities and determines resource allocations.

The key organizational and operational unit of the State Department is the geographic bureau. Geographic bureaus are organized on subregional, multiple country, and/or individual country bases much as the foreign ministry is organized. The structure is designed to allow for the regrouping of countries whenever necessitated by changes in workloads, crises, or other operational factors.

Heading each geographic bureau is an assistant secretary who can be either a career Foreign Service officer or a political appointee. Assistant secretaries generally change with a change of administration. The assistant secretary is the bureau officer in closest contact with the secretary of state and is his principal adviser on policy problems affecting the bureau's area of responsibility. The assistant secretary stays in close touch with the ambassadors in his geographic area in order to be informed concerning any emerging crises, and he maintains close working relations with his counterparts in the Pentagon, National Security Council, and other departments with foreign policy interests and responsibilities. He chooses his deputies, is influential in selecting ambassadors for posts in his area, and is the chief policy officer for his bureau.

The Bureau of East Asian and Pacific Affairs will serve as an example of a key geographic bureau. In addition to the assistant secretary, this bureau has four deputy assistant secretaries; three preside over a group of countries in the area as defined by the assistant secretary, and one heads the major economic unit of the bureau. The deputy assistant secretaries supervising the various country directorates play an important role in choosing the chiefs of these country directorates.

A country director for an assigned country or countries is the sole person responsible for the coordination of departmental and interdepartmental activities within his assigned country or countries. In the Bureau of East Asian and Pacific Affairs, in addition to the senior officers already noted, there is a country director for Australia and New Zealand affairs; for Thailand affairs; for Indonesia, Malaysia, Burma, and Singapore affairs; for Japan affairs; for Korea affairs; for Vietnam, Laos, and Kampuchea (Cambodia) affairs; for Pacific Island affairs; for Philippine affairs; and for China affairs, as well as a Taiwan Coordination Staff. There is also a Regional Affairs Office, usually headed by a senior Foreign Service officer (as are the country directorates) with responsibility for regional political matters, including multicountry problems within the region. The director of this office also supervises and coordinates the activities of the regional planning adviser, the political-military adviser (usually a military officer on temporary detail from the Department of Defense under the State–Defense Department Exchange Program), the United Nations adviser, the labor and human rights adviser, and the bureau's narcotics coordinator. The director also serves as the staff director of the NSC Interdepartmental Subgroup for the bureau. These are all "line" directorates or offices that have decision-making responsibility.

In addition, the bureau has a staff consisting of the following individuals. The executive director supervises budget preparation, personnel matters, and resource allocation for the bureau and for Foreign Service posts in the region. The staff assistant to the assistant secretary is usually a young Foreign Service officer who directs the flow of action and information documents to and from the various country directorates and the Regional Affairs Office; he also ensures that there is proper coordination and that necessary action is taken on active issues. The public affairs adviser, who is the chief assistant to the assistant secretary on public affairs and information matters, provides information and policy guidance to the United States Information Agency (USIA) and other U.S. agencies and assists in the development of the State Department's public information policy. The public affairs adviser can be a Foreign Service officer or a member of the USIA staff. The labor and human rights adviser in the Bureau of East Asian and Pacific Affairs advises on labor, manpower, and social aspects of U.S. foreign relations relative to the bureau's area of responsibility. The political-military adviser works closely with the Bureau of Political-Military Affairs and advises the assistant secretary on political-military issues, especially on matters concerning important Defense Department interests. (The political-military adviser, who generally has had previous experience in the Office of the Joint Chiefs of Staff, provides a valuable link between the relevant regional bureau and important offices in the Department of Defense.) The regional planning adviser participates in studies on current and long-range foreign policy planning and programming and maintains useful contacts with members of the State Department's Policy Planning Staff. Finally, the United Nations adviser (in the Bureau of East Asian and Pacific Affairs, a civil service employee) advises on and coordinates the bureau position in support of the Bureau of International Organization Affairs on matters affecting the region that arise in international organizations, principally the United Nations and its specialized agencies.

Organization of a U.S. Overseas Post

In a U.S. Embassy, the ambassador has full authority. He is the personal representative of the president and, if he has sufficient status and clout, reports directly to the president on crucial foreign policy problems. However, a wise ambassador will also keep in close touch with the secretary of state, the assistant secretary of state, and the country director and will coordinate his actions with them. He needs the support of these officers as well as the confidence of the president if he is to carry out his responsibilities successfully.

If he is to manage his post efficiently, the ambassador must be able to discipline and coordinate all constituent elements. With so many Washington departments and agencies represented at an embassy, this is often difficult. Sometimes it is necessary for the president to send an official letter to all posts and government departments reinforcing ambassadorial authority. Infighting is as common in the U.S. bureaucracy as in the Japanese bureaucracy, and these bureaucratic struggles are often transplanted from Washington or Tokyo to an embassy. This situation creates additional problems for the ambassador, especially when the departmental or agency bureaucrat concerned reports directly to his office in Washington through back-channel messages or informal official letters without clearing them with the ambassador or deputy chief of mission.

A large U.S. Embassy, or class A post, is organized along traditional lines. In Tokyo (a class A post), for example, the ambassador has several assistants and depends heavily on the deputy chief of mission for day-to-day management and for advice on problems affecting relations between the United States and Japan. The embassy also has a political section headed by a senior Foreign Service officer (usually a Japanese language officer) and divided into three branches that cover Japanese domestic political developments, Japanese relations with other countries, and political-military affairs, especially concerning the United States–Japan Security Treaty and Status of Forces Agreement and liaison with Headquarters U.S. Forces Japan.

Another major unit is the economic section, headed by a senior economic specialist, usually a Foreign Service officer with the title of economic counselor or economic minister. This section is responsible for following all aspects of economic and commercial relations (including trade problems) between the United States and Japan and Japanese economic policies toward third world countries. It has representatives from the Treasury Department, Commerce Department, Agriculture Department, the Maritime Commission, and other U.S. government agencies.

A major part of the economic section is the Commercial Attaché's Office, which promotes U.S. business interests in Japan, supervises the operation of the large U.S. Trade Center in downtown Tokyo, and maintains a close relationship with the U.S. Chamber of Commerce in Japan, an organization composed of representatives of U.S. companies doing business in Japan.

Other organizations represented in the embassy include the Internal Revenue Service, the National Science Foundation, the Atomic Bomb Casualty Commission, and the Federal Bureau of Investigation.

The public affairs officer, who represents the USIA (he is usually a senior career official of that agency with broad Japanese experience), is another key adviser to the ambassador. He supervises media relations, cultural centers, press and publications, and Voice of America activities and advises on all aspects of information policy.

The military offices of the embassy are headed by the U.S. Army, Navy, and Air Force attachés. These three officers are mainly responsible for following the activities of the Japanese Self-Defense Forces and assisting members of the political-miltary branch of the political section in interpretation of the United States–Japan Security Treaty. They also assist the ambassador during special military conferences (such as the United States–Japan Security Consultative Committee) and in meetings between the ambassador and senior U.S. and Japanese military commanders.

The heads of these major units of the embassy are brought together in an organization called the Country Team, and it is here that the ambassador can listen to the reports of his assistants, advise them of his views on current policy problems, and exert leadership over the multiplicity of embassy units. The Country Team usually meets on a weekly basis; when the ambassador is absent, it is chaired by the deputy chief of mission. The Country Team can be as effective as the ambassador wishes it to be. It is a tried and tested forum for exchange of views between the senior officers of the embassy and the ambassador, but it has proven somewhat unwieldy for dealing with crisis situations. On these occasions, the ambassador usually consults with several of his top aides in arriving at decisions.

Supporting the activities of both the State Department and its overseas posts is a budget that in FY 1980 called for the expenditure of almost $1.4 billion: 61.3 percent for administration of foreign affairs, 36.3 percent for international organizations and conferences, 1.9 percent for international commissions, and 0.5 percent for other activities (see Figure 5 for a breakdown of the budget request). Even though the department's budget proposal for FY 1980 was in excess of $1 billion, it was still one of the smallest budgets in the federal government that year. (Similarly, in Japan, the ministry's budget is usually only about 0.6 percent of total government expenditures.)

Personnel Structure

Categories of personnel in the Japanese Ministry of Foreign Affairs and the U.S. Department of State differ in significant respects.

Japan

The Ministry of Foreign Affairs is organized into eight grades and the Designated Class. Employees are classified into three groups: career officers or *jōkyū*, noncareer language and area specialists (*senmon-shokū*, or *chūkyū*), and noncareer administrative and clerical personnel or *shokyū*. An em-

Figure 5
State Department Budget Request, FY 1980

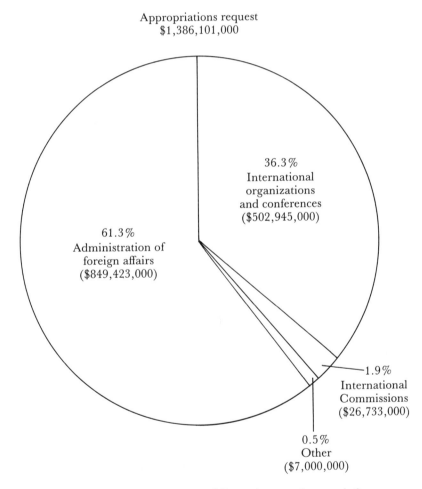

Appropriations request
$1,386,101,000

36.3%
International
organizations
and conferences
($502,945,000)

61.3%
Administration of
foreign affairs
($849,423,000)

1.9%
International
Commissions
($26,733,000)

0.5%
Other
($7,000,000)

(Figures supplied by Subcommittee of Committee on Appropriations,
House of Representatives, April 3, 1979.)

ployee's classification is determined by the examination he takes, and he usually remains in that class throughout his career.

As of January 1, 1981, the foreign ministry (Tokyo and overseas) had approximately 3,440 employees, of whom about 690 were career officers, 1,000 were language and area specialists, and 1,770 were clerical and administrative personnel. Since 1980, a five-year manpower expansion program has been under way, with a target of 5,000 ministry personnel by 1985.

Approximately 24 percent of the career officers are in grade 4, 15 percent are in grade 3, 13 percent are in grade 5, and the remaining 48 percent are clustered at the three top and bottom grades. The configuration of the service thus shows slight swelling in the middle.

No position classification exists in the ministry or, in fact, anywhere in the Japanese government bureaucracy. There is no precise method by which an officer's rank and salary level can be equated to his job responsibilities. The rules and regulations that do exist reflect more the influence of tradition and custom than a systematic effort to develop job descriptions that are relevant to an officer's grade and that serve as a basis for judging his work performance.

Career officers generally understand that when they reach a certain rank or level in the service, they will be assigned to certain jobs. The system is fluid, one senior personnel officer said, and is influenced in large measure by what has gone before. He reminded me that the career service is small, and this not only simplifies personnel administration but introduces an element of informality into procedures. He explained that an officer who was promoted to grade 4, for example, would expect to be assigned as deputy director of a division or as first or second secretary at an embassy. Because the responsibilities of a deputy director or a first secretary are well established by tradition and custom, there is no need to spell them out in detail—all officers know what they are. To be explicit about them would cause unnecessary and undesirable rigidity in the system. Besides, he said, it is relatively easy to evaluate an officer's performance because important weight is given to such elements as character, personality, and the ability to promote office harmony.

The United States

The Department of State, on the other hand, has only two basic categories of personnel as a result of the Foreign Service Act of 1980; the Foreign Service and the civil service. Within this dual structure, there is a Senior Foreign Service and a Senior Executive Service (part of the civil service); the two components have a common pay schedule.

Figure 6

Changes in State Department Personnel Structure Effected by the Foreign Service Act of 1980

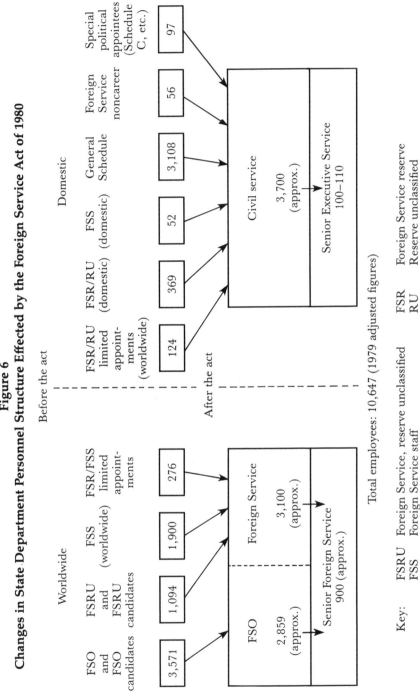

Total employees: 10,647 (1979 adjusted figures)

Key: FSRU   Foreign Service, reserve unclassified   FSR   Foreign Service reserve
       FSS   Foreign Service staff   RU   Reserve unclassified

The U.S. Foreign Service includes career and noncareer Foreign Service officers, specialists, secretaries, communications officers, and security officers. The personnel structure before and after enactment of the Foreign Service Act of 1980 is shown in Figure 6.

Officers having any of the basic cone-structured skills are normally referred to as "generalist" officers. (Japanese language officers would be included in this group.) The "specialist" group within the Foreign Service includes auditors, budget and fiscal specialists, communication officers and communication engineers, diplomatic couriers, foreign buildings officers, general services officers, medical officers, medical technologists, narcotics officers, nurses, personnel officers, psychiatrists, science officers, secretaries, security engineers, and security officers.

There is a position classification for each job in these categories. The classification system enables personnel managers to know how many positions there are at each grade level and how many officers are available at that level. Each March the positions are reviewed by functional specialty and grade, from the top grades in the Senior Foreign Service down to the junior ranks, and the number of positions is compared with the number of officers in each grade and specialty. Through this process, the number of promotions to the next higher grade is determined. If it is decided, for example, that 40 officers can be promoted from the minister counselor grade to the career minister level, this decision has a cascade effect down to the junior levels and 40 is established as the basic promotion figure, although the number can be adjusted within cones as the needs of the service require.

The criteria for establishing the position or grade level at an embassy are generally determined by the category of the embassy (class A, B, or C). At a class A post, the deputy chief of mission and the section chief positions (political, economic) are normally classified as minister counselor.

The dual structure established by the Foreign Service Act of 1980 has greatly simplified the administration of the Foreign Service. Whereas before 1980 there were eight subcategories of personnel, there is now only one, with the simple designation of FS, or Foreign Service. In the civil service there is one system, with the designation GS, or general schedule. Table 3 shows the equivalent FS and GS rankings.

The Senior Foreign Service category, which includes counselor (old FSO-2), minister counselor (old FSO-1), and career minister, is comprised of officers from the following organizations: State Department, the Agency for International Development, the United States Information Agency, the Foreign Agricultural Service, and the Foreign Commercial Service. As of December 31, 1981, the number of officers from each organization was as follows:

State Department	703
Agency for International Development	211
United States Information Agency	163
Foreign Agricultural Service	13
Foreign Commercial Service	10
	1,100

After enactment of the Foreign Service Act of 1980, personnel officials were confronted with the problem of Foreign Service personnel classified as "domestic" Foreign Service employees. The act provided for the conversion to the civil service from the Foreign Service of current members not available or not needed for service overseas if they chose to remain in government employment at the conclusion of the three-year conversion period (February 14, 1984). The act preserved the status and benefits of those who converted from the Foreign Service to the civil service.

Table 3
Changes in Personnel Categories
Effected by the Foreign Service Act of 1980

Before 1980 Act	After 1980 Act	
FSO–3, FSR–3, FSRU–3, or FSS–1	FS–1,	GS–15
FSO–4, FSR–4, FSRU–4, or FSS–2	FS–2,	GS–14
FSO–5, FSR–5, FSRU–5, or FSS–3	FS–3,	GS–13
	FS–4,	GS–12
FSO–6, FSR–6, FSRU–6, or FSS–4	FS–5,	GS–11
FSO–7, FSR–7, FSRU–7, or FSS–5	FS–6,	GS–9
FSO–8, FSR–8, FSRU–8, or FSS–6	FS–7,	GS–7
FSS–7	FS–8,	GS–6
FSS–8	FS–9,	GS–5
FSS–9	FS–10, GS–4	
FSS–10	FS–10, GS–4	

SOURCE: *Special Report*, Bureau of Personnel, Department of State, January 1982.

In 1980 there were 471 domestic Foreign Service employees who had to decide whether to convert or to leave the federal service. As of January 1982, approximately 10 percent had converted to the civil service (Senior Executive Service, designated GS); nearly 25 percent appealed their designation, seeking to remain in the Foreign Service. As of February 1982, 369 persons were deferring conversion as permitted by the law. Conversion status of the 471 employees as of December 31, 1981, was as follows:

Accepted, converted to GS or SES (Senior Executive Service)	50
Appealed, retained in the Foreign Service	30
Declined conversion, agreed to separate by 2/15/84	15
Unresolved appeals	4
Deferred conversion to GS/SES	372

During the House Committee hearings on the Foreign Service Act of 1980, the committee requested statistics on the number of employees classified as Foreign Service personnel by grade and number (including women and minorities) for the twelve-month period December 31, 1977, to December 31, 1978. The categories of employees reflected the single personnel system, which was in effect at the time. Since 1980, basic numbers have changed very little; they have merely been rearranged under new categories to reflect the mandate of the act. As of December 31, 1978, the proportion of women in the Foreign Service was 20.2 percent in the junior ranks, 9.2 percent in the middle ranks, and 2.9 percent at the senior levels. In the Foreign Service as a whole during 1978–79, the proportion of minority officers was 4.7 percent; 2.6 percent held the rank of career minister.

Managers of the System

All of the principal managers of the system who serve in the Ministry of Foreign Affairs are career officers; in the State Department, only a few managers have career status, and their numbers change with different administrations. In terms of the functions of top-level management, however, there are striking similarities. In both services, senior officers handle the important political, economic, and administrative matters. Greater diversification of duties and responsibilities exists at the lower levels of management, principally because of the difference in size and global mission of the two services.

Japan

The top career official and senior Foreign Service officer in the foreign ministry, the number two man under the foreign minister who is in overall charge of the personnel system, is the vice-minister, or *jikan*. He generally serves for about two years and is then assigned to a top ambassadorship (usually in Washington) before retirement. A seasoned diplomat with a high reputation among his colleagues, he had reached the top by virtue of seniority[2] and performance, although he was probably earmarked for the top position in the ministry years before the actual appointment. The vice-minister's elevation to the top career post was, in effect, decided by the consensus of his superiors that he was the best qualified in his class to assume the responsibilities of that position.

The vice-minister is the chief foreign policy adviser to the foreign minister. He is also the principal link between top government and party officials and the foreign ministry. Because of his rank and prestige, he is normally involved in high-level policy discussions within the government on urgent international problems that often include the chief Cabinet secretary, the foreign minister, and the prime minister. The vice-minister's effectiveness depends not only on his skill as a negotiator but also on the strength of his personality and the breadth of his experience as a diplomat. There have been strong and persuasive vice-ministers, as well as some who have chosen to play a quieter role. Takashima Masao, the vice-minister who resigned in July 1981, was active in many important negotiations such as the reversion of Okinawa, the normalization of relations with China, and the return of Kim Dae Jung.[3] He also played a key role in formulating the policy discussed by Prime Minister Suzuki Zenko and President Reagan at their summit meeting in May 1981 and was considered a strong and effective leader by his colleagues.

The vice-minister is responsible for the selection of top ministry officials, including important ambassadors. In consultations with the deputy vice-minister for administration and his staff and with other key officers in the ministry, he orchestrates a consensus on who, for example, should be appointed ambassador to the United States, the Soviet Union, China, France, or Great Britain. While these intraministerial deliberations are going on, he has informal discussions with the foreign minister, the chief Cabinet secretary, the prime minister, and top Liberal Democratic Party officials to elicit opinions and recommendations as to the best candidates. This process can extend over several months or more, but when general agreement has been reached on the best choice, the official recommendation is made and is swiftly approved by the Cabinet. The choice is almost always a career officer. (The former Japanese ambassadors to Kuwait, Imai Takakichi, and Denmark, Takahashi Nobuko, were appointees from outside the career Foreign Service.)

Tradition often plays a role in the selection process. For example, when the vice-minister leaves his post after the usual two-year assignment, he is generally the top choice for assignment as ambassador to Washington. (Shimoda Takeso, Ushiba Nobuhiko, and Togo Fumihiko were all appointed ambassadors to Washington after leaving the post of vice-minister.) However, in July 1981, vice-minister Takashima chose to resign from the ministry rather than accept an assignment to Washington, probably, in part, because the incumbent ambassador to Washington, Okawara Yoshio, was his junior and was also his candidate for that position. It is unusual for a senior to replace a junior in an important ministry position.

Parallel to the jikan in the organization chart, but having relatively little influence on policy, is the Liberal Democratic Party member assigned to the ministry to act as liaison with the Diet. He usually does not participate in the making of crucial policy decisions but generally considers his assignment as an important step in his career in the party.

Another senior ministry official heads the Minister's Secretariat (in charge of administration) and has the title of deputy vice-minister for administration, or *kambōchō*. He plays an important role in selecting career officers for the top posts in the ministry in Tokyo and overseas, acts as policy coordinator when problems encompass several bureau jurisdictions, and supervises day-to-day personnel operations.

The other top ministry positions are the deputy vice-minister for political affairs and the deputy vice-minister for economic affairs, created in the 1970s to handle the ministry's growing work load. These two senior officers perform essentially staff functions, advising the vice-minister and foreign minister on policy problems, representing the ministry at special international conferences, and/or undertaking special fact-finding missions. Like the vice-minister, they normally serve about two years and are then appointed to senior ambassadorships.

The deputy vice-minister for administration and his staff assist the vice-minister in overall administration of the ministry. The deputy vice-minister is in direct charge of daily operations and wields considerable influence because of his power to select important officials. Very few, if any, top positions are filled without his recommendation.

The three units under the deputy vice-minister for administration that are headed by midlevel managers and are pertinent to this study are the General Affairs Division, the Financial Affairs Division, and the Personnel Division. Figure 7 shows the lines of authority extending from the vice-minister to senior officials in the ministry. Line responsibility for policy decisions runs from the vice-minister to the deputy vice-minister for administration. The deputy vice-ministers for political affairs and economic affairs are considered staff positions—they are merely supportive of the vice-minister.

The chief of the General Affairs Division is the principal assistant to the deputy vice-minister in dealing with coordination and administrative problems within the ministry, especially in cases where several geographic bureaus find it hard to resolve jurisdictional differences. Division personnel examine legal documents that go to the Cabinet to ensure compliance with Cabinet rules, act as a liaison with the Diet to coordinate ministry policy statements to be used in Diet interpellations, and evaluate and recommend changes to improve the effectiveness of the administrative structure.

The chief stressed to me the importance of "not sticking the division's neck out too far" in mediating interbureau problems and complaints. He also said that whatever success was achieved in such mediation was attributable in part to the principle of hierarchy. When he spoke for the deputy vice-minister, he said, his statement carried weight with his own colleagues, and they, in turn, tried hard to persuade him on a particular issue, knowing that he might have influence with his superior.

The chief of the Financial Affairs Division is in charge of the general budgetary process for the ministry. A subsidiary office provides special budget support to overseas posts.

The size of the ministry's budget is miniscule compared with that of other ministries of the Japanese government, and it has never exceeded 1 percent of the total government budget. The activities of the Economic Cooperation Bureau absorb about two-thirds of the budget.

The fiscal year is from April 1 to March 31. To prepare for budget debates in the Diet in February and March, the various ministries develop budget estimates and submit them to the Ministry of Finance by the end of August. This means that the Financial Affairs Division must obtain budget

Figure 7
Office of the Japanese Foreign Ministry Vice-Minister

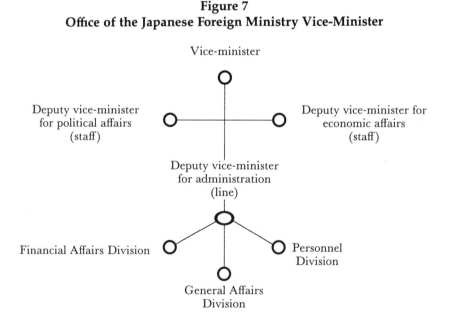

requests from the various bureaus in June in order to meet the finance ministry's August 31 deadline. The division sends budget experts to the various bureaus to assist in preparing budget estimates. These officials often remain in a particular bureau for several years and are sometimes sent to Japanese posts abroad as budget and fiscal officers.

The division chief plays an important role in the discussions of budget estimates. He is the pivotal officer around whom bureau activities range, and has important budget input covering administrative and personnel costs (including training estimates).

When bureau budget estimates are completed, they are submitted to the Financial Affairs Division for study and further processing. At this stage, the Financial Affairs Division makes recommendations to the deputy vice-minister for administration on how to meet budget ceilings for the ministry established by the Cabinet for a particular year. If decisions are contested by a bureau, negotiations recommence between the bureau and the Financial Affairs Division until agreement is reached. When all differences are reconciled, the ministry submits its budget to the Ministry of Finance.

During the budgetary process, important ministry officials meet with sympathetic Diet members to gain their support for increases in the budget. About 100 Diet members have organized themselves into the Group of Liberal Democratic Party Members to Help the Gaimushō, and it is to this group that senior ministry officials take their requests for assistance and other ministry officials address their efforts to gain support for ministry policies and programs.

The chief of the Financial Affairs Division has the authority to disburse funds in about 60 percent of the cases. In the other 40 percent (for example, how much money should be contributed to various United Nations agencies), he must submit disbursement proposals to his superiors for approval. Decisions on these questions are made by a committee under the chairmanship of the deputy vice-minister for administration. The chief of the Financial Affairs Division indicated that the foreign minister does not usually get involved in budgetary matters.[4] Tight centralized control of the budgetary process is possible because of the relatively small size of the ministry.

The chief of the Personnel Division, the third major unit under the deputy vice-minister for administration, was in 1982 a career officer with extensive experience in U.S. affairs. This division is divided into various sections dealing with such matters as general affairs and the training and assignment of career and noncareer officers and clerical and administrative personnel. It also provides general policy guidance and outlines personnel requirements to the Foreign Service Training Institute and has specific responsibility for recruitment, assignment, promotion, and performance evaluation. Its structure reflects the distinction in the ministry between career and noncareer employees.

The chief of personnel assigns career officers up to and including the division chief level. He is assisted by a deputy chief of the division, who is also a career officer. For assignment of officers above the division chief level (deputy directors general, director general of bureaus, and senior officers at overseas posts, including ambassadors), the division chief normally makes recommendations to the deputy vice-minister for administration, who then discusses them with the vice-minister and other senior officers. Before doing so, the division chief may hold informal discussions with the director general of a bureau if the assignment involves the bureau, or with other officers as necessary. He communicates with an ambassador if the assignment concerns a senior officer scheduled to be posted to that ambassador's embassy. When he senses that agreement has been reached with the concerned bureau or ambassador, he discusses the matter further with his superiors, and if all agree, he makes a formal recommendation.

This is the general pattern, but it varies with assignment requirements. The chief of the Personnel Division is a powerful figure in the ministry and generally is a man earmarked by his seniors for more important responsibilities. The past three Personnel Division chiefs (1970–1980) have all moved on to more influential duties.

The pattern of administration in the ministry reflects not only the traditions and mores of the service but the clear dominance of the career Foreign Service. The ministry operates efficiently and without undue discord because of its relatively small size and the dedication and loyalty of its members.

The United States

By contrast, the Department of State has a large, sprawling bureaucracy complicated by layering and imbued with few of the elements of cohesion that characterize the Japanese foreign ministry. The top official is the secretary of state, usually a prominent U.S. citizen who is personally appointed by the incumbent president. The secretary relies on the deputy secretary for the coordination of foreign affairs activities and for advising the State Department and allied agencies as to the allocation of resources. The deputy secretary is also responsible for the overall management of the department, including planning, evaluation, and resource allocation.

The under secretary for political affairs is the third ranking officer (see Figure 4) and is responsible for political-military, intelligence, and arms control and disarmament matters, and for relations with other departments and agencies on such matters.

The under secretary for economic affairs coordinates all economic policies and programs, chairs the Operations Group of the Council on International Economic Policy (CIEP), and represents the State Department at meetings of interagency groups concerned with major issues of international economic policy.

The under secretary for management has responsibility for the State Department's personnel and financial resources, the inspection and evaluation process, new policy analysis, and resource allocation.

These four senior managers carry the major load in directing affairs and advising the secretary of state on management of foreign policy. Other important officials in the hierarchy are the under secretary for security assistance, science, and technology; the counselor, who serves as a special adviser and consultant to the secretary of state, the deputy secretary, and the under secretaries on major problems of foreign policy and handles special assignments; and the executive secretary and his staff (the Executive Secretariat), who coordinate the flow of documents and telegrams between the secretary of state and all principal officers and the bureaus and offices of the State Department and act as a formal liaison with the White House, the National Security Council, the Department of Defense, the Central Intelligence Agency, and other agencies concerned with foreign affairs. The executive secretary has the rank of assistant secretary. Ambassadors-at-large assist and advise the secretary of state on a variety of foreign policy problems and may be called upon to serve anywhere in the world to help with emergent crises, to conduct special and/or intensive negotiations, or act in other capacities as requested by the secretary of state or the president. Ambassadors-at-large are generally distinguished former government officials or business or professional leaders. Elliot Richardson, who was an ambassador-at-large to the Law of the Sea Conference, was formerly an under secretary of state and attorney general and also held other Cabinet posts.

Key officers in the management of the department's personnel system are the under secretary of state for management (usually a political appointee recommended to the president by the incoming secretary of state), the director general of the Foreign Service, the inspector general of the Foreign Service, two deputy assistant secretaries for personnel and their staffs, the director of the Foreign Service Institute, the chairman and members of the Grievance Staff attached to the director general's office, and the chairman of the autonomous statutory body known as the Foreign

Service Grievance Board. Figure 8 shows the principal units of the State Department's personnel system.

The inspector general has a rank equivalent to that of an assistant secretary and serves under the direct supervision of the under secretary for management. He and his staff are responsible for evaluating the activities of the State Department and its missions abroad; furnishing senior officials with information, analyses, and recommendations on personnel policies; evaluating the effectiveness of U.S. policies and programs and of the organization and management of the State Department and its posts abroad in achieving their policy and management goals; evaluating the allocation and efficient use of U.S. resources, including the personnel required to support U.S. policies and programs; and recommending adjustments as necessary in order to fulfill the audit responsibiities of the department.

In carrying out these functions, the inspection corps usually divides itself into teams of two inspectors each, one inspector to investigate the general substantive affairs of an office in the department or at a post abroad and the other to inspect administration. A team's visit to an embassy, for example, is usually preceded by a letter to the ambassador outlining the general aspects to be inspected and requesting certain information to facilitate the inspection. After arrival at the post, the inspectors probe into the operations of the mission and evaluate the efficiency and correctness of the organizational structure to determine whether the post is meeting its responsibilities in a manner that fully supports U.S. policy objectives in the area. One of the team's important tasks is to interview each Foreign Service officer to hear his complaints and criticisms and his general feeling about his career, his job, and his role in the embassy. The inspector then prepares a report on that officer, giving his own evaluation of the officer's performance and any recommendations he wishes to make regarding the officer's future assignments, prospects for promotion, and potential for a leadership role in the service. The report is placed in the officer's official file and is considered important by Selection Boards evaluating the officer for promotion and by assignment panels. This report, plus the annual efficiency report, are the bases for judging an officer's performance and have a profound influence on his prospects for advancement.

The inspection corps tries to inspect a post or office in the State Department once every several years, but the growing number of posts and departmental offices sometimes makes this impossible. Inspectors are generally senior Foreign Service officers with extensive experience within the State Department and at overseas posts. They are tough and realistic in their appraisals, and their continuing efforts to improve efficiency and to make the department more responsive to the president in the management

Figure 8
State Department Bureau of Personnel

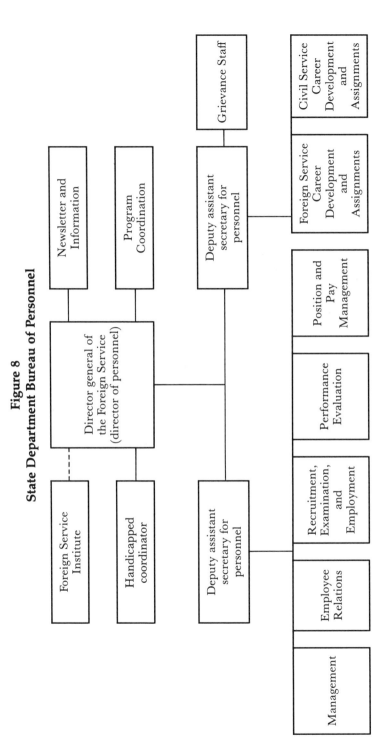

of U.S. foreign policy provide a valuable service to the department and to the Foreign Service.

The Bureau of Personnel is headed by the director general of the Foreign Service, who also has the title of director of personnel. The director general is a senior Foreign Service officer with a distinguished record as a substantive policy officer, as well as broad administrative experience. Since early 1975, two women occupied this position; both served as ambassadors, and both had outstanding records as Foreign Service officers.

The director general directs the formulation and implementation of personnel policies and programs in consultation with the under secretary of state for management, serves as chairperson of the Board of Examiners for the Foreign Service, has general supervisory responsibilities for the Foreign Service Institute, and coordinates and directs the sections of the bureau that have responsibility for administering personnel programs.

The director general's principal assistants are the deputy assistant secretary for personnel and the deputy assistant secretary for management. The deputy assistant secretary for personnel supervises the work of the Office of Career Development and Assignments and the Office of Civil Service Career Development and Assignments. In addition, he is responsible for supervising the activities of the Grievance Staff and for public affairs.

The Office of Career Development and Assignments of the Foreign Service will be discussed in the section on assignment procedures in Chapter 4; here I wish only to point out some of the more important features of that office. It is organized to counsel and place officers at various grade levels and in the four cones (functional groups). The senior officers' section counsels officers in the Senior Foreign Service (those who are in the program direction/executive "cone," with officers who retain their conal affiliation as political, economic, administrative, and consular officers, and with specialists, such as labor, security, and science officers) and arranges assignments for these officers by holding discussions with interested bureaus. Formal action is then taken by assignment panels.

The midlevel officers' section is administered by officers who handle various grade levels with different conal affiliations much as is done in the senior officers' section. For example, a Foreign Service officer in the political cone at grade 1 has an officer with whom he can discuss his career problems and assignment preferences. These career development and assignment officers also participate in the assignment panels.

The chief of the Office of Career Development and Assignments is usually a senior career Foreign Service officer, and he and his staff direct and coordinate all programs concerned with career development, career projections, counseling, training, and assignments. The staff members coordinate their activities with regional and functional bureaus, compile lists of prospective candidates for important positions under the open assignment procedure introduced in 1980, and identify certain officers, especially those in the Senior Foreign Service, who can be detailed to other departments and agencies seeking personnel with special qualifications in the field of international relations.

The other important responsibility of the deputy assistant secretary for personnel is to supervise the activities of the Grievance Staff, which is headed by a lawyer who has had extensive experience within the federal government. Assisting him are a number of investigators who are Foreign Service officers. The chief and his staff investigate, review, and prepare recommendations for the resolution of grievances of State Department and Foreign Service personnel, maintain liaison with the Foreign Service Grievance Board, process the remedial orders issued by the board in formal grievance cases, and represent the State Department at formal grievance hearings. The staff also handles the grievances of former Foreign Service employees seeking administrative review outside the Foreign Service grievance system.

The other senior manager of the personnel system under the jurisdiction of the director general of the Foreign Service is the deputy assistant secretary for management. This officer, usually a senior Foreign Service officer with broad administrative experience, directs the work of the Office of Employee Relations, the Office of Performance Evaluation, the Office of Position and Pay Management, and the Office of Recruitment, Examination, and Employment. He is also responsible for supervising programs involving local employees of the Foreign Service (citizens of the country in which a particular Foreign Service mission is located).

The director of the Office of Performance Evaluation, one of the key units of the Bureau of Personnel, is in charge of the promotion system. He prepares the precepts for the Selection Boards, plays an important role in the selection of members for those boards, and monitors the performance evaluation system to ensure that annual efficiency reports are prepared in accordance with departmental regulations. He also participates in determining how many career Foreign Service officers can be promoted to the next higher grade on the basis of conal affiliation.

Another major unit of the director general's office, whose activities are closely correlated with those of the Bureau of Personnel, is the Foreign Service Institute. The director of the institute establishes the basic procedures to be followed by the institute, plans its programs of training and instruction, and coordinates these programs with the training activities of the State Department and other government agencies.

The FSI provides training and instruction to officers and employees of the Foreign Service, the State Department, and other government agencies.

It also provides orientation courses and language training for members of families of officers and employees of the federal government. The institute has a School of Professional Studies, a School of Language Studies, and a School of Area Studies; it also administers an executive seminar in national and international affairs. A new training program for midlevel Foreign Service officers was begun in 1981.

PERSONNEL SYSTEMS IN OPERATION

T HE PERSONNEL SYSTEMS IN THE FOREIGN MINISTRY AND THE STATE DE-
partment, although they have similar responsibilities (to recruit, examine, assign, and promote), must contend with different problems resulting
from different management styles, attitudes toward career objectives, foreign policy responsibilities, and manpower goals. The two systems must
operate in a manner dictated in part by their differences in size and in
bureaucratic ambience. The policies and procedures described in this
chapter reflect some of these differences.

Recruitment and Examination

Japan

In Japan, recruitment of employees for the foreign ministry is a key
function of the Personnel Division. Officers are sent to college campuses to
talk with students who are about to graduate regarding a career in the
Foreign Service. The division also prepares recruitment material and nomi-
nates ministry officials and university professors to participate in the examination process.

There is strong competition for the top graduates. As Japan's economy
continues to expand, companies and banks are stepping up their recruitment efforts to meet their growing manpower needs. Other government
ministries also compete for outstanding young men. This places increasing

pressure on the foreign ministry to find the best candidates for career appointments.

Career officers are recruited mainly from three public universities (Tokyo, Kyoto, and Hitotsubashi) and from two leading private universities (Keio and Waseda). Most candidates come from the law faculties of these schools. Between 1958 and 1960, over 75 percent of the career appointees were University of Tokyo graduates. By 1980, the percentage had dropped to 50 percent, largely because candidates from other universities had been increasingly successful in passing the ministry's career examination and the examinations of other government ministries, especially the Ministry of Finance and MITI. The finance ministry usually gets the top 5 graduates of the University of Tokyo, and MITI and the foreign ministry usually split the remaining top 10. Large banks and corporations take about 200 high-ranking college graduates annually.

The Personnel Division asks career officers with five or six years' experience to return to their own universities to talk with prospective candidates. One such officer told me that when he returned to the University of Tokyo and met with about 50 seniors, he was struck by their lack of knowledge about and interest in foreign affairs; they had given little thought to the foreign ministry or to a career in the Foreign Service. The experience of talking to these young people frustrated and disappointed him. He said that an undergraduate with aspirations to become a diplomat must begin preparation early in his university years. The examination is difficult and the life of a diplomat is demanding; not everyone can pass the intellectual and emotional test.

A number of professors who participate in the examination panels, in discussing the growing competition on their campuses for top graduates, said that the private sector and some other government ministries appear to have considerable attraction for young people. Unlike the foreign ministry, they allow employees to work in Japan throughout most of their careers and to enjoy living standards that are comparable to those in other advanced countries.

The finance ministry has always had an allure for college graudates. Powerful and prestigious, its senior officials often move to top positions in business or politics. Several of Japan's postwar prime ministers were formerly career officials in the finance ministry. The Ministry of International Trade and Industry is increasing its power and influence, particularly with regard to Japan's economic development and international trade policy.

The foreign ministry, however, appeals to the young recruit because it offers a diplomatic career with challenge, excitement, and prestige. In attempting to attract the best candidates, the ministry is sometimes at a disadvantage because of the effect of a Foreign Service career on the education of children and on the family as a whole. (This consideration is often worrisome to officers of companies and banks serving abroad as well.) Families sometimes have to be split up, the wife returning to Japan to supervise the education of the children while the husband remains abroad. But because the Japanese business and professional world is not yet ready to fully accept the credentials of young men and women educated in foreign countries, families feel pressured to enroll their children in Japanese schools.

In times of great social or economic change or when there are real or potential threats to national security, the impulse to serve the nation is strong, and careers in public service appear to be more popular than careers in the private sector. The great economic surge in postwar Japan attracted young people to both the private and the public sectors, especially to the Ministry of Finance and MITI. The restoration of national self-confidence inspired young people to enter the public service. (Franklin Roosevelt's New Deal also inspired young people to enter public service, in the hope of accelerating the nation's economic recovery.)

Recruitment statistics for the foreign ministry covering the period 1960 to 1980 indicate that the number of individuals taking the career examination rose from 395 in 1960 (15 were women) to 1,213 in 1980 (114 were women). This is an increase of over 300 percent in twenty years, a very enviable record. Although it is arguable that the quality of applicants is a very different matter from the number of individuals taking the examination, personnel officials have expressed satisfaction with the quality of the recruits.

I was particularly impressed when I met and spoke with the class of 1980 in the Foreign Service Training Institute. I found these young officers (24 men and 3 women) quite optimistic about their career prospects. Most had made up their minds about becoming diplomats as undergraduates, because they wanted to go into public service, or they had long had an interest in foreign affairs, or they thought the life of a diplomat would be exciting and challenging, or they believed that a diplomat held a high position in Japanese society, or because a relative or close friend had been in the ministry.

Most of these young officers had graduated from Tokyo University, but many more were graduates of other universities than in previous years. For example, for the first time, a young male officer was a graduate of Soka University, the institution associated with the large lay Buddhist organization, Soka Gakkai.

These young officers believed there would always be a group of highly qualified university students interested in becoming Foreign Service officers and that public service would always have an attraction for many young

Japanese because of the increasing importance of Japan's role in foreign affairs.

The ministry has a reasonable chance of obtaining its share of bright young college graduates. Interest in public service has not diminished, as reflected in the recruitment statistics. In 1980, the ministry began a five-year personnel expansion phase requiring flexibility in personnel management, and there are clear indications that top officials of the Personnel Division and the deputy vice-minister for administration are aware of the challenges and are prepared to meet them with typical Japanese patience and hard work.

The foreign ministry is the only government agency that prepares and administers its own written and oral examination to prospective career Foreign Service officers and language and area specialists.[1] (Applicants for clerical and administrative positions must take the governmentwide National Public Service Examination.)

In April of every year, the ministry makes a public announcement, which is carried in the *Official Gazette* and in all major Japanese newspapers, that an examination will be held for career positions. Each candidate is required to submit an official application form furnished by the ministry and a photograph to the examination section of the Personnel Division. Candidates must be at least 20 years of age and not older than 27 as of April 1 of the year of the career examination (*jōkyū shiken*). Only Japanese nationals are eligible to take the examination; those who possess dual nationality or whose spouses are of foreign nationality are not eligible.

The chief of the Personnel Division selects two or three examiners for each subject from among senior ministry officials and professors who are recognized authorities in their fields. Those selected are officially appointed by the foreign minister as members of the examination board. The professors selected as examiners by the Personnel Division prepare the written examinations. Those professors who prepare a particular section also grade that section; grades are averaged and candidates with grades in the 50 range generally fail. Some professors who prepare the written portion of the examination also participate in the orals.

The 1980 examination board for career officers included, in addition to senior ministry officials, five professors from the University of Tokyo, three from Kyoto University, three from Hitotsubashi, two from Sophia, one from Waseda, one from Keio, and one from Gakushuin University.

A senior editor of a Tokyo newspaper who has covered the foreign ministry for over twenty years said that professors, especially those at Tokyo University, not only prepare and grade the career examination but help their students get ready for it. A Keio professor told me that the special help given by professors, especially at Tokyo University, to young men or women who have decided upon a career in the Foreign Service might include individual instruction and counseling—specifically, suggestions for intensive study in a subject to be covered in the career examination. This may be one reason, he said, why graduates of Tokyo University comprise the majority of successful candidates.

The attention given to prospective candidates for the Foreign Service examination by professors at Tokyo University and other universities undoubtedly helps these young men and women pass the examination. A strong relationship usually develops between student and professor in this situation, because both have a vested interest in the student's performing well. But it is also a fact that passing the examination for entry into Tokyo and Kyoto universities is, in itself, a very painful and exacting experience for many young Japanese, and those who succeed are generally not only intellectually gifted but highly motivated. These are traits that in the end generally explain why so many Tokyo and Kyoto University graduates are accepted into the career Foreign Service.

The written exam, which takes two to three days, is held in Tokyo and Kyoto in the latter part of June and covers liberal arts, the Japanese Constitution, international law, principles of economics, diplomatic history, administrative and civil law, and public finance, as well as a foreign language translation (into and from Japanese). Candidates who fail the liberal arts section of the examination are automatically disqualified from further consideration.

Of the more than 1,200 candidates who took the written examination for the career service in 1980, about 60 passed and thus qualified for the oral examination. The week-long oral examination, administered in early August, covers the Japanese Constitution, international law, and principles of economics and includes a written essay, a group discussion on a particular subject, preparation of a composition in a foreign language, an examination to assess the personality and character of the candidate, and a physical examination. The 27 members of the class of 1980 were notified in October. The successful candidates are given a document with a foreign ministry seal stating that they have been appointed career officers in the Japanese Foreign Service.

Candidates for the language and area specialist corps are given the same general oral examination but also have to take a difficult oral test in one of 40 languages. Fifty of the candidates who pass the oral examinations are chosen to enter the specialist group. After receiving their appointments, they are assigned to four months of basic training at the Foreign Service Training Institute and then to a one-year assignment in a division of the ministry for on-the-job training. They are then sent abroad for intensive language training that can last from one to three years, depending on language difficulty. (Arabic, for example, is generally a three-year course.)[2]

Since the early 1970s, from 23 to 27 career officers have been appointed annually. Factors influencing the number in a particular year include the ministry's budget and what one ministry official termed "management considerations." He explained that the system must be kept in balance. Many young applicants not only wish to devote their careers to foreign affairs, but expect ultimately to be assigned to senior positions in the service. If too many officers are appointed to the career service in a particular year, it will be difficult to find senior positions for them when their class becomes eligible for such positions. Thus pressures are building for some limit to the number of career officers recruited each year. Counterpressures are also present to expand the career corps to meet the growing manpower needs of the ministry.[3] There seems to be a consensus that recruitment levels for career officers should not exceed 30 to 35 annually, but there is uncertainty that recruitment at this level could preserve the needed balance. No clear guidelines have yet been established under the five-year manpower expansion program as to how many officers should be recruited for the three groups (career, noncareer, and clerical/administrative) within the ministry.

The United States

The Bureau of Personnel in the Department of State has essentially the same functions and responsibilities as its counterpart in Japan, with some variations in procedure and method. In the recruitment and examination processes, the department leans toward the use of more modern techniques.

Recruitment for the State Department means ensuring a steady flow of highly qualified young men and women into the career Foreign Service. Each December, the written part of the Foreign Service Entrance Examination is given throughout the United States and abroad. About 20,000 individuals apply each year, and generally between 12,000 and 15,000 actually take the examination. The examination is so designed that a candidate can choose a particular functional cone (political, economic, administrative, or consular) in which to be rated. He must obtain a general passing score and a rating high enough in his functional cone to move on to the next stage in the examination process.

From 2,500 to 4,000 pass the written examination annually, and those who do must then take an oral examination conducted in the Assessment Center (discussed later in the chapter) as part of a program of employee analysis and evaluation instituted by the State Department in 1979 and patterned after the pioneering efforts of the American Telephone and Telegraph Company. Candidates who successfully pass through the Assessment Center must have a physical examination and a security check. If the results of both are affirmative, they are given probationary appointments as Foreign Service officers in their skill cones.

The political cone register has almost three times as many candidates as can be appointed FSOs. Therefore, the prospects for appointment from the administrative, economic, and consular registers are much more favorable. Normally, the department wishes to have a register with twice the number of candidates that can actually be appointed. When appointment offers are made, only about 50 percent accept. This means that in order to get 40 new officers from a particular register, 80 offers must be made.

Timing is one reason why candidates do not accept appointments. Some individuals who are given offers of appointment cannot accept because they cannot resign from their present job; housing and financial considerations preclude others from accepting an appointment; still others do not wish to create schooling problems for their children. The department has tried to ameliorate this situation by inducting one new Foreign Service officer class every two months for a total of six inductions a year.

Candidates whose names are on registers established as a result of the examination for any one year retain their eligibility for eighteen months. If no offer is forthcoming from the department during that period, the candidate's name is removed, and he must take the examination again.

About 200 FSOs are appointed every year. This number tends to balance the 160 FSOs who annually leave the service, on the average.

In addition to the regular recruitment-examination program for Foreign Service officers, there is a minority program for Asian Americans, Hispanics, and Native Americans, American Indians, and Eskimos. These candidates must be college graduates and must submit their grade transcripts in lieu of taking the written examination. Personnel officers then evaluate the candidate's college record, and if they find it acceptable, recommend the Assessment Center examination. To ensure fairness, examining officers in the Assessment Center are not informed whether the minority candidate took the written examination or was passed by an evaluation of college performance.

A serious bottleneck to efficient appointment procedures is the length of time (nine months to a year) required for the necessary security clearance. Some candidates prefer not to wait out the investigation and seek other employment. The long delay in processing results from the heavy work load in the Office of Security caused in large part by the need for security officers to protect visiting foreign dignitaries and senior State Department officials.

In order to make a career in the Foreign Service as attractive as possible, the department provides annual leave and sick leave, group life and medical insurance, and membership in the Foreign Service retirement system. It also reimburses the travel expenses of employees and their families to Washington for appointment, for any subsequent temporary duty assignments in Washington, and for travel to and from assigned posts abroad.

The department supplements the basic salaries of Foreign Service personnel serving overseas by shipping their automobile and personal effects to and from these posts, supplying living quarters or a housing allowance, providing government furniture and storage of personal furniture or shipment of personal furniture, and providing home leave (for which travel expenses are reimbursed), and hospitalization benefits.

An educational allowance and educational travel for dependent children to visit their parents during an academic year, temporary lodging allowance upon arrival at post, separate maintenance allowance, cost of living allowance, and hardship post salary supplements are also provided when appropriate.

Over 750 U.S. colleges and universities are represented in the Foreign Service. Most of the officers have educational backgrounds in history, political science, economics, and management, but many officers are being recruited with backgrounds in science, systems analysis, language and area studies, business and industrial development, environmental science, transportation, and communication because of the growing need for expertise in these fields. Before entering the service, some officers were teachers, lawyers, businessmen, scientists, or journalists, and some worked in the military and the federal government.

Because the value of much of an officer's work depends on his ability to speak and write effectively and to analyze and defend policies and proposals, high priority is given to these qualities in selecting officers and evaluating their performance. Knowledge of a foreign language is not required for appointment, but once hired, new officers must demonstrate professional competency in at least one foreign language before they can be tenured. Those officers who enter with proven and tested language ability in one of the "hard" languages receive a higher salary.

The written examination, the first hurdle for the applicant, takes about half a day and consists of a section testing for general knowledge required for work in the Foreign Service, an English Expression Test, and a Functional Background Test. The general knowledge section is designed to measure a candidate's breadth of understanding of the institutions and concepts that have been fundamental to the development of the United States and other countries, as well as knowledge of important scientific principles, geography, international relations, and the literary, artistic, and philosophical heritage of the United States and other nations. The Functional Background Test measures a candidate's knowledge concerning the four principal functional cones of the Foreign Service (political, economic, consular, and administrative), as well as the work habits (such as diligence and accuracy) required to perform effectively in each of those areas. The English Expression Test measures writing skill and consists of a series of questions that test ability to correct sentences, express ideas clearly and accurately, and revise sentences according to instructions.

To pass the written examination, candidates must achieve passing scores in each of the three parts of the examination. The names of candidates who achieve passing scores in more than one area-specific segment of the Functional Background Test are placed on one or all of the four cone registers, depending on how many segments they pass. The multiple-register candidate has a better chance of being reached for appointment than does a candidate whose name appears on only one cone register, unless the latter's name is near or at the top of the register. (Names do not appear on any register, of course, unless candidates have not only passed the written examination but performed successfully in the Assessment Center and passed their physical examination and security background check.)

In the Assessment Center, candidates are given a day-long examination that includes a variety of job-related simulations and interviews. A panel of trained Foreign Service examiners judges the candidates against a uniform and consistent set of standards and then discusses and scores their observations of each candidate.

The assessment procedures are based on up-to-date job analyses of Foreign Service work and measure the knowledge, abilities (such as oral communication skills, administrative/problem-solving skills, and leadership skills), and personal characteristics (such as interpersonal awareness, cultural awareness, sensitivity, stability, and adjustment) considered necessary to perform that work. Candidates are asked for a personal inventory, in which they provide information on their interests, attitudes, and motivation, as well as an assessment of their areas of strength. They are given a written "in basket" test of managerial skills that is designed to measure ability to plan and organize work, decision-making and problem-solving abilities, interpersonal awareness, and quality of judgment. Candidates have a personal interview with two Foreign Service officers who evaluate their oral communication skills, analytic ability, and breadth of knowledge. They submit a writing sample that is used to measure the effectiveness of their written expression, and they participate in a two-part group exercise that is used to evaluate oral communication skills; ability to analyze and synthesize; interpersonal awareness and skills; ability to lead, negotiate, represent, and mediate; and ability to adjust readily to changing situations. Part one consists of a short oral presentation of a proposal to the group by each candidate, based on material furnished to him; part two is a leaderless group negotiating session in which the various proposals are discussed and an attempt is made to agree on which should be accepted.

A candidate must participate in the assessment process within twelve months after passing the written examination. The names of those candidates who successfully complete the entire examination and assessment process are placed on registers according to the specialty (cone) or specialties in which they have been judged qualified. Each register lists qualified candidates in order of their combined grades in the various phases of the examination and assessment process.

Once their names are placed on a register, candidates are given probationary appointments as career candidates for a period of four years. Appointments are made at the FS-6 through FS-4 levels, depending on previous educational and work experience.

Table 4 gives annual recruitment estimates for FY 1982 to FY 1986 for various categories of Foreign Service employees. Table 5 provides data on the number of men, women, and minorities who passed the written and oral examinations from 1975 through 1978.

In looking at the broad recruitment and examination picture, it is important to remember that the Foreign Service places certain demands on individuals and families that are peculiar to overseas work (such as ensuring adequate education for children, and coping with physical hardships, danger, and inadequate medical facilities). To adjust to these challenges requires discipline and sacrifice. Furthermore, the competition that is so intense throughout the process of recruitment and examination will persist without abatement for the remainder of the officer's career. Promotions are often hard won, especially in the political cone, where there are many more officers than there are positions to be promoted into at a particular grade level. Getting to the top of the Foreign Service, like advancement to the summit in business or the professions, is a stressful experience; only a few succeed. Appointment as an FSO is but the first step in a long journey.

Assignment Procedures

Japan

Because of the differences in size of the personnel systems in the foreign ministry and the State Department, there are some dissimilarities in the methods used to assign officers. For example, categories of positions have a special significance in the assignment of Japanese FSOs. Basically there are two kinds of positions: management (*kanrishoku*) and nonmanagement. In the former category are: (1) positions established by law, including vice-minister, bureau director general, and division chief (line positions); (2) positions established by Cabinet order such as bureau deputy director general and counselor (staff positions); and (3) positions established by ministerial ordinance, including regional coordinator and senior assistant attached to a bureau or division (staff positions).

An officer eligible for any of these positions must be at the class 2 level or above. A young career officer is generally assigned to the general affairs section (*somuhan*) of a division, the section that normally coordinates the division's work. The young noncareer officer works in the planning and analysis and administrative sections of the division.

As a general rule, changes of assignment for junior, midcareer, and senior officers take place in January, April, July, and October. The Personnel Division keeps a list of vacancies and a list of officers, both career and noncareer, who are eligible for reassignment. These lists are kept current and are referred to during the quarterly reassignment period.

The salary level of a career officer and the class to which he belongs are two important considerations in making assignments. The salary or grade

Table 4
State Department Annual Recruitment Estimates, FY 1982–FY 1986

Category	Estimate
Generalist (FSO)	127–194
Auditor	0–2
Budget and fiscal officer	1–5
Communications officer	26–40
Communications engineer	2–8
Diplomatic courier	2–8
Foreign buildings officer	0–2
General services officer	2–6
Medical officer	0–2
Medical technologist	0–2
Narcotics officer	0–1
Nurse	1–5
Personnel officer	1–5
Psychiatrist	0–1
Science officer	0–2
Secretary	68–102
Security engineer	1–5
Security officer	14–20
Total	245–410

Source: *Special Report*, Bureau of Personnel, Department of State, January 1982.

Table 5
Candidates Passing U.S. FSO
Written and Oral Examinations, 1975–1978

Examination	Total	Men	Women	Minorities	Nonminorities
December 1975					
Applications	20,807	14,660	6,147	—	—
Took written	13,744	9,883	3,861	—	—
Passed written	1,508	1,347	161	—	—
	(11)	(14)	(4)	—	—
Took oral	1,094	965	129	—	—
Passed oral	330	289	41	—	—
	(30)	(30)	(32)	—	—
December 1976					
Applications	18,760	13,486	5,274	—	—
Took written	11,814	8,673	3,141	—	—
Passed written	1,729	1,510	219	—	—
	(15)	(17)	(7)	—	—
Took oral	1,276	318	70	—	—
Passed oral	388	318	70	—	—
	(30)	(29)	(41)	—	—
December 1977					
Applications	18,022	11,943	6,079	—	—
Took written	11,531	7,789	3,742	1,339	10,319
Passed written	2,373	1,679	694	60	2,274
	(21)	(22)	(19)	(4)	(22)
Took oral	1,696	1,183	513	23	1,696
Passed oral	353	279	74	8	353
	(21)	(24)	(14)	(35)	(21)
December 1978					
Applications	17,904	11,296	5,798	—	—
Took written	10,123	6,804	3,319	1,382	8,803
Passed written	2,370	1,735	635	89	2,195
	(23)	(25)	(19)	(6)	(25)

SOURCE: U.S., Congress, House, *Hearings on the Foreign Service Act of 1980* (H.R. 4674), 96th Cong., 1st sess., 1979, p. 901.

NOTE: Parentheses indicate percentages; dashes indicate data not available. The statistics resulting from the 1978–79 assessment process are not yet complete. However, an analysis of data for the first 971 candidates to be assessed indicates an overall pass rate of 22 percent. The pass rate for men is 22.4 percent; that for women is 21.3 percent. The pass rate for all minority candidates is 17 percent. The pass rate for minority examination passers (in the assessment process) is 41.7 percent.

level (they are the same) generally determines the broad category of positions to which the officer can be assigned. The class to which he belongs determines the rate of his promotion. When officers reach a certain grade level, they become eligible for positions that traditionally have been assigned to officers at that grade level.

As the members of a class reach grade 4, for example, they become eligible for assignment as a deputy chief of division, a position for which grade 4 officers have traditionally been considered. It is a comfortable system to administer, according to one official in the Personnel Division, because everyone understands that he will be assigned to a certain type of position when he reaches the grade level for which such an assignment is appropriate.

When a particular class reaches grade level 2, its member are, in effect, eligible for assignment to the position of division chief or to an equivalent position abroad (such as counselor of an embassy). The weeding out process begins at this stage and competition (Japanese style) begins to determine the course of an officer's career. Not all class 2 officers are appointed division chiefs. Some, because of their mediocre performance, are sent abroad and usually stay there for the rest of their careers. Failure to be assigned as a division chief may also be a signal from the system that the officer's career has peaked.

The general assignment pattern just described is the visible, more formal pattern followed in day-to-day operations. However, a subsystem exists that is less visible but is nevertheless important to the career development of officers and to the smooth functioning of the assignment process. A good deal of informal discussion takes place between personnel officials and division chiefs and bureau directors general over plans to assign particular officers to particular divisions. The Personnel Division does not usually force an assignment on a reluctant division chief or bureau director general. Sometimes, the division or bureau chief has his own candidate, most likely an officer with whom he has worked in the past and whose qualifications he knows well. In these circumstances, the two sides discuss the assignment; generally a solution is found that is acceptable to both parties. If this is not possible, the Personnel Division may withdraw its nomination and begin a search for a new candidate. Such a search may take three or four months, during which the concerned bureau may be without a needed officer. In this way the Personnel Division can exert subtle pressure on the division or bureau to accept its candidate.

One director general of an important geographic bureau told me that although he theoretically had veto power over an assignment proposal, he was most reluctant to use it and favored seeking a compromise. He did not like to request a particular officer for his bureau because it might cause morale problems and put the concerned officer "on the spot." If bureaus were allowed to select their own officers, he said, the system would be in complete disorder. He was therefore usually willing to accept the proposals of the Personnel Division, and where differences did exist, to attempt to resolve them through discussion and compromise.

The subsystem appears to be effective in determining the future assignments of young career officers. When an officer approaches time for reassignment, he either takes the initiative and discusses his preferences for future assignments with the division chief or the deputy (both fellow career officers), or he waits for one of his superiors to initiate the discussion. After the discussion, the chief of the division or his deputy relays the young officer's desires for his next assignment to the Personnel Division, and presents his division's recommendations. If the division chief or deputy succeeds in getting an attractive assignment for the young officer, it not only enhances the reputation of his division, tending to draw promising young officers there, but encourages newly assigned officers to work hard so they can increase their chances of securing choice assignments.

Thus, the subsystem meets the needs of bureaus and divisions, whereas the more formal system supports overall personnel requirements by providing a mechanism for the assignment and rotation of officers in accordance with tradition and custom.

Some interesting statistics are available concerning other aspects of the personnel system. There are no regulations governing the length of time officers can be assigned in Tokyo. The average length of an overseas tour of duty is about two years and eight months.

For assignment purposes, officers in grades 7 and 6 are usually considered to be at the junior level, those in grades 5 to 3 are in midcareer, and those in grades 2 and 1 and the Designated Class are the seniors. About 37 percent of the officers are in the geographic bureaus, 20 percent are in the Economic Affairs Bureau, 35 percent are in the Minister's Secretariat, and 8 percent are in the Consular Department.

At any one time about 40 to 70 officers are awaiting assignment. If an officer is assigned as a division chief or as a deputy director general or director general of a bureau, it usually indicates that the officer will eventually obtain an important ambassadorial post. One ambassador awaiting assignment to another ambassadorial post told me that the critical point in a career officer's professional life is his assignment as a division chief; that appointment may be the springboard for his advance to the top of the service, but it does not always assure he will get there. Some kachō do not gain the coveted ambassadorial assignments to the United States, Great Britain, China, the Soviet Union, or France or become directors general of bureaus, but have to settle for lesser posts. They are sometimes unhappy, but they accept the reality of competition at the senior levels.

By examining careers of successful Foreign Service officers, one gains a better picture of the kinds of assignments that contributed to their success. The careers of five of them are summarized in the following paragraphs.

Former Vice-Minister Sunobe Ryozo, appointed to that post in July 1981, was born in Saitama Prefecture, graduated from Tokyo University, and entered the foreign ministry in 1940. He has served as minister to the Soviet Union and to the United States, director general of the Asian Affairs Bureau, and ambassador to the Netherlands, Indonesia, and Korea. Ambassador Sunobe, when he was chief of the Personnel Division (a position that seems to assure further advancement), had to deal with an officer complaining about a particular assignment. When the officer became agitated and slapped Sunobe on the left side of his face, Sunobe reportedly reacted by inviting the complainant to strike him on the right cheek as well. This story has been handed down in the foreign ministry as indicative of Sunobe's physical endurance and stoic nature.[4]

Katori Yasue, formerly a deputy vice-minister, was appointed ambassador to China in August 1981. He was born in Sendai City in 1921, studied at Tokyo University, and entered the foreign ministry in 1943. Katori has served as chief of the Finance Division, minister to India, chief of the Minister's Secretariat, director general of the Economic Cooperation Bureau, and ambassador to Austria.[5]

Yanagiya Kensuke was formerly deputy vice-minister for administration and was appointed deputy vice-minister to replace Katori in August 1981. Born in Tokyo in 1924, he graduated from the law faculty of Tokyo University, and entered the foreign ministry in 1948. He has been assigned as chief of the Financial and Accounting Division, minister to China, and director general of the Public Information and Cultural Affairs Bureau and the Asian Affairs Bureau.[6]

Date Muneoki, the former director general of the Treaties Bureau, was appointed deputy vice-minister for administration in August 1981, replacing Yanagiya. He was born in Tokyo in 1918, graduated from the law faculty of Tokyo University, and entered the foreign ministry in 1950. Date has served as chief of the Northeast Asian Division, counselor of the Public Information and Cultural Affairs Bureau, deputy chief of the Cabinet Research Office, and counselor in charge of Central and South American affairs.[7]

Kuriyama Takakazu, formerly deputy director general of the Treaties Bureau, was appointed director general of that bureau in August 1981, replacing Date. He was born in Tokyo in 1931, studied at Tokyo University, and entered the foreign ministry in 1953. His positions have included chief of the Treaties Division of the Treaties Bureau, counselor of the Japanese Embassy in Washington, chief of the Personnel Division, and deputy director general of the North American Affairs Bureau.[8]

The careers of these officers have followed a common path: education at Tokyo University and service in key functional posts such as economics, finance, and personnel, and in substantive positions in the major geographic bureaus. I talked with two of these officers and found them highly intelligent, pragmatic, and dedicated. They were both aware of the need for some change in the personnel structure to improve resource allocation and had given much time to analyzing the ways in which such change might successfully be accomplished.

It would be a mistake to ignore the role of politics in the assignment process. Intense competition exists for top positions, but it is subtle because of the traditional Japanese practice of masking true feelings and intent and avoiding open confrontation or a show of excessive ambition. Such behavior is comfortable and workable in a service that is relatively small, compact, and influenced by history.

There is some temporary exchange of personnel between the foreign ministry and other agencies of the Japanese government. As international relations grow in complexity, so does the need for this exchange. Assignments to the ministry under the exchange program are generally for a two- to three-year period. At the conclusion of their assignments, the officers return to their parent agencies—the ministry does not recruit officers from other agencies for permanent positions in the career service. Lateral entry into the career service at the middle or senior grades, which sometimes happens in the U.S. Foreign Service, is relatively unheard of in Japan. The Japanese system is so finely balanced and so influenced by custom and tradition that an integration policy of this kind would be unworkable. The temporary exchange program meets current needs and educates the personnel of participating agencies about important aspects of foreign affairs.

Assignment patterns vary. Career and noncareer officers are assigned to such agencies and organizations as the Executive Office of the House of Representatives and of the House of Councillors, and the Secretariat of the Cabinet. They may be appointed secretaries to the prime minister or to the deputy director general of the Cabinet, or made public relations officers in various government agencies or officers in the legislative bureaus. Senior and middle-level officers are assigned to such agencies and ministries as the International Cooperation Agency, the Overseas Economic Cooperation Fund, the International Exchange Fund, the Japan External Trade Organization, the Administrative Management Agency, the Economic Planning

Agency, the Defense Agency, and the Ministries of Finance; Agriculture, Forestry, and Fisheries; Justice; Education; and International Trade and Industry. The foreign ministry stipulates that most officers from other ministries who are assigned to Japanese embassies and consular posts abroad must have passed the High National Public Service Examination, a policy prompted by a desire to give other nations a favorable impression of Japan.

An interesting mix of agencies sends officers to the foreign ministry. Over 440 such officers were on temporary detail to provide needed expertise as of September 1980. They came from such organizations as the Prime Minister's Office, the National Personnel Authority, the National Police Agency, the Defense Agency, the Economic Planning Agency, the Cabinet, the House of Representatives and House of Councillors, and the Ministries of Justice; Finance; International Trade and Industry; Agriculture, Forestry, and Fisheries; Education; and Health and Welfare.

The presence of these officers abroad has sometimes created certain communication and administrative problems. The regular personnel at embassies must give administrative support to representatives of other government agencies, and this places a heavy burden on the staff. But a more serious problem, denounced strongly by one foreign ministry official, is that many representatives of other agencies bypass the ambassador and high embassy officials and deal directly with their home offices in Tokyo. Under the law, the foreign ministry in Tokyo is the "spokesman" for Japan, and official communications from all embassies must go to that ministry before being distributed to the other agencies concerned. Unfortunately, the official said, this does not always happen, and the result is a weakening of the position of the foreign ministry.

The United States

Aside from determining the careers of Foreign Service officers, the assignment process—the matching of officer qualifications to position requirements—plays a key role in the State Department's ability to carry out its mandate. One might at first conclude that the process has become too mechanical, too computerized, too regulated, too indifferent to the needs of officers, too circumscribed by labor union demands, too compartmentalized, and too subject to management manipulation. In some ways this is so, but there has also been innovation, including the adoption of procedures to ensure more equity. The open assignment process, discussed later in this chapter, is an example of management's efforts to show more fairness in making assignments. However, much of the assignment process remains unchanged. The irresistibility of the "buddy-buddy" system in the selection of officers for important positions has not lessened, and although not institutionalized, it is still almost a bureaucratic law of nature. Its chief exponents are the senior departmental officials, ambassadors, and assistant secretaries.

In one sense it is important for top managers and policymakers to select as their own assistants officers they know well as a result of past working relationships. If a top official wants a particular FSO for his office, the Bureau of Personnel can do little to challenge the assignment, even if it has a strong case. "Rank has its privileges" is a well-entrenched principle, and those Foreign Service officers who are selected by their seniors for important positions on the basis of this principle are guaranteed a generally bright future.

The selection process often works this way. An ambassador in a certain country who is well served by the country director in charge of that country will request that the officer be made his deputy chief of mission. Even if the country director is becoming too specialized in an area and needs an out-of-area assignment for the purpose of career development, there is little the Bureau of Personnel can do about it. The relationship may not end there. If the ambassador is assigned to a high State Department position, he may ask for the same officer again, provided they still share mutual respect and trust. This is very much like the oyabun-kobun (patron-client) relationship in Japan. Young officers are especially eager to have such assignments, as they consider them a good way to advance rapidly in their careers—and they often do, provided their performance is of high quality.

These machinations by senior officials often cause difficulty for the assignment system. I recall the case of a certain young officer who was a protégé of a senior officer. He was assigned to an embassy in Asia, but the assignment was changed and he remained in the State Department. The Bureau of Personnel made several attempts to move the FSO to an overseas post, but each time the effort failed. There are not many cases as flagrant as this one (one senior personnel officer observed that the buddy-buddy system is affecting a smaller range of positions), but the fact that they are possible is frustrating to personnel officials and demoralizing to FSOs.

The assignment process is also affected by the tug-of-war that often exists between the central personnel organization and the regional and functional bureaus—the struggle of centralization versus decentralization. The contest appears to have reached a standoff, with the Bureau of Personnel attempting to look after the personnel needs of the Foreign Service on a departmentwide basis, and the regional and functional bureaus trying to fill their personnel needs by transferring officers who have developed bureau identifications.

Both units are becoming more aware of the need to work together. The central personnel organization, with its near monopoly of the personnel data necessary for assignment, career development, promotion, and training, does not arbitrarily make assignments without consultation with the bureaus. The latter often know more than the Bureau of Personnel about the requirements for a particular position in a regional bureau or at an embassy or consulate in its area of jurisdiction. The byplay between the central organization and the regional bureaus before formal actions are taken by the assignment panels goes a long way toward resolving differences.

Selection of Ambassadors

Ambassadors are selected from among career Foreign Service officers and from citizens in the private sector. The selection procedure reflects the realities of the political system in the United States where the administration in power rewards its backers in the private sector with choice diplomatic posts. On the average, about 65 percent of the ambassadorships are awarded to career officers and 35 percent go to those outside the State Department. Table 6 gives a breakdown of career and noncareer ambassadorial appointments from 1961 to 1981.

This dual selection method has posed a persistent morale problem for management. All young Foreign Service officers have their career sights set on an ambassadorship as the cap to their professional careers. The level of expectation has changed little over the years; neither has the ratio of career appointees to political appointees. Congress has made several efforts to limit the number of ambassadorships given to political appointees, including the introduction in 1982 of legislation by a senator from an eastern state to limit the ambassadorships awarded to persons outside the Foreign Service to 15 percent. (The bill did not pass.)

As one former Foreign Service officer wisely pointed out, it is misleading to give the impression to every young FSO that he might become an ambassador. There are simply not enough ambassadorships to go around, even if all FSOs were qualified for such assignments—and all are not. The time has come, he said, to be frank with entering FSOs concerning the realities of a competitive service and to assure them that a career can be considered successful without attainment of an ambassadorship. An attempt is being made in this regard and it is reportedly having a therapeutic effect on officers' morale.

Officers who are selected for ambassadorial assignments must pass a careful screening process that begins in the Bureau of Personnel with the

Table 6
U.S. Ambassadorial Appointments, 1961–1981

REAGAN ADMINISTRATION APPOINTMENTS AS OF NOVEMBER 20, 1981

Type of Appointment	Career	Noncareer
Bilateral Missions		
Remaining at post	40	2
Newly chosen	39	26
Subtotal	79 (74)	28 (26)
Multilateral Missions and Ambassadors-at-large		
Remaining at post (NATO)	1	0
Newly chosen	4	10
Subtotal	5 (33.3)	10 (66.7)
Total	84 (68.9)	38 (31.1)

APPOINTMENTS TO BILATERAL MISSIONS, 1961–1980

Year	Career	Noncareer
1961	67 (72)	26 (28)
1962	63 (64)	35 (36)
1963	66 (65)	36 (35)
1964	74 (73)	27 (27)
1965	79 (72)	30 (28)
1966	80 (75)	26 (25)
1967	73 (71)	30 (29)
1968	71 (66)	36 (34)
1969	68 (68)	32 (32)
1970	72 (68)	34 (32)
1971	73 (68)	34 (32)
1972	72 (68)	27 (27)
1973	72 (68)	29 (29)
1974	80 (68)	36 (31)
1975	80 (68)	32 (28)
1976	82 (68)	35 (30)
1977	86 (68)	24 (22)
1978	92 (68)	30 (25)
1979	91 (68)	30 (25)
1980	94 (68)	30 (24)

MINORITIES AND WOMEN

Group	New Appointees	Incumbents
Women	5	4
Blacks	4	2
Hispanics	4	1

SOURCE: *Foreign Service Newsletter*, December 1981.
NOTE: Parentheses indicate percentages.

preparation of a list of six to ten officers considered qualified for a particular ambassadorial vacancy. This list is given to the appropriate assistant secretary of the relevant geographic bureau for his recommendations. The assistant secretary arranges his top three or four choices in rank order and may add some names of his own. A departmental committee chaired by the deputy secretary of state and composed of the under secretary of state for political affairs, the director general of the Foreign Service, the under secretary of state for management, the executive secretary of the State Department, the counselor of the State Department, and the special assistant to the secretary of state then considers the nominations of the Bureau of Personnel, the rank-order list of the geographic bureau's assistant secretary, and other nominations from committee members. In its deliberations, the committee has traditionally given major weight to the choice of the assistant secretary because the latter must work closely with the new ambassador and have confidence and trust in the ambassador's ability to perform his duties. The committee sends its recommendation to the secretary of state, who decides what name should go to the president for nomination.

The general officer assignment process of the State Department differs markedly from that of Japan's foreign ministry in both style and function. The main differences are the use of open, stretch, and tandem assignments, the mechanics of the assignment process, and, to some extent, the tour-of-duty policy.

Open Assignments. The "open" method of assignment, introduced in 1981, is an innovation in the personnel process designed to give all FSOs an equal chance at assignments. It was strongly endorsed by AFSA as a remedy to what the union called a haphazard approach to assignments. The Bureau of Personnel prepares a list of positions that will become available during a certain period and sends it to all FSOs who are available for reassignment, requesting that they bid on the positions desired. Each FSO can submit from six to fifteen ranked bids, which must fall into at least two geographic areas. After the bids have been returned, they are consolidated and given to the regional and functional bureaus for comment. The executive director of each bureau sends his bureau's response to the Bureau of Personnel, and when differences exist, representatives of Personnel and of the relevant bureau try to arrive at a mutually satisfactory decision.

According to several officials in the personnel organization, open bidding on assignments has both good and bad points. On the plus side, it provides FSOs who are eligible for reassignment with a list of positions that will become available in a certain period and allows them to bid on the positions for which they wish to be considered. On the minus side, it has resulted in even more politicking by FSOs who, aware that a particular position will become available, ask colleagues to intercede on their behalf. Furthermore, the open bidding process often results in imbalances. Few FSOs bid for assignment to hardship posts, and these positions often go unfilled for unacceptable lengths of time. Competition for desirable posts is heightened because more officers know of their availablity. Sometimes FSOs believe they are qualified for an important position when they are still lacking in the necessary experience and skills. The net effect is that it is becoming more and more difficult to fill essential positions and to get the job done. At a certain point, the State Department sends a message to all posts listing overbid, underbid, and unbid positions, requesting officers to reconsider earlier bids in order to take action on those posts that have few or no applicants. Management sometimes has to resort to forced assignments, but with reluctance because ambassadors do not want FSOs who have expressed opposition to an assignment at their post. Forced assignments to the unfilled positions in embassies and consulates can be made only if certain steps, prescribed under labor-management arrangements to safeguard the rights of FSOs, are followed.

The process of compiling lists of available positions, sending them to all FSOs eligible for reassignment throughout the world, and processing the bids is also time-consuming. Even with this assignment method, assistant secretaries still play a major role in selecting country directors and other key officers for their bureaus. If, per chance, there is a coincidence between an assistant secretary's choice and the bid of an officer who is up for reassignment, the position is filled swiftly—but this does not happen often.

"Rank has its privileges" with regard to the assignment process has as much vitality today as ever and is an operative principle in the upper echelons of the State Department. Political officers are favored over the FSOs in the other three skill cones. For example, political officers obtain most of the deputy chief of mission assignments, most of the country director positions, and most of the important officer slots at consulates. Consular, administrative, and, to a lesser extent, economic officers are excluded from these choice positions on the grounds that they are not qualified to assume "program direction" responsibilities. This argument has a hollow ring to those excluded because they have never had a chance to gain the necessary experience.

As I listened to the complaints of consular and administrative officers while visiting the State Department in January 1982, I could not help recalling my many conversations with noncareer officers in the Japanese foreign ministry in 1980–1981, who were unhappy at not obtaining more important and challenging work, and with the career officers who explained that noncareerists were not put into important positions in the ministry because they were unqualified.

It is probably too early to pass judgment on the effectiveness of the open assignment process, even though it is generally acknowledged to be time-consuming, cumbersome, a headache to management, and of questionable cost-effectiveness. This innovation has not eliminated what it was intended to eliminate—the politicking and favoritism of the past—but it has given officers a greater range of choices and the opportunity to bid on positions that they want and believe will contribute to their career advancement. In effect, it has given the FSOs a greater stake in their own futures by involving them more intimately in the assignment process.

Stretch Assignments.   The term "stretch assignment" simply means that promising new FSOs at grade 1 are assigned to senior positions, mainly at the counselor level, thus giving these officers an opportunity to demonstrate their capability to perform at senior levels and their potential for pro-motion. The stretch assignment also provides a mechanism by which a new assistant secretary, for example, can promote his own choice for a country director, often a new FSO, by utilizing a slot that would otherwise go to a senior officer. In 1982, about 25 percent of the senior positions were held by new officers. As a consequence, there are senior officers who have no as-signments.

One problem related to stretch assignments is what is known as senior officer holdback—the reduction in promotion opportunities for the senior class in order to provide senior officer assignment opportunities for midlevel officers. Historically, management has assigned midlevel officers to senior positions in order to satisfy the desires of senior officials and to reward ambitious officers with important senior assignments. Such a policy was not called "stretch assignments," but the effect was the same—junior officers displaced senior officers in senior positions, causing a glut of senior FSOs with no assignments. The tradition appears to be continuing and has now been given a name.

Tandem Assignments.   Tandem assignments, or the posting of husband and wife to the same embassy or consulate, are increasing because couples, for economic and career reasons, wish to stay together. In 1982, tandem assignments comprised about 5 percent of total overseas assignments. The State Department is making reasonable efforts to assign working couples to the same post in positions appropriate to their class levels and qualifications. If such assignments are not feasible, the husband and wife may be assigned to positions at different posts, or either spouse may be granted leave without pay for the duration of the other's tour of duty. The couple is consulted on the alternatives. If both spouses are at the same post, one cannot exercise supervisory authority over the other, and this includes serving as a rating or reviewing officer, giving instructions on assignment of work, or initiating discipline.

Tour-of-Duty Policy.   In general, rotation policy for nonhardship posts is two years, followed by home leave and return to the same post for two years, or a straight three-year assignment and transfer. For hardship posts, usually in Africa, the policy is eighteen months and transfer, or eighteen months, home leave, and return for eighteen months.

The so-called three in fifteen rule has been broadened somewhat by the Foreign Service Act of 1980. All FSOs are now required to spend at least three out of each fifteen years of service in the United States. Exceptions to this rule are based on the needs of the service. Any continuous period of more than 120 days is counted toward the three years.

Normal tours of duty in the United States for FSOs are limited to four years, and extensions of more than one year beyond that limit require the approval of the director general of the Foreign Service. This is not a significant departure from past practices but merely a reaffirmation of the four-year domestic tour-of-duty policy, a policy that was being stretched by the granting of exception after exception for "personal" reasons. The trend toward longer tours of duty in the United States has made it increasingly difficult to maintain satisfactory staffing levels at embassies and consulates.

Language-designated Positions.   There has long been a policy of designating certain positions in embassies for officers with a required level of competence in the language of the country in which the embassy is located. Recommendations for such designation are initially made by the post after a determination of how many officers with required language proficiency are needed to support the basic mission of the post. The recommendations are then sent to the Personnel Bureau, where they are processed. An inventory of officers with required language proficiency is maintained, and these officers are assigned to language-designated positions under a normal tour-of-duty policy.

Officers with language competence below the level of R4 (reading), S4 (speaking), who have not been tested in the preceding five years, must be retested by the Foreign Service Institute prior to proceeding to a post. If a new test shows results below R4, S4, a period of special language instruction has to be scheduled in order for the officer to regain the required level of competence.

The numbers of language-designated positions at the U.S. Embassy in Tokyo and at U.S. consular posts in Japan, have usually been considered insufficient to satisfactorily carry out the mission of the embassy. This has been especially true in the economic section, where there has usually been a dearth of Japanese-speaking officers who were also skilled economists.

Japanese is a very difficult language and officers with only an R3, S3 level of competence have usually had to study for two years at the embassy language school in Tokyo/Yokohama. These officers, who were normally in the political cone (which contains most of the language-designated positions), were expected to spend several tours of duty in Japan after finishing such training. Economic officers, by contrast, because they have had to undertake considerable economic study at the Foreign Service Institute or in a university in the United States before assuming their economic duties in Tokyo, have had little time left for Japanese language training.

As economic and trade relations between the United States and Japan become increasingly important, economic officers with a competence in Japanese are becoming increasingly necessary in Tokyo, and the State Department, apparently in recognition of this need, is assigning more economic officers to Japanese language training.

Mechanics of Assignment. The two assignment periods are the summer cycle, when most transfers take place, and the so-called off cycle—the remainder of the year. During the summer cycle, there are approximately 1,000 position openings and about the same number of officers available for reassignment.

As mentioned, the cost-effectiveness of the assignment process is questionable. For example, there are about 80 officers on the various assignment panels, and they make about 4,000 assignments a year (50 assignments per panelist annually, or 40 man-hours per assignment). This is considered too heavy a manpower cost by some senior officials in the director general's office. But the panel assignment system is well entrenched, having been used for many decades, and no one has yet come up with a better, more cost-effective idea.

Seven panels exist, one for each functional cone (political, economic, administrative, consular), one for secretaries, one for communicators, and one called an interfunctional panel, which handles the difficult decisions and senior assignments. All panels meet once a week. The interfunctional panel is chaired by the chief of the Office of Foreign Service Career Development and Assignments. Represented on this panel are officers from the five geographic bureaus, a training and liaison officer, an officer responsible for junior assignments and one responsible for senior assignments, and one officer representing each of the four cones. Each geographic bureau representative prepares an agenda for discussion. The panel makes assignments to positions that are not designated by cone and also handles all assignment problems and policies that require the consideration of representatives of all grades and functions, including issues that cannot be settled by subpanels. It often merely takes formal action on personnel decisions that have been the subject of informal discussions between the central personnel organization and the bureaus, such as the assignment of hard-to-place officers or officers sought by more than one geographic bureau, and exceptions to the tour-of-duty policy.

Of inestimable value to the personnel officer in making assignments is what is known as the "corridor reputation" of an officer—his peers' opinion of him, his weaknesses and strengths, his personality, his character, and his behavior under stress. Much of this information is, of course, contained in the officer's official dossier, but some information that is of a "corridor" variety never finds its way into an officer's official file. The personnel officer must be scrupulous in his investigation of rumor and innuendo and not allow unsubstantiated hearsay to influence his judgment; he must be sagacious in order to preserve the equity of the system. Having sat on many panels and having engaged in many informal discussions regarding officers' assignments, I know that officials in the Bureau of Personnel do their utmost to be fair and to promote an officer's career interests while trying to satisfy the needs of the service. It is sometimes a difficult balancing act, but the rewards are a well-staffed mission or office and high officer morale.

The Senior Officer Division in the Bureau of Personnel is responsible for the management of the careers of officers at the levels of counselor, minister counselor, and career minister, and for the staffing of all Foreign Service positions at these levels. It prepares lists of candidates for the positions of chief of mission, assistant secretary, and the equivalent of both, and must pay special attention to what are known as key positions in the State Department and overseas. In the State Department, these positions are deputy assistant secretary, special or staff assistant to an assistant secretary or to another senior officer of the department, secretary to an assistant secretary or to another senior official, senior watch officer in the Operations Center, and staff officer in the Executive Secretariat. Overseas, such positions include the deputy chief of mission, the special or staff assistant to the ambassador, and the secretary to the ambassador.

The Senior Officer Division often has the difficult tasks of protecting senior officer positions from the intrusion of "stretch assignment FSOs" and of finding suitable work for senior officers who, because of their seniority and experience, have placed certain valuations on their skills that they believe require recognition in their next assignments. It is not always possible to do so, and officers in this division are frequently frustrated in their attempts to deal with the chronic problem of senior officer surplus. Some believe that the surplus problem will become manageable only if there is strict enforcement of the TIC regulations established in 1981 and if limited extensions for senior officers facing TIC are granted prudently.

The Career Development Officer. The career development officer (CDO) has essentially two functions: he participates in the activities of the assignment panel, and he determines the career development preferences and needs of career Foreign Service officers. The CDO's objective is to make the most efficient use of the Foreign Service human resource pool—that is, he evaluates FSO assignment preferences against position requirements, assesses the present and potential qualifications and career development needs of FSOs, and suggests one or more candidates for each position becoming available, attempting to identify the best-qualified candidates for the priority jobs.

A most important and often the most difficult task of the CDO is to counsel an FSO as to his career potential; to provide realistic and objective answers to such questions as: Why have I not been promoted in the past several years? Have I a future in the Foreign Service? As a CDO, I often had to sit across the table from a discouraged FSO and explain to him why I believed his career had peaked, as well as some of the reasons why I felt that he had not been promoted.

I recall the case of one midlevel FSO who had been in the same grade for seven years and who was very disheartened because his friends were passing him by on the career ladder. He asked why his career was in trouble. This particular officer was diligent and careful, but cautious and rather dilatory in making decisions. He was also in the highly competitive political cone where such a career profile could be a liability rather than an asset. In counseling this officer, I had to determine whether his expectations were inflated and unrealistic; whether his reputation in his parent geographic bureau was such that he would have difficulty securing a position in the bureau that could lead to promotion; and whether the pattern of performance revealed in his official record would predictably cap his career at midlevel. I told him that I had reluctantly come to the conclusion, based on my own evaluation of his career and my discussion of it with other officers in the Bureau of Personnel and in his geographic bureau, that if he stayed in the political cone, he would run the risk of involuntary retirement as a result of TIC. His options were few. He could either stay in his present cone, or he could switch to another, less competitive cone and attempt to rebuild his career. He chose the latter option, was promoted within the consular cone, and became a first-class consular officer.

This FSO had early in his career misjudged his abilities and had opted for the more glamorous political cone, whose members, he felt, were all slated to become ambassadors. When the competition became more intense as he moved to the middle level of the Foreign Service, his career stalled. The responsibility of the CDO was to explain the situation to him and to present him with career options. In this case, all turned out for the best. However, when the CDO does not succeed in persuading a disgruntled FSO to re-evaluate his career, the officer continues to stumble ahead in a career filled with more disappointment than satisfaction.

Performance Evaluation and Promotion: Japan

The system for evaluating and promoting officers is more flexible, informal, and traditional in Japan than in the United States, in general because the two services differ in size, in the attitudes of their FSOs, and in the professional milieus in which they operate. Security, harmony, and class identification are important characteristics of the professionalism of the Japanese FSO. (Intense competition, the "up or out" philosophy of personnel management, and a concern for self and for promotion determine the actions of the U.S. Foreign Service officer.)

In the foreign ministry, an officer's performance is evaluated annually by his immediate superior, whose report is reviewed by a senior officer—either the director general of the bureau to which the officer is assigned or, if he is overseas, by the chief of mission or his deputy. The completed report is then sent to the Personnel Division for further review; particular attention is given to evaluating the evaluator to ensure that fairness and objectivity are maintained and to preserve the credibility of the system.

In one section of the efficiency report the rating officer checks either "excellent" or "insufficient" in judging such factors as drafting ability, personal relations, promptness, thoroughness, initiative, and loyalty. A narrative section provides rating and reviewing officers with opportunities to expand on checked items. I observed several evaluation reports on career officers and noted that "excellent" was checked for all factors relating to work performance, personality, and character. Commenting on this, an official of the Personnel Division said that with only two standards of evaluation, there is considerable margin for error. Therefore, the Personnel Division attaches considerable importance to the narrative part of the efficiency report. If the director general of a bureau or the chief of mission, as a reviewing officer, disagrees with the evaluation, he can explain his reasons in writing and present his own evaluation of the officer's performance and potential. Even though this option is open to the reviewing officer, it is seldom used. Rather, the rating and reviewing officers consult with each other to arrive at a common understanding.

There are four ways in which a career officer is evaluated: (1) the annual efficiency report, (2) informal letters from supervisors to officers commenting on their work performance, (3) achievement cards sent to all departments in the foreign ministry and to overseas posts to record noteworthy accomplishments (these cards are checked carefully in the Personnel Division for bona fides), and (4) information gained from unofficial sources (word of mouth and corridor gossip) and Personnel Division inquiries of former supervisors regarding a particular officer.

The information compiled on an officer is maintained in a large register in the Personnel Division and used for assignment and promotion purposes. In addition, the division has a file on each officer showing his assignment and training history, language skills, class, and salary grade. This information and his efficiency report file comprise the officer's record.

The small size of the career corps makes the evaluation process, both formal and informal, simple and manageable. There is quick access to information about officers' strengths and weaknesses, which provides the basis for decisions on key assignments. In a broader sense, the flow of such information determines not only an officer's standing in his own class but the reputation of the class as a whole.

The Personnel Division is working to improve the record-keeping system and administrative operations, but there is no apparent haste to modernize, according to one official, because the division's system of performance evaluation and assignments works well. He said that the service has its own way of doing things, with informality and fluidity the hallmarks of the system. Change for the sake of change will not be considered, but change to improve efficiency where such improvement is clearly called for will be implemented. In this regard, he said, the Japanese are studying the application of computers to the system.

The rate of promotion for career officers is approximately as follows:

Class 7 to class 6	1 year (apprentice training)
Class 6 to class 5	3 years
Class 5 to class 4	3 years
Class 4 to class 3	4 years
Class 3 to class 2	4 years

The rate of promotion from class 7 to class 2 is determined by foreign ministry regulations. Each ministry in the Japanese government has a somewhat different time span between promotions, but the salary structure is uniform throughout.

Performance Evaluation and Promotion: United States

At the heart of the U.S. Foreign Service career system is the promotion process, which, since the Rogers Act of 1924, has been based on the merit principle. Most officers in the Foreign Service, even those who are sometimes selected out for substandard performance, acknowledge that the system is perhaps as fair as can be devised. The centerpiece of the promotion process is the Selection Board, a group of outstanding individuals from inside and outside the Foreign Service (including at least one public member and with a good representation of women and minorities) who evaluate the performance of officers and rank them for promotion purposes.

The cornerstone of the evaluation process is the annual efficiency report, an evalution of an officer's performance by his supervisor. This report is reviewed by a more senior officer and then is sent to the officer's official file in the Bureau of Personnel, where it is carefully examined to see that all regulations regarding its preparation have been complied with.

The charter for Selection Boards is called the precepts. The State Department prepares the precepts in collaboration with AFSA prior to each Selection Board session; both parties negotiate and usually come to an agreement on the major articles. Under an executive order that was codified by the Foreign Service Act of 1980, AFSA has the right to review the proposed precepts three months before a Selection Board convenes and to submit its views and comments on potential Selection Board candidates.

Precepts are prepared for the Intermediate Foreign Service Selection Boards, which evaluate officers in classes FS-2 through FS-8, and for the Senior Foreign Service Selection Boards (the Senior Threshold Selection Boards), which evaluate career ministers, minister counselors, counselors, and FS-1 officers being considered for promotion to the senior ranks. A Senior Specialist and Specialist Threshold Board evaluates officers in the specialist category (labor, communication, security, medicine) for promotion to or within the senior ranks. The senior boards also determine who will receive limited career extensions through a rank-order process. Junior officers compete on a classwide basis because there are not enough reports in their files to evaluate them on a skill code basis. The basic philosophy of the promotion system is that boards determine merit and management determines need. An FS-1 political cone officer competes in the political cone as well as on a classwide basis for program direction. He thus has two chances for promotion to the Senior Foreign Service (in the political cone, and classwide as a program direction officer) and is ranked by the board in both categories. If management decides to promote ten political officers and five program direction officers, and if he is ranked seventh in the political cone but eighth in the program direction category, he will be promoted on the basis of his rank in the political cone, even though he has failed in the program direction category. About 90 percent of junior officer candidates are tenured as a result of their performance on the junior officer threshold examination. Most candidates make tenure on the second review of their file. By then, they are class 4 officers and can expect to have a 25-year professional career without worrying too much about promotions until they face mandatory retirement. Selection out and TIC become serious considerations only when officers reach the senior levels.

An important problem with regard to promotion is what groups of senior officers should compete against each other, that is, what competitive groups should be established. For example, should specialists and generalists in the senior ranks compete in one group or in separate groups? Are there enough common criteria for evaluation of both groups together or are their functions so different that they should compete separately? Can a labor specialist of counselor rank compete fairly against a generalist of similar rank, or should he compete against other labor officers? Would his chances of promotion be better in the counselor rank if he competed in the labor specialty or if he competed across the board? These difficult questions are being studied and debated in the service.

The 1981 Senior Threshold Selection Board Precepts stipulated that FS-1 generalists and specialists be judged by separate boards. Generalists were defined as career officers with program direction or with generalist (administrative, consular, economic, or political cone) primary skills; they would compete both classwide and by cone for promotion opportunities, based on estimated vacancies in multifunctional and functional positions at the counselor level. Specialists were to be considered by occupational category for available promotion opportunities in their fields. Those promoted to the senior ranks would retain their occupational skill code and would be expected to fill senior positions in their fields. Statistically, more promotions would be available for generalists, but the competition among specialists would be more severe and therefore these positions would probably be less appealing.

When evaluating officers with generalist skill codes who are competing classwide, the Selection Boards look for evidence of the leadership and managerial qualities necessary to carry out executive responsibilities that span more than a single function. Judgment of conal competition and of competition of specialists within their occupational categories is based on demonstrated expertise and leadership in the functional area of career concentration. In evaluating all groups, the boards look particularly for evidence of accomplishment and potential in those aspects of leadership, intellectual development, interpersonal and managerial skills, and substantive knowledge that have been identified as important for superior Foreign Service performance.

The composition of competitive groups is determined by the employees' pay plans and skill codes and is based on negotiated agreements with AFSA:

Class to Which Promoted	Nature of Competition
Career minister	Classwide
Minister counselor	Classwide
Counselor	Functional and classwide
Class 1	Functional
Class 2	Functional
Class 3 (FSO)	Classwide
Class 3 (specialist)	Functional

The performance of all career officers eligible to request promotion consideration (those who have been in a grade one year or more) is reviewed by Selection Boards for possible selection out because of the officers' failure to maintain the standard of performance of their class, whether or not they have applied for promotion consideration. Cases in which an officer is identified for possible selection out are decided by the Performance Standards Board. The performance of all FS-1 officers with career appointments, whether or not they were previously subject to selection out for unsatisfactory performance, is similarly reviewed.

Now that all officers are subject to being selected out, involuntary retirement, which is what selection out really is, has become a more important consideration in the career calculations of FSOs, especially senior officers. The threat creates apprehension for many FSOs, especially those with mediocre performance records. The victim feels discouragement or despair, humiliation, anger, and resentment. It is also an unpleasant experience for the board members who have to make the decision, especially those who are colleagues of the FSO. As a result, selection out has been honored more in the breach since the 1970s.

The Foreign Service Act of 1980 emphasized anew the importance of selection out as a means of cleaning out the service. Skeptics continue to wonder, however, whether management will be any more willing now than in the past to resort to it for this purpose. There is reason for such skepticism. More attention is being given to due process for officers who perceive an injustice. Formerly, when an officer was low-ranked and recommended for selection out, there was no appeal procedure, no right to a serious hearing. A Performance Standards Board and a Special Review Board have now been established to consider appeals. Additionally, AFSA is taking an active role in safeguarding the rights of Foreign Service personnel who have been marked for selection out. It is too early to predict whether management will hesitate to use the process in the future. One young AFSA official voiced the conviction that "selection out is dead in the department." This forecast is probably premature, but there is little doubt that the emphasis on due process has made selection out more difficult for management.

The State Department's performance evaluation system relies on the written record as the primary basis for judging an officer for promotion and assignment. Supervisor and employee usually work out a series of job requirements, and the employee is evaluated on how well his performance meets them. Nothing in the efficiency report is confidential; an officer can examine his entire file. He is required to comment on the rating given him by his supervisor, especially concerning his career potential. The so-called open efficiency reports have sometimes led to inflation, and supervisors tend to "pull their punches" in rating officers, sometimes damning them by faint praise. Distinctions between officers often have to be made by interpreting nuances, and this sometimes leads to errors in judgment.

In evaluating performance, Selection Boards can easily discern the top 20 percent and low 20 percent of the officers. It is in the middle that boards sometimes have difficulty making distinctions. In any system where performance is judged by a supervisor, there is bound to be an employee tendency to try to get along with the supervisor and satisfy his wishes. This appears to be less true in the Foreign Service, however; the service encourages constructive dissent.

Management's role in the promotion system, particularly in allowing a senior officer surplus, drastically reducing the number of promotions in a particular year, and frequently failing to insist that rating officers be more frank in their assessments of the strengths and weaknesses of the officers they evaluate, has adversely affected the credibility of the system. Ambassador Robert Neumann touched on several of these points in the prepared statement he presented to the two House committees holding hearings on the Foreign Service Act of 1980 during the period June–October 1979.[9]

One of the problems that management has confronted over the years has been a variation in number of promotions from year to year. Under the Foreign Service Act of 1980, the State Department must report to Congress annually on promotions realized and projected and must share this information with AFSA. (The practice of management is to give AFSA, the State Department's labor union, a sealed envelope with the number of foreign service officers to be promoted before the Selection Boards convene. An AFSA representative opens the envelope and checks to see that management's number coincides with AFSA's announced number of promotions. If not, management must explain or be subject to a grievance. This practice is

Table 7
State Department Projected Generalist Promotions, 1981–1986

Class to Which Promoted	Projected Annual Promotions	Actual, 1981	Actual Average, 1973–1981
Career minister	7–10	7	8
Minister counselor	33–57	41	54
Counselor	55–97	69	68
Class 1	100–124	114	111
Class 2	124–151	138	133
Class 3	130–160	147	138
Total	449–599	516	512

SOURCE: Department of State projection, Bureau of Personnel, January 29, 1982.

intended to forestall additions to or subtractions from the promotion lists by managment after the boards have concluded their work.) The annual number of promotions is affected by such factors as the rate of attrition at the senior levels, the number of limited career extensions given to senior officers, the number of officers selected out, and the size of the State Department's salaries and expenses budget. Promotion projections for generalist FSOs are given in Table 7.

Management has given increasing attention to the promotion of women and minorities, and Congress has expressed interest in the progress made in the recruitment, assignment, and promotion of minority and women officers. The trend is for greater participation by these two groups in the career Foreign Service.

Training

Training programs in the foreign ministry and the State Department are designed to meet these agencies' special needs in managing diplomacy. Both agencies concentrate on language and area studies, and both introduce training programs at various stages in an FSO's career to prepare him for assuming more responsibility. A Japanese Foreign Service officer is less reluctant than a U.S. Foreign Service officer to accept a two- or three-year training assignment because he has a greater sense of job security and is less preoccupied with competition for promotion, and also because more prestige is attached to training.

Japan

Training in the foreign ministry is carried out mainly by the Foreign Service Training Institute, established in February 1946. It provides language and substantive training for career and noncareer officers and for officials of other government ministries who are assigned abroad. Training for newly appointed career and noncareer officers begins in April and lasts about four months. (There were 70 officers in the 1980 class—about 40 noncareer and 30 career trainees.) The institute has four (originally five) divisions.

The original purpose of division 1 was the training and career development of midcareer and senior officers, but because of the acute shortage of officers at these levels, training activities have had to be suspended.

Division 2 is responsible for training young career officers who have just entered the service. Courses cover general orientation and the functions and responsibilities of the ministry bureaus and overseas posts. Seminars are held on diplomacy and lectures are given on such diverse subjects as Western and Oriental culture; Japanese economic and commercial policies and practices; and domestic problems in the areas of agriculture, labor, fisheries, welfare, and defense. There is even special instruction on wine selection and serving, ikebana (flower arrangement), tea ceremony, and how to comport oneself in various social situations.

Division 3 trains noncareer personnel, and because administrators are trying to de-emphasize the difference between career and noncareer status in training programs, its curricula are much the same as for career officers in division 2. In most cases, career and noncareer officers attend the same lectures and go on the same field trips. Language classes are separate because noncareer officers take a more concentrated language program.

Division 4 provided specialized training to a limited number of officials for a few months but was deactivated in the late 1970s.

Division 5 provides language training to midcareer officers in other government ministries to prepare them for temporary duty at Japanese overseas missions. About 100 students attend the course, held once a year for five to six months.

After completing a year of on-the-job training in the foreign ministry, career officers are generally sent to a foreign university for two or three years of general study. They are then assigned to an embassy, or they return to the ministry in Tokyo to work in one of the geographic or functional bureaus.

The wives of these young career and noncareer officers cannot join their husbands abroad until they have completed one year of training. The ministry wants young officers to devote full time to the training assignment and considers the first year critical. This policy apparently does not present special problems, because very few of the young officers are married at the time of their first overseas training assignment. Training at the institute is available to wives of foreign ministry officials and of officers of other ministries. Special instruction is given on personal and post security, including protection of official documents and embassy buildings. Security reports prepared by Japanese overseas missions are used for instructional purposes.

Language training is compulsory for all new officers, career and noncareer. The Personnel Division decides what languages officers will study, based on the needs of the service determined through consultation with officials in the geographic bureaus. English is most frequently studied, but some officers are assigned to study other languages, especially Arabic. If a young officer would prefer not to take Arabic or another hard language, he must negotiate with the Personnel Division to get the decision changed. Complaints are seldom made and orders are seldom changed, but unhappy officers do have recourse to an appeal procedure. The ministry tries to be flexible in establishing a career pattern in language and area training for noncareer officers because many of these officers, at least in the training phase of their development, are uncertain about the future.

After training, officers can indicate their assignment preference on a special form provided by the Personnel Division. They sometimes complain that their first substantive assignment bears little relationship to the training program; a similar comment was made to me by several junior noncareer officers. An officer's post preference and the needs of the service may sometimes conflict. For example, many career and noncareer officers desire advanced English language training because it will give them more flexibility in career development by qualifying them for assignments to English-speaking countries. They think they will have a better chance to advance to key senior positions if they can work in areas that have special significance for Japanese foreign policy.

In developing training policies, the institute and the Personnel Division closely coordinate their efforts; in particular, there is mutual consultation on the selection of instructors for the institute. Prominent professors from Japanese universities, as well as ex-ambassadors, are usually recruited on a temporary basis. Unfortunately, there is little coordination among instructors, and students often complain about overlaps in lectures. A permanent coordinator of academic instruction is needed, but because of budget difficulties the institute is unable to hire one.[10]

United States

The Foreign Service Act of 1980 emphasized training and called for a revised and accelerated professional development program to improve the core skills of Foreign Service officers. The revamped training program is administered by the State Department's Foreign Service Institute. About 17,500 individuals enroll in institute courses annually—about two-thirds in the United States and one-third abroad—in full-time, part-time, and extension programs. State Department employees constitute about two-thirds of the enrollment, with the balance made up of individuals from 39 other departments and independent agencies (principally the Agency for International Development, the United States Information Agency, and the Department of Defense).

The institute's library has about 40,000 volumes and subscribes to approximately 300 periodicals. The basic collection emphasizes political science, economics, history, languages and linguistics, geography, international law, and sociology. Special collections have been established to support the institute's Executive Seminar on National and International Affairs and the School of Area Studies.

Because of the added impetus training has received as a result of the 1980 act, the State Department has begun to budget and schedule training as a normal and sometimes mandatory part of the assignment process for Foreign Service officers. Additional teaching positions have been established at the institute as part of the revised professional development program.

The heart of the institute's program is professional training at three key points in an FSO's career: junior officer/entry, midlevel, and threshold to the Senior Foreign Service. Additional courses at the middle level and senior threshold level are expected to produce a 50 percent increase in professional training.

The language and area program is also undergoing change. In the 1970s, the aim of this program was to provided FSOs with general knowledge of a particular language and region. Training now focuses on those skills essential to working and living in a particular country. This is an important innovation that is being carefully evaluated for effectiveness. The institute has few programs that are as important, in my judgment, as the language and area program. Foreign Service officers spend most of their professional careers abroad, and if they are to perform with a high degree of effectiveness, a command of the language of the country to which they are assigned is essential.

The institute's Japan program, for example, lasts for two years, is comprehensive, well balanced, effectively integrated with the daily responsibilities of a Foreign Service officer, and very difficult. When the officer completes his training, he is usually at a level of S3, R3, can read a Japanese newspaper, especially those articles relevant to his area of specialty (toward the end of the language training, an officer is exposed to political vocabulary if he is a political officer, or to economic words and phrases if economics is his skill cone), and can converse with Japanese newspapermen, politicians, businessmen, and government officials in Japanese. The training enables him to gain a clearer perspective on issues that concern U.S.-Japan relations, eliminates his dependence on interpreters (something important may be lost in the interpretation), and helps him to handle emergency situations (such as demonstrators at the embassy gate demanding to see the ambassador on a security issue), and to explain U.S. policies to Japanese friends and associates. He is also able to gain greater cultural and social knowledge of Japan because he has the ability to speak and read the language.

More needs to be done by management to reduce the career risks of a training assignment that are perceived to exist despite the increased importance placed on training. As mentioned, the highly competitive nature of the Foreign Service puts great pressure on individual FSOs to remain in the mainstream and to avoid assignments that do not lead to promotion. Some officers believe that an efficiency report covering the period they are in training cannot compete with the efficiency report of an officer in a substantive assignment. They are convinced that training will hold them back for one or two years on the promotion track, and they may never catch up— even though studies and statistics tend to refute these allegations. As a result of the tightening of TIC regulations in the senior ranks, there is even greater pressure for senior officers to obtain the kinds of assignments that will help them gain limited career extensions, and this means avoiding training assignments. Similarly, the eagerness of younger FSOs to be appointed ambassador before age 40 prompts them to avoid training assignments in order to stay in the mainstream.

Management could ensure that the precepts prepared for the Selection Boards allow board members to give the same weight to a training assignment as to a substantive assignment on a score of one to ten. If the promotion lists were to reflect this policy, and officers in training were to gain promotions in approximately the same numbers as those in substantive assignments (everything else being equal), some of the concern about training would probably diminish. This is admittedly a sensitive and difficult issue, dealing as it does with the career aspirations and professional lives of FSOs, but if proper incentives are devised, the prospect of a training assignment might be made much more attractive.

One incentive is certainly the provision in the Foreign Service Act of 1980 for salary increases for study of and acquired proficiency in a difficult language (such as Arabic, Bengali, Farsi, Thai, Turkish, Korean, Lao, Tamil, Burmese, and Nepali). Foreign Service personnel who begin study of a designated incentive language receive one within-class salary increase effective at the beginning of the first pay period following completion of sixteen continuous weeks of full-time intensive training upon certification by the Foreign Service Institute. Furthermore, FSOs who receive an institute-tested rating of R3, S3 in an incentive language receive three within-step salary increases. These salary increases can be effective if applied consistently over a considerably period. Salary increases are no substitute, however, for the assurance that a training assignment is not a disadvantage in the continuing competition for promotion.

Retirement

A Japanese diplomat is not required by law to retire at a certain age, whereas a U.S. Foreign Service officer must usually retire at age 65. The foreign ministry appears to be more involved than the State Department in helping a retired FSO find postretirement work, but both agencies, because of weak constituencies, have difficulty assisting their retiring FSOs. In the foreign ministry, there is a greater sense of appreciation for the years of loyal service given by the retired FSO than in the State Department. The philosophy that employment is for a lifetime is partially responsible for this attitude.

Japan

Japanese ambassadors generally retire between ages 62 and 65, after having served in several ambassadorial assignments. Upon retirement, they normally get 80 percent of their last salary as a pension, which is taxable. Because the wife of an ambassador often comes from a wealthy family, her resources may supplement her husband's pension.

The Personnel Division carefully monitors ambassadorial assignments to avoid inordinate congestion at the top. There is constant upward movement in the service, and when class members become eligible for assignment to ambassadorial posts, the Personnel Division must have the positions available. At the same time, the division (and especially the deputy vice-minister for administration) attempts to locate postretirement employment for retiring ambassadors; a strong feeling exists at all levels that the ministry should protect the interests of its officers. (Retirement from a government position to a civilian position is often called *amakudari*, or "descent from Heaven," reflecting the high status in which bureaucrats are held.) But unlike the finance ministry or the Ministry of International Trade and Industry, the foreign ministry has few constituents in the private sector, and therefore, large companies and banks usually show little interest in

Table 8
State Department Retirement Projections, 1981–1985

Rank	1981	1982	1983	1984	1985	Average	Estimated Range
Career minister	4	5	5	5	5	5	4–6
Minister counselor	25	27	39	39	39	34	27–41
Counselor	20	21	33	32	32	28	22–34
Class 1	41	41	41	41	41	41	33–49
Class 2	22	20	20	20	20	20	16–24
Class 3	15	14	13	13	13	14	11–17
Class 4	13	13	14	13	13	13	10–16
Class 5	7	6	5	4	4	5	4–6
Class 6	1	1	1	1	1	1	0–1
Total	148	148	171	168	168	161	127–194

SOURCE:: *Special Report*, Bureau of Personnel, Department of State, January 1982.

employing ministry personnel. Because it is hard to find good positions in the private sector, some senior officials try to stay on as long as possible.

However, as a result of Japan's increased role in world affairs, Japanese companies and banks are hiring experienced diplomats to advise on various policy questions. Some retired ambassadors also find jobs with large hotel chains, in semiautonomous government organizations, and on faculties of well-known Japanese universities.

A number of ambassadors admitted to me that it would have been easier for them to get good jobs had they retired in their mid-50s, but one said that he had worked all his life to be an ambassador and did not want to retire on the threshold of such an assignment. The ministry discourages early retirement, however. Each officer of each class is a part of the system with a role to play, and because the system is understaffed, officers are vitally needed. It wants to preserve the experience of the senior officer group in order to continue to staff missions abroad with qualified and experienced ambassadors.

An ambassador, being guided by custom and tradition, knows that a certain ambassadorial assignment carries with it the clear signal that he should retire at the end of his tour. (As he nears retirement, he becomes vulnerable to what the Japanese call *katatataki*, or a "tap on the shoulder," indicating that it is time to consider retirement.) If he heeds this signal, he will have ample time to make retirement plans and transfer from active to retired status with dignity.

United States

A U.S. Foreign Service officer usually must retire by age 65 if he has not been separated earlier for TIC. In order to estimate the attrition rate in the senior ranks, which impacts importantly on the promotion rate further down the line, the State Department has established certain variables to be used in its calculations. They include:

1. Attractiveness of annuity compared with present salary (inflation increases compared to actual salary and pay cap, a ceiling placed by Congress on senior pay)
2. Effect of lifting the current pay cap
3. The impact of the TIC rules for senior officers
4. Whether employment ceilings are static or follow an upward or a downward trend

Using these variables, management has estimated that approximately 150 to 160 officers will retire annually from 1981 through 1985 (see Table 8).

Retirement benefits for U.S. Foreign Service officers are generous. An officer receives a substantial percentage of the average of the three highest years of his salary, plus a government insurance policy and health benefits. If disability occurred as a result of official duty, additional benefits are provided.

Because of the nature of Foreign Service work and because of the academic and employment background of most FSOs, retirement usually means work in the field of education, in foundations, and in organizations involved with international affairs (such as the World Affairs Council and the Council on Foreign Relations). Some retirees become advisers to companies having large international business interests; for others, retirement may mean selling houses or operating a travel agency.

The average age of a retiree is 57 years, and the average length of service is 28 years. About 10–12 percent of the senior officers retire annually. In 1982, there were about 7,300 retired Foreign Service officers. Each spring, the State Department sponsors a Foreign Service Day. Retired officers are invited to Washington to attend the festivities and to reminisce with old friends and renew old ties. The event is always well attended.

5

DECISION-MAKING

I N THIS CHAPTER I WILL EXAMINE THE IMPORTANCE OF THE HUMAN FACTOR and of the organization and operation of the diplomatic management systems in decision-making in the United States and Japan.

The Japanese FSO must follow certain rules of order in decision-making, and a paramount one is adherence to the staff and line system and observation of the division of authority between division and bureau. Considerable formality surrounds decision-making in the foreign ministry; the mode of operation is firmly entrenched in tradition and custom.

Decision-making by the U.S. Foreign Service officer is not as structurally confined, although the country directorate in the State Department, like the division in the foreign ministry, plays a key role in the process.

The relationship of the U.S. Embassy to the foreign ministry and that of the Japanese Embassy to the State Department is another element in the decision-making process, and it has an important influence on the outcome of negotiations. In this section, two actual negotiations between the U.S. Embassy and the foreign ministry will be discussed as examples of how the two organizations carry out their responsibilities.

Impact of Structure on Decision-Making in Japan

Any serious study of the Japanese Foreign Service must take account of the role of the FSO in developing policies and the structure within which he must work to carry out the ministry's primary mission of formulating, implementing, and coordinating foreign policy. One structural element in the decision-making process is the staff and line system, a command arrangement common to military organizations. The line of authority flows downward from the vice-minister to the deputy vice-minister for administration to the directors general of bureaus to the chiefs of bureau divisions. The deputy directors general are considered staff, and they do not issue orders to bureau division chiefs. However, in actual practice, the deputy director general plays an influential role in policy matters, the extent of which is defined by the forcefulness of his personality.

The staff and line system assures a dominant role for the division chief in the decision-making process and confirms the key position of the division as the hub of the wheel—the matrix for policy formulation. The power of the division chief derives mainly from his knowledge of his area and his near monopoly on information. All action and information cables come to him for processing. Replies to embassy inquiries regarding a particular policy issue are prepared at the division level and move up the chain of command as the situation warrants. The division chief originates policy recommendations and guides the decision-making process as it moves both horizontally and vertically.

He is responsible for all the work of his division. For example, he decides what clearances are needed for a particular policy recommendation or action on a cable going to his embassy. He must negotiate with division chiefs in other ministries on issues of interdepartmental significance. Being the line officer directly under the bureau director general, he keeps the director general advised on particular policy issues. He must prepare briefing papers for the director general, vice-minister, or foreign minister for Diet interpellations or press conferences. (It seems almost axiomatic that the more controversial the issue, the fewer officials are involved. Often, if the matter carries a high classification, the division chief may have to deal only with his bureau director and the vice-minister.)

The chief, his deputy, and the career officers in the general affairs section of the division are the only ones empowered by regulation, tradition, and custom to issue orders. The most junior career officers can give orders to the noncareer members of the division, originate policy recommendations, and offer opinions or advice on specific policy issues to the division chief and his deputy. The chief can either send these recommendations to the bureau director general or can prepare his own recommendations after consultation with his staff. In either case the chief will deal directly with the director general, but he also may discuss various aspects of a problem with the deputy director general. Final authority for sending recommendations to the director general rests with the chief. Figure 9 shows the foreign ministry line of authority.

Figure 9
Japanese Foreign Ministry Line of Authority, 1981

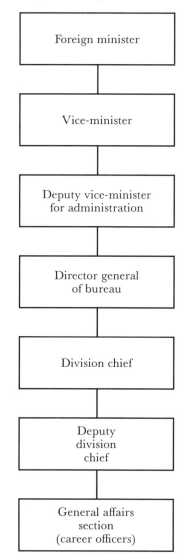

To allow the ministry to deal with the critical shortage of midlevel career officers, additions to and subtractions from the staff complement are less tightly regulated than are changes in line positions, which are closely controlled by regulation. (The two exceptions are sanjikan and shingikan, which are governed by strict regulations similar to those governing the positions of division chief and director general.) If additional personnel are needed to fill line positions, they must be taken from another division.

Staff personnel, especially the deputy directors general (sanjikan), who are free from line responsibility, can be assigned to consultative and negotiating duties, thus relieving line officers of these burdens. For example, a former deputy director general of what was then the American Affairs Bureau headed the Japanese delegation to the civil aviation negotiations with the United States in 1977. (This appears to be a customary assignment for the deputy director general of the bureau.) He presided over the Japanese negotiating team and was the final authority on matters pertaining to Civil Aviation Treaty interpretations and other legal aspects of the negotiations. Representatives of the transportation ministry and of the other organizations concerned advised and recommended; officials of these organizations and of the foreign ministry consulted on various questions arising in the negotiations. A unified policy position was established and was conveyed to the U.S. side by the deputy director general. He performed a policy coordinating role for the team much as members of his ministry had in developing a unified policy position in Tokyo.

Crisis management is a difficult and lingering problem, and it is here that the scarcity of careerists is most keenly felt. Problems often must be handled on a case-by-case basis. When senior officials are involved in an important policy matter that is controversial, it is difficult for them to give equal attention to another important policy issue in a different part of the world. To lessen the strain on the career corps, the ministry, as noted, has not only created two staff positions at the senior level (deputy vice-minister for political affairs and deputy vice-minister for economic affairs), but has adopted a plan for crisis management by committee. A deputy vice-minister for administration (the official who is responsible for coordinating crisis management), explained to me that a committee had been formed to handle various aspects of the problem of the U.S. hostages in Iran, and to it he had appointed representatives from the North American Affairs Bureau and the Middle Eastern and African Affairs Bureau. The vice-minister assigned the Middle Eastern and African Affairs Bureau primary responsibility for handling the general problem insofar as Japanese interests were concerned.

Depending on the seriousness of the issue, the deputy vice-ministers for political and for economic affairs, in addition to the deputy vice-minister for administration, may get involved in the work of a crisis management committee. In the Iranian crisis, the responsibility for handling daily developments rested primarily with lower-level officers in the Middle Eastern and African Affairs Bureau and the North American Affairs Bureau. These officers would consult on one or two aspects of a problem and prepare a position paper for consideration by division superiors. If the issue was serious and had implications for U.S.-Japanese relations (such as the United States asking Japan to enforce sanctions against Iran), the directors general of the two bureaus, as well as the vice-minister, became involved. The vice-minister also consulted with the chief Cabinet secretary, the foreign minister, the prime minister, and leading LDP political leaders in order to get a "feel" for how these top politicians viewed the crisis. Each crisis seems to evoke its own strategy, but in general, the committee approach appears to be gaining greater acceptance as the best method of crisis management. It is an ad hoc arrangement and not a deviation from the more traditional practice of assigning primary line responsibility for handling a crisis to the geographic bureau most intimately involved.

Personalities are important in the management of Japan's foreign relations. A strong vice-minister can leave his imprint on the decision-making process. Most individuals I spoke with outside the ministry thought that the strong postwar vice-ministers have been Shimoda Takeso, Ushiba Nobuhiko, Hogen Shinsaku, and Takashima Masao; all have left their mark on some aspect of Japanese foreign relations. Shimoda, with his legal background, played a dominant role in negotiating many of the postwar treaties that led to the establishment of normal diplomatic relations between Japan and its wartime adversaries. Ushiba gave Japan's foreign policy a strong economic thrust. Hogen and Takashima were brilliant strategists and contributed significantly to important negotiations with the Soviet Union and China. More examples could be cited, but it seems clear that strong leadership can overcome serious manpower deficiencies in the career ranks by mobilizing the ministry's personnel resources to safeguard and advance Japanese foreign policy interests.

These personnel resources are normally "in-house" resources, that is, Japanese government personnel. Unlike the State Department, which uses experts from the private sector (business, the academic community, and the professions), the foreign ministry does not often move outside the bureaucracy for input in the decision-making process. The Japanese bureaucracy considers itself the main repository of foreign affairs information and expertise and therefore believes it unnecessary to go "outside" for assistance. This is one reason, according to a former senior official in the Japanese United Nations delegation, that the establishment of a National Security Council with outside experts as members has not been seriously considered as a mechanism for achieving more efficient decision-making in Japan.

Even members of the Research and Policy Planning Staff do not play significant roles in the decision-making process. The staff is viewed with some suspicion by the major geographic bureaus as presenting a potential threat to their jurisdictional independence.[1]

The attitude of young FSOs toward staff work is generally negative. When I asked a number of them whether they would seek an assignment on the staff to advance their careers, all but one demurred and indicated they would accept such an assignment but would not seek it. They said the surest way to success is to work in an active capacity in a major geographic bureau, not as a policy researcher or planner outside the bureau. The one exception was a young man who rather modestly explained that although he recognized that the choice assignments were in the geographic bureaus, he believed that ministrywide policy planning was necessary and was willing to devote a tour of duty to staff work.

The Security Division in the foreign ministry and the country directorate in the State Department play key roles in the decision-making process, especially regarding U.S.-Japanese security relations. An analysis of their operations will provide an understanding of how FSOs contribute to the process.

The Security Division: Japan

The cornerstone of Japanese foreign policy is Japan's relationship with the United States, and the basis of that relationship is the United States–Japan Security Treaty. The Security Division of the North American Affairs Bureau has primary jurisdiction over security arrangements with the United States. This division is responsible for such general security matters as determining the status of U.S. military personnel in Japan under the Status of Forces Agreement; resolving problems arising from the entry and exit of U.S. military vessels, aircraft, and military supplies; acting as executive secretary for the Japanese side in meetings with U.S. officials (such as the United States–Japan Consultative Committee) on security and defense-related questions; and negotiating with U.S. officials on cost-sharing of weapons systems in close association with the Defense Agency. The division has no precise antecedents, and in the early postwar period, senior officials had to comb the career corps for officers to assign to it. Fortunately for U.S.-Japanese relations, such officers were available, and the foreign ministry has since developed a cadre of security experts in the career corps to handle the many complex problems arising between the two countries. The division has experts who can produce the right answers for government leaders in Diet interpellations on security issues respond to statements by

U.S. political leaders and government officials on U.S.-Japanese defense issues and to media comments (often hostile) on aspects of the United States–Japan security relationship, handle military incidents that result from the presence of U.S. military personnel in Japan, and prepare ministry officials for bilateral negotiations with the United States on special security matters. Efficient operation of the division is enhanced by continuity in division personnel, recruitment of outstanding career officers with a background in or some knowledge of military affairs, an accurate filing system, and a computerized memory bank to record information concerning past critical issues in the security relationship.

To facilitate and support the work of the Security Division, the State Department has organized a similar office (the political-military section) in the U.S. Embassy in Tokyo. A close working relationship has developed between these two organizations, and many difficult problems have been solved by the two offices, working closely with the Japanese Defense Agency and Headquarters U.S. Forces Japan.

One forward step in organizing the foreign ministry to undertake broader operations in the security field was the establishment in 1980 of the Security Policy Planning Committee, composed of a senior member of each major geographic bureau under the chairmanship of the vice-minister. The committee meets from time to time to discuss not only major security issues involving Japan and the United States but also multilateral problems affecting Japan's security in Northeast Asia. It seeks to formulate general recommendations for the government on critical security issues and is given valuable assistance by the Security Division.

Another aspect of decision-making with regard to the United States–Japan security relationship is what might be termed the psychological dimension. It is here that the more subtle elements in the relationship come into play: hierarchy and the dependency syndrome. Since the end of World War II, the Japanese have regarded the United States with respect and with some awe. The United States has held a superior position to Japan in the eyes of many Japanese, and only since the early 1970s has Japan's national pride begun to grow, with the growth of its economic power. The Japanese have been experiencing *taikoku ishiki*, or "big-country consciousness," and this has prompted feelings of equality with the United States, at least in economic terms.

Kitamura Hiroshi, a career Foreign Service officer and, since 1982, director general of the North American Affairs Bureau, wrote a paper entitled *Psychological Dimensions of U.S.-Japan Relations* for Harvard University's Center for International Relations in August 1971, in which he pointed out that although the Japanese admire many aspects of life in the United States, they are concerned lest Japan's relations with the United

States become too close. Many Japanese place the United States on a pedestal, and this sometimes leads to a sense of disillusionment or even betrayal. Security, trade, and other relations are frequently affected by these feelings.[2]

The Japan of the 1980s is not the Japan about which Kitamura wrote. Japanese influence throughout the world is increasing; its economic power is awesome and its technological progress enviable. The average Japanese citizen, and especially the country's leaders, find great satisfaction in these accomplishments; pride and self-confidence have been restored. But there are lingering doubts about Japanese security. Article 9 of the Constitution (in which war is renounced as an instrument of national policy), memories of defeat, a desire not to jeopardize the good life, uncertainty about the international role Japan should play, tenuous relations with the Soviet Union, worry that a closing of the sea-lanes might prevent access to essential resources—all combine to create some psychological blocks to formulation of a more positive and resolute foreign policy. It is in the areas of security and the decision-making process as it pertains to the relationship between the United States and Japan that some of Kitamura's conclusions about the psychological relationship between the two countries have continuing validity.

Country Directorate: United States

Decision-making in the country directorate has a certain methodology of its own. In the United States, the "chain of command" or "going through channels" philosophy is followed carefully, and each member of the decision-making team knows what role he must perform. There is a certain amount of rigidity in the process (although less than in the Japanese system), but flexibility is allowed in the handling of crisis situations.

If a U.S. Foreign Service officer has an interest in Japan, having an input in policy formulation and being a player in the decision-making process as it affects the relationship between the United States and Japan are twin goals that he seeks with undiminished drive and enthusiasm. Assignments involving decision-making are always of value for his career development, however, for they challenge his intellect, his judgment, and his analytic powers. They allow him to develop his ability to move successfully within the Washington bureaucracy and to persuade and maneuver to obtain the coveted bureau assignment.

The decision-making process in the State Department can be viewed from a number of perspectives, but it will be useful for the purposes of this study to focus on the country director and the assistant secretary of the

Figure 10
State Department Bureau of East Asian and Pacific Affairs

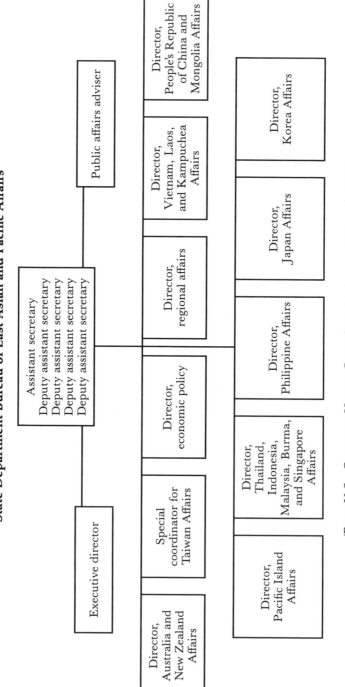

(From U.S., Congress, House, Committee on Appropriations for 1980,
Hearings; State Department Budget, April 1979, p. 176.)

bureau. Figure 10 shows the organization of the Bureau of East Asian and Pacific Affairs; Table 9 gives statistics on the bureau's budget and on personnel in various posts under the bureau's jurisdiction.

The country director for Japan plays very much the same role in the decision-making process as the chief of the First North America Division of the North American Affairs Bureau of the foreign ministry. The country director has a "line" responsibility that flows upward through the deputy assistant secretary to the assistant secretary of the bureau. He is generally chosen by the deputy assistant secretary or the assistant secretary on the basis of his knowledge of Japan, his experience working and living in Japan, the relationships he has developed with the assistant secretary and the deputy assistant secretary over the years, and the strengths he has shown in working in the Washington bureaucracy.

The country directorate is generally divided along functional lines that mirror the organization of the political section of the U.S. Embassy in Tokyo: domestic Japanese politics, third country relations, and political and military affairs. The directorate also has an economic component that follows economic and commercial relations between the United States and Japan and works closely with the deputy assistant secretary for economic affairs and the economic divisions of the State Department.

The country director usually is an individual who has been associated with Japan for a large part of his professional life. He knows the language and has firm contacts in the Japanese bureaucracy, the academic community, the media, and professional and business circles. He is proud of his membership in the "Japanese language officer" clique and of his stature as a Japanese expert. The country director runs the directorate very much as he would if he were chief of the political section in the U.S. Embassy in Tokyo. In fulfilling his function of central coordinator for Japanese affairs, he and his staff must maintain close working relations with key staff members of the National Security Council, with officers in the Directorate for International Security Affairs in the Office of the Secretary of Defense (especially the Asian directorate of that office), with officers in the Treasury and Commerce Departments with responsibilities that pertain to Japan, and with offices in the State Department that are responsible for Japanese political, economic, trade, and military affairs. The country director must be a master at working within the Washington bureaucracy; he must be tough where toughness is required, be accommodating where such accommodation will further the policies of the State Department, and be alert to trends and attitudes toward Japan, both in and out of government, that could affect relations between the United States and Japan.

The director must be prompt and judicious in keeping his superiors informed of important developments in his area; he must also anticipate

Table 9

State Department Bureau of East Asian and Pacific Affairs: Budget and Personnel

BUDGET AND PERMANENT STAFF: DOMESTIC

Unit	1978 ACTUAL		1979 ESTIMATED		1980 ESTIMATED	
	No.	Net Cost	No.	Net Cost	No.	Net Cost
Office of the Assistant Secretary	46	$1,255,800	46	$1,330,747	46	$1,350,210
Office of Regional Affairs	15	432,675	15	458,202	15	465,075
Special Coordinator for Taiwan Affairs	6	124,824	6	132,188	6	134,170
Australia/New Zealand Affairs	3	113,395	3	120,185	3	121,886
Japan Affairs	8	230,212	8	243,794	8	247,450
Korea Affairs	7	219,002	7	231,923	7	235,401
Pacific Island Affairs	6	147,831	6	156,553	6	158,901
People's Republic of China and Mongolia Affairs	12	289,676	12	306,766	12	311,367
Philippine Affairs	6	165,590	6	175,359	6	177,989
Thailand/Indonesia/Malaysia/Burma/Singapore Affairs	10	309,327	10	327,577	10	332,400
Vietnam/Laos/Kampuchea Affairs	6	229,468	6	243,006	6	246,651
Total	125	$3,517,800	125	$3,726,300	125	$3,781,500

POST INVENTORY: OVERSEAS

TYPE OF POST	1978 ACTUAL	1979 ESTIMATED	1980 ESTIMATED
Embassy			
Class 1	3	4	4
Class 2	4	4	4
Class 3	2	2	2
Class 4	5	5	5

Liaison Office	—	1										
Subtotal	15	15										
Consulate General	6	6										
Consulate	8	11										
Consular Agency	3	3										
Trust Territory, Pacific Islands	1	1										
Total	33	36										

STAFFING SUMMARY BY POST: OVERSEAS

Post	1978				1979				1980			
	Officers	Clerks	Foreign Service Nationals	Total	Officers	Clerks	Foreign Service Nationals	Total	Officers	Clerks	Foreign Service Nationals	Total
Australia												
Canberra	22	7	20	49	22	7	20	49	22	7	20	49
Brisbane	3	—	6	9	—	—	—	—	—	—	—	—
Melbourne	7	1	15	23	7	1	15	23	7	1	15	23
Perth	3	—	5	8	3	—	5	8	3	—	5	8
Sydney	11	1	23	35	11	1	20	32	11	1	20	32
Total	46	9	69	124	43	9	60	112	43	9	60	112
Burma												
Rangoon	13	4	50	67	13	4	50	67	13	4	50	67
Mandalay	1	—	3	4	—	—	—	—	—	—	—	—
Total	14	4	53	71	13	4	50	67	13	4	50	67
China												
Peking	22	6	19	47	22	6	19	47	22	6	19	47
Fiji												
Suva	5	1	8	14	5	1	8	14	5	1	8	14

Table 9 (continued)

STAFFING SUMMARY BY POST: OVERSEAS

Post	1978				1979				1980			
	Officers	Clerks	Foreign Service Nationals	Total	Officers	Clerks	Foreign Service Nationals	Total	Officers	Clerks	Foreign Service Nationals	Total
Hong Kong	35	10	113	158	35	10	102	147	35	10	102	147
Indonesia												
Jakarta	33	10	42	85	33	10	42	85	33	10	42	85
Medan	3	—	8	11	3	—	8	11	3	—	8	11
Surabaja	3	—	7	10	—	—	—	—	—	—	—	—
Total	39	10	57	106	36	10	50	96	36	10	50	96
Japan												
Tokyo	60	16	146	222	60	16	136	212	60	16	136	212
Fukuoka	3	—	14	17	3	—	14	17	3	—	14	17
Naha	4	1	13	18	4	1	13	18	4	1	13	18
Osaka-Kobe	7	1	29	37	7	1	28	36	7	1	28	36
Sapporo	2	—	6	8	2	—	6	8	2	—	6	8
Total	76	18	208	302	76	18	197	291	76	18	197	291
Korea												
Seoul	41	8	77	126	41	8	78	127	41	8	80	129
Laos												
Vientiane	8	1	41	50	8	1	41	50	8	1	41	50
Malaysia												
Kuala Lumpur	16	5	29	50	16	5	29	50	16	5	30	51

New Zealand												
Wellington	11	4	20	35	11	4	20	35	11	4	20	35
Auckland	3	—	7	10	3	—	7	10	3	—	7	10
Total	14	4	27	45	14	4	27	45	14	4	27	45
Papua New Guinea												
Port Moresby	5	2	9	16	5	2	9	16	5	2	9	16
Philippines												
Manila	61	14	203	278	61	14	194	269	61	14	194	269
Cebu	2	—	4	6	2	—	4	6	2	—	4	6
Total	63	14	207	284	63	14	198	275	63	14	198	275
Saipan	1	—	—	1	1	—	—	1	1	—	—	1
Singapore	16	4	29	49	16	4	29	49	16	4	29	49
Taiwan	29	7	60	96	29	7	60	96	29	7	65	101
Thailand												
Bangkok	44	12	81	137	44	12	81	137	44	12	81	137
Chiang Mai	2	—	7	9	2	—	7	9	2	—	7	9
Songkhla	1	—	4	5	1	—	4	5	1	—	4	5
Udorn	2	—	4	6	2	—	4	6	2	—	4	6
Total	49	12	96	157	49	12	96	157	49	12	96	157
Bureau Total	479	115	1102	1696	472	115	1053	1640	472	115	1061	1648

SOURCE: U.S., Congress, House, *Hearings* by Subcommittee of Committee on Appropriations for 1980; State Department Budget, April 1979, pp. 177–81.

certain actions by other elements in the bureaucracy and forewarn his superiors regarding them. Above all, he must keep the U.S. Embassy in Tokyo abreast of developments in Washington that relate to issues of importance to the embassy, arm the embassy with pertinent information on policy issues, and at all times be ready to combat those who would intrude on his area of responsibility.

The country director for Japan can expect to participate in most crucial policy discussions, but not all of them. If the issue is highly controversial, with strong political overtones (such as trade and defense issues), the director may or may not be invited to the seventh floor to meet with senior State Department officials. If he is not present, it is reasonable to assume that his views and recommendations on the issue at hand will find their way into such discussions—generally transmitted by the bureau assistant secretary or deputy assistant secretary. The country director helps to identify and shape policy issues and makes recommendations as to what should be done in particular situations. He passes these recommendations to the deputy assistant secretary, who either accepts them, modifies them, incorporates them in his recommendations to the assistant secretary, or sends them back to the country director to be reworked. The director is often a close confidant of the deputy assistant secretary; they probably have served together at several posts or in the State Department and respect each other's expertise and judgment. Therefore, they can discuss informally and frankly any differences they may have regarding the handling of issues.

An example of a complicated policy issue that concerns Japan and the United States is defense. In developing a policy position on this issue for discussion with the Japanese, the Bureau of East Asian and Pacific Affairs has to coordinate its actions with the State Department's Bureau of Political-Military Affairs and Policy Planning Staff, as well as with the Defense Department's Directorate for International Security Affairs. Each office approaches the problem from a different point of view, and these views have to be reconciled before discussions can take place with Japan. It is a time-consuming process that tests the patience, endurance, and intellectual discipline of the participants. Again, the country director plays a crucial coordinating role; he is responsible for achieving an initial consensus before the issue moves to discussion at a more senior level.

An important weakness in this process insofar as relations between the United States and Japan are concerned is the lack of Japanese experts at the levels of the U.S. government where policy is made. The dearth of Japanese language officers has made it difficult to fill language-designated positions in Japan and in the East Asian and Pacific Affairs Bureau, as well as other top positions in governmental departments responsible for Japanese affairs. The record of the assignment of FSOs with Japanese language capability to top positions in the State Department and the U.S. Embassy in Tokyo is spotty. John Allison and U. Alexis Johnson were the only career FSOs with Japanese language capability to be assigned as ambassadors to Japan in the postwar period. (Edwin Reischauer was not a career FSO but an academic specializing in Japan.) The record for the deputy chief of mission is somewhat better; most deputy chiefs of mission have a Japanese language capability. Japanese language officers have been conspicuous by their absence as assistant secretaries of state for East Asian and Pacific affairs, although there have been several deputy assistant secretaries of state with Japanese language ability. The State Department has likewise had difficulty finding Japanese language specialists to fill important economic positions in the East Asian and Pacific Affairs Bureau and the Tokyo Embassy, despite the growing importance of U.S.-Japanese trade relations. (Ironically, Japanese language officers have sometimes been neglected or their advice has been ignored in the decision-making process.)

Several high Japanese officials and elder statesmen have commented on the dearth of Japanese experts in the U.S. government. Both Chief Cabinet Secretary Miyazawa Kiichi and former Ambassador to the United States Ushiba Nobuhiko were quoted in the *Sankei Shimbun* of April 22, 1981, as deploring the fact that so few individuals in the U.S. government were knowledgeable about Japan. Ambassador Ushiba emphasized this point to me in conversations on June 29, 1981.

Each new administration brings in its own policy team, and this team has to be educated as to Japanese security, political, and economic policies; the ethics and values of Japanese society; and why the Japanese act and react as they do. Policymakers should be more disposed to listen to Japanese language and area experts in the U.S. Foreign Service, and outstanding Japanese experts should be elevated to policy-level positions in the State and Defense departments. A greater effort should also be made to treat Japanese officials as equals and not as "little brothers." (Condescension has no place in foreign policy.) Any or all of these steps would improve understanding between the two governments, promote the formulation of policies that have more relevance to political realities, and make the decision-making process more effective.

The country directorate is usually staffed by midlevel and junior FSOs who have had some exposure to Japan, either at a university or as a result of assignments to the U.S. Embassy in Tokyo or to one of the U.S. Consulates in Japan. The Bureau of Personnel and the East Asian and Pacific Affairs Bureau try to staff the country directorate with several officers who have language and area expertise or with one or two junior officers who have indicated a preference for Japan in career development projections.

Assignments to a country directorate are generally prized because they guarantee rapid career advancement. Most of the officers so assigned are in the political cone; a few are economic officers. The political officer (and to a lesser extent the economic officer) is thus given an advantage over officers in the administrative and consular cones for assignments to positions that are regarded by the system as prerequisites to ambassadorships and to the positions of assistant secretary and deputy assistant secretary. As long as the geographic bureaus maintain their pre-eminence in the power structure of the State Department and insist that their directorates be staffed predominately by political officers, there seems to be little likelihood that officials in other cones can play a useful role in the decision-making process.

The Negotiating Process

Negotiations usually reveal the problems, both internal and external, that influence the decision-making process and provide an opportunity to analyze the role played by FSOs in managing negotiating sessions.

I became aware of some of these problems when I sat across the table from my counterparts in Tokyo to negotiate the consular convention that was signed in Tokyo on March 22, 1963, and the entry of the first U.S. nuclear-powered submarine into Sasebo Harbor on November 12, 1964.

The Sea Dragon

When Foreign Minister Kosaka Zentaro visited the United States in June 1961, the U.S. government asked Japan to allow U.S. nuclear-powered submarines to call at Japanese ports. The Ikeda government turned down the request, fearing hostile public reaction. Japan was just recovering from the security treaty demonstrations of 1960, and the Ikeda government was determined to assume a low profile in foreign and domestic affairs. When the United States repeated the request in January 1963, the Japanese government indicated its acceptance "in principle" but informally requested that consultations with the U.S. government on safety and other matters precede a final decision. For the next 21 months, negotiations took place between officials of the U.S. Embassy and the foreign ministry over various aspects of the submarine's visit. In early November 1964, the U.S. Embassy received an *aide-mémoire* from the Japanese government formally agreeing to the visit, and on November 12, 1964, the nuclear-powered submarine *Sea Dragon* entered Sasebo Harbor, the first such submarine to visit Japan. Other nuclear-powered submarines subsequently visited Yokosuka and Sasebo harbors with increasing frequency.[3]

The main focus of the Diet debate on port calls by nuclear-powered submarines had been the allegation by the opposition that they were attack types that normally carried Subroc (nuclear-armed torpedoes), and thus their entry would be subject to prior consultation under the security treaty. The U.S. government responded that *Sea Dragon*–type submarines, although nuclear powered, carried only conventional weapons. However, when pressed by the opposition, U.S. officials admitted that such submarines might carry Subrocs, but these weapons were removed before the vessels entered Japanese ports.

Subroc and the safety question were the principal topics of discussion in the Diet, in the media, and between the U.S. Embassy and the foreign ministry. The ministry's role, especially the Security Division of the then American Affairs Bureau, was to coordinate discussions among the various parts of the Japanese government in an attempt to reach a decision. The embassy's function, especially the political/military unit of the political section, was to respond to the ministry's request for information. The pace was slow. The Security Division held discussions with the Science and Technology Agency, the Defense Agency, and other concerned departments of the Japanese government over the safety and nuclear weapons issues. Japanese fishermen were especially worried about contamination of fishing grounds by discharge from nuclear-powered submarines. The Japanese government, anticipating heavy questioning in the Diet from opposition parties, was anxious to defuse any such debate by eliminating Subroc as an issue and by allaying Japanese fears about nuclear safety. To do so, it had to get answers to a number of questions concerning the technical operation of a nuclear-powered submarine.

The foreign ministry presented a series of such questions to the U.S. Embassy, and the embassy submitted them to Washington, at the same time consulting with officers of U.S. Forces Japan. When Washington responded, the embassy forwarded the response to the ministry, and the chief of the Security Division discussed it with several members of his staff and a member of the political and military unit of the embassy. A number of issues were resolved, but others soon surfaced. Often, the chief of the Security Division would present new questions that obviously had had their genesis in earlier discussions between the ministry and the Science and Technology Agency, the Fishermen's Association, or the Defense Agency, or had resulted from queries from the Liberal Democratic Party or opposition parties. Some questions regarding safety could be answered on the spot, based upon background information already furnished by Washington, but other questions had again to be sent to Washington. The U.S. government could provide very little on Subroc because of the sensitive nature of that particular weapons system.

This pattern of negotiation continued for over 21 months. As the proposed submarine visit gained greater publicity, arguments in the press and the Diet became more heated. The Security Divison also had to respond to a plethora of statements, demands, warnings, protests, and denunciations from scientific, academic, and political circles. The mayor of Sasebo wanted answers to his questions, student groups (especially the Zengakuren) threatened demonstrations, and fishermen continued to express their fears about water contamination. (Water-testing stations were established in parts of Sasebo Harbor to monitor discharge from the submarine.) Newspaper articles appeared casting suspicion that the submarine's visit was the opening thrust in a campaign by the United States to introduce nuclear weapons into Japan, and scientists warned about the safety aspects of the visit.

As the negotiations progressed, greater understanding developed on both sides. The Japanese representatives appreciated the lengths to which the U.S. Embassy was going to obtain answers to the endless line of questions, and the embassy understood the pressures being exerted on the ministry by those opposing the submarine's visit. Both sides worked hard to lessen the pressures.

The final decision, however, had to be a political one—a decision the Japanese government felt it could live with. In early November 1964, the ministry sent an *aide-mémoire* to the embassy agreeing to the submarine visit.[4] Discussions were then held between Minister John Emmerson and Yasukawa Takeshi, director general of the American Affairs Bureau; November 12, 1964, was agreed on as the date for the *Sea Dragon*'s visit (see Appendix C for the exchange of documents). There were demonstrations on land and sea on the day of the visit, contained by the efficient work of the Japanese police and the Maritime Self-Defense Force.

During the negotiations, the Security Division had borne the brunt of the effort. It had coordinated all aspects of the issue as viewed by the Japanese side, supplied answers to nervous government representatives who had to deal with Diet interpellations by opposition members on an almost daily basis, set the policy line for the ministry's response to media questions, and worked tirelessly to satisfy the demands of special-interest groups and ordinary Japanese concerning the safety issue. A camaraderie developed between embassy representatives and members of the Security Divison, born of mutual respect for the sincerity and honesty shown in the process of achieving another milestone in the evolution of U.S.-Japanese security relations: the visit of the first nuclear-powered submarine to Japan. Such visits eventually became fairly routine, but the basic course had been charted during the long negotiations over the *Sea Dragon*.

The United States–Japan Consular Convention

The consular convention was signed by the United States and Japan in Tokyo on March 22, 1963, culminating nearly two years of off and on negotiations. The main burden for the final negotiations was carried by the Legal Division of the Treaties Bureau in the foreign ministry and the consular section of the U.S. Embassy in Tokyo.

Like the negotiations over the visit of the *Sea Dragon*, the discussion and study of issues involved were the responsibility of a small nucleus of embassy and foreign ministry officials. The final lap of the negotiations centered on discussion of the meaning of certain phrases and words and how they could and would be interpreted by each side. For example, when a U.S. citizen was arrested by the Japanese police, the U.S. side requested that the embassy be notified "promptly." The Japanese side responded by asking what length of time was meant by "promptly." The issue was finally resolved when both sides agreed that appropriate authorities of the "receiving" state should, upon the request of the national concerned, inform the consular officer of the "sending" state "immediately" of the detention of the national. The consular officer was also allowed to visit the detained national "without delay." Both phrases concerned the Japanese negotiators. In an attempt to clarify their meaning, the officer in charge of the negotiations for the Legal Division had lengthy discussions with the ministry officials, police officials, and officers of the Ministry of Justice.

Countless issues of varying importance required clarification by both sides, and they usually had to be referred to Washington by the embassy and to various government departments in Tokyo by the ministry before negotiations could continue. Topics discussed and studied during the final stages of negotiations included legal rights and immunities, financial privileges, estates and transfer of property, shipping, general consular functions, and definition and application of terms.

Because the convention applied to citizens of both countries in equal measure, great care had to be given to mutual understanding of key points. For example, legal rights and privileges had to be the same for Japanese citizens in the United States as for U.S. citizens in Japan. Any translator of documents from Japanese to English or from English to Japanese knows the difficulty of ascertaining precise meanings in translations; obviously, this was a major hurdle. But patient work and perseverance enabled the consular convention to be hammered into final form and submitted to both governments for approval.

During the nearly two years that passed from beginning to end of negotiations, the Japanese and U.S. negotiating teams developed a spirit of mutual trust and respect that greatly facilitated their work. The Legal Division was very sensitive to the need for close collaboration with appropriate ministry units and with departments and agencies of the Japanese government as the negotiations progressed, and it often had to ask for patience and understanding from the U.S. side as the Japanese drew together to reach consensus on an important negotiating point. The embassy negotiators likewise had to request understanding as they waited for the Legal Adviser's Office in the State Department to furnish an official opinion on a salient issue under consideration. Both sides understood that the key to a successful and workable consular convention was agreement concerning the rights and privileges of the citizens of both countries.

Not only did these negotiations end in success, but the principal negotiators for both sides learned a great deal about one another and about the complexities of negotiating a document that not only established the tone of U.S.-Japanese consular relations but provided a basic format for Japan's negotiations of consular conventions with other countries.

The Issue of Defense

The defense issue raises many questions that are testing the viability and strength of the decision-making process in both the United States and Japan. Several ministries and agencies of the Japanese and U.S. governments have jurisdiction over defense matters, and it is a challenge to the ability of both sides to gain a better understanding of these matters, especially at a time when the United States is increasing its pressure on Japan for a greater defense effort.

Discussion of the issue of defense also provides opportunities for both sides to expound their views about the threat from the Soviet Union and what to do about it; to explain the rationale for policy actions taken and contemplated in the defense field; to examine essential elements in the security relationship between Japan and the United States; and to propose measures to broaden understanding and achieve agreement on fundamental issues of security. It is an important and stressful leadership task for the State Department and the foreign ministry, one handled with competence and skill by the country directorate for Japan and the Security Division.

The two countries have had different perceptions of the threat to Japan. James Reston noted in a 1981 report filed from Tokyo that the basic difference was that officials in Tokyo, as well as leaders of public opinion in the news media and in the universities, did not accept the Reagan administration's estimate of the Soviet menace. They did accept the argument that the Soviet Union was increasing its military power faster than the United States and that Washington and Tokyo must do something to redress the balance. But the Japanese were clearly uneasy with the U.S. military solution to the problem they referred to as "the so-called Soviet menace"; they insisted it should be met, not with arms alone but with a policy that would provide more "comprehensive security." This means increasing the defense budget moderately. Whatever is left over, the Japanese believe, should go into foreign aid to relieve the hunger and social tensions that might lead to war. "And when President Reagan talks . . . about 'limited nuclear war' they [the Japanese] give you a present—a book titled: *Hiroshima and Nagasaki—The Physical, Medical, and Social Effects of the Atomic Bombings.*"[5]

The problem of whether increased Soviet forces in the Far East constitute a threat to Japan has been thoroughly discussed in the Japanese press, with reports of differing opinions between the Defense Agency and the foreign ministry. The ministry has argued that the presence of Soviet forces posed no threat because to constitute a threat, military capabilities must be coupled with aggressive intent. The Defense Agency, on the other hand, declared that the presence nearby of any powerful military force threatened Japanese security. The government considered these opposing views and decided to adopt the "potential threat" doctrine in reference to Soviet forces in the Far East.[6]

However, as a result of harsh threats from the Soviets in 1982–83, the increase in their forces and weapons strength on the disputed northern islands, and the not-so-subtle suggestion that SS-20 missiles might be moved to within range of Japan, Japanese officials are taking a harder look at the military menace posed by the Soviets. The Japanese people, however, remain generally indifferent and the finance ministry still resists substantial increases in the defense budget. As one U.S. scholar put it, Japanese attitudes on defense fall into three categories: minimalists (the public), who want a minimum of expenditures for defense; gradualists (most government officials), who want the defense buildup to continue at a moderate pace; and Gaullists (conservatives in the LDP and right-wing groups), who want a rapid defense buildup with growing independence from the United States in security matters.[7]

Soviet belligerence is beginning to move Japan and the United States closer on security matters, although disagreements continue to exist concerning the magnitude of the threat and what to do about it. Japan does not want to antagonize the Soviets or cause concern in Association of Southeast Asian Nations (ASEAN) countries over Japanese rearmament. It wants to do more for its own defense but within the scope of domestic political realities. It is wary of responding to U.S. pressures for greater defense outlays yet recognizes that more needs to be done. The situation poses a dilemma for the government.

The Soviet invasion of Afghanistan on December 27, 1979, prompted the United States to begin a buildup of its military forces and to ask its allies to do the same. Former Defense Secretary Harold Brown, visiting Tokyo on January 14, 1980, requested then Prime Minister Ohira Masayoshi to increase Japan's defense efforts. He repeated the request several months later to then Japanese Foreign Minister Okita Saburo when the latter visited Washington. President Carter also raised the matter with Ohira in May during the prime minister's visit to Washington.

After the Reagan administration came to power in 1981, high officials in the State and Defense departments repeatedly urged Japan to allocate more resources for defense. Secretary of Defense Caspar Weinberger was most insistent in this regard and asked the Japanese to spend more on such activities as patrol and reconnaissance of lines of communication up to 1,000 miles from Japan and antisubmarine warfare.

In a forum held under the auspices of the Japan Society in New York on November 2, 1981, to discuss "Changing Perceptions of National Security in Japan and the United States," Japan was again requested to do more. As reported by the *New York Times*, a senior official of the National Security Council said that although the United States was not applying public pressure on the Japanese for a military buildup, and although the United States recognized that decisions on how Japan should deal with threats to its security should be made in Tokyo, not Washington, both Japan and the United States were aware that as soon as domestic constraints were removed (he pointed out that the Japanese have argued that they need to balance their budget and cannot sacrifice social welfare programs for sharp increases in military spending), Japan should assume a larger defense burden.[8] A U.S. senator participating in the seminar said that no Congress will long tolerate a situation in which the United States provides the defense while Japan prospers.[9]

A professor from Kyoto University said that he favored a gradual increase in military spending but thought that the key need for his country was a "psychological breakthrough" on military affairs, for although the Japanese economy has surged, the nation retains a feeling of isolation to almost the same extent as in the early 1960s.[10]

The Japanese react with outward patience and some irritation to these veiled threats. At the Honolulu Conference of June 1981 (one of a series of conferences of U.S. and Japanese officials on security matters held periodically under an agreement between the two countries), the United States presented Japan with a list of demands for a buildup of its armed forces that caught some Japanese officials by surprise—a reaction caused not so much by the general thrust of the proposals as by the cost of the items recommended. An official of the foreign ministry explained that by recommending a military program of such dimensions, the U.S. side clearly showed that it had no real understanding of what the Japanese government was able to do in the defense field, given not only its budgetary constraints but, more importantly, the politics of the issues involved. The Japanese public was not yet ready to accept the heavy burdens of an increased defense effort. The U.S. requests, he pointed out, should have been tempered by an awareness of the political risks involved for the ruling Liberal Democratic Party, were it to endorse and push through a military budget to support these requests. We can only conclude, he said, that you either do not understand or are not sympathetic to our problems.

Pressure from the United States will undoubtedly continue (especially if economic conditions in the U.S. do not improve), and Japan will attempt to parry these demands by giving ground slowly on budgetary and specific military issues so as not to incur unacceptable political risks. It will be a delicate balancing act, one made more difficult by the Japanese trade surplus with the United States; care will have to be exercised not to force the issue to a point that places the Japanese government in political jeopardy.

The defense issue continues to be the subject of much debate among officials of the foreign ministry, the Ministry of Finance, MITI, the Defense Agency, and other departments of the Japanese government. It is never far from their thoughts as one intergovernmental conference after another deliberates on how to respond to the latest U.S. proposals. The heavy manpower burden it has placed on the Security Division has prompted one former vice-minister to suggest that the division be made a bureau to deal more effectively with it.

6

PROBLEMS IN DIPLOMATIC MANAGEMENT: JAPAN

T HE TWO FOREIGN SERVICES HAVE ENCOUNTERED DIFFERENT PROBLEMS IN
developing the organizational structure and assembling the manpower
resources required to accomplish the task of managing diplomacy.

For Japan, the manpower problem—the shortage of career officers—is
real and vexing and has ramifications that have spread throughout the
diplomatic establishment. Probably nothing about the Japanese Foreign
Service is less understood in the United States than the manpower difficulties the Japanese face in the management of diplomacy, both in the foreign
ministry and at overseas posts. It is hoped that this discussion will help
Americans gain a deeper appreciation of these difficulties.

In this chapter I will also analyze some of the other main difficulties
faced by the Japanese diplomatic establishment, explain how Japanese
traditions make diplomatic operations difficult, and describe the solutions
the Japanese have proposed for their problems.

As Japan's international role grows and as interest in its position as a
world economic power increases, the demands on ministry personnel to find
solutions to their problems steadily increase. The staff that exists is insufficient to accomplish the mission of the ministry, yet there is resistance to an
increase in personnel on the part of FSOs because of the threat such an
increase would present to their career goals.

The Setting

Serious questions are being raised inside and outside the foreign ministry as to how to solve the manpower problem. Why does Japan have a foreign affairs establishment only one-fourth the size of that of the United States, one-third that of Great Britain, one-half that of France, and smaller still than the establishments of West Germany, Italy, and India? Why do the staffs of over 54 Japanese overseas posts have fewer than five persons each? In the 1970s, the volume of Japanese telecommunications increased more than 10 times, support activities increased 6.08 times, and there was a threefold increase in the number of treaties negotiated. Yet the number of personnel (both domestic and overseas) increased only 1.27 times. How can one of the world's leading economic powers continue to conduct foreign affairs with such a small staff?

Discussion of the five-year plan (1980–1985) to increase the number of personnel has produced no clear decisions as to how the augmented resources will be distributed or whether, in fact, the plan's goal can be fully accomplished. A number of factors affect these decisions: the balance between recruitment and retirement in the career system, the impact of increased work loads on the three categories of personnel (career, noncareer, and clerical/administrative), the extent to which noncareer personnel can be integrated into the career service, and a new type of entrance examination being considered for career and noncareer aspirants.

How did the ministry get into this situation in the first place? Why is it facing such a serious personnel problem? A deputy director of a major geographic bureau told me that he thought the manpower situation of the 1980s was caused by the failure of senior officers in the past to anticipate future personnel needs. Steps should have been taken to expand the career service between 1960 and early 1970, a period of rapid economic growth when there were fewer constraints on government spending.

Since then it has become clear that ministry personnel are overworked and there are too many missions for the number of personnel available to man them. A former ambassador has said that the ministry should make more of an attempt to explain its predicament to the Japanese people (as mentioned in the Introduction) in order to gain support for an increase in personnel. He pointed out that Japan has been eminently successful in selling products abroad, but now the government needs to sell the ministry to the Japanese people, to awaken them to the significance of foreign policy problems. "It is ridiculous to put a number limitation on a Ministry that must deal with so many countries," he said.[1]

However, there are important obstacles to achieving the desired personnel increases by 1985. A major difficulty is the emphasis on a reduction of government spending by Japanese Cabinets. The Administrative Management Agency, which oversees the personnel system of the Japanese government, has been reluctant to approve personnel ceiling increases for the foreign ministry when other ministries are being directed to reduce their staffs. To obtain additional personnel under the five-year expansion program requires not only protracted discussions with AMA and finance ministry officials and the intercession of important prominiistry Diet members but, if necessary, an amendment to the 1980 law authorizing the requested personnel increases. Once agreement has been reached and/or the necessary amendment passed, the finance ministry will allocate the required funds. Part or all of this process must be repeated annually in order that the objectives of the expansion program can be fulfilled.

Even before announcement of the prime minister's austerity budget in 1981, it was difficult to increase the number of personnel. A 1970 law limits the number of government employees to 506,571. The AMA has authority under that law to enforce this policy. The ceiling allows for flexibility and maneuverability, however, and the ministry is constantly seeking ways to augment its staff and still comply with AMA regulations. In order for the foreign ministry to establish a new bureau it must eliminate a bureau or the equivalent. When the foreign ministry established the Central and South American Affairs Bureau in 1979, it had to abolish the Cultural Affairs Department, the Osaka Liaison Office, and one deputy director position in the Asian Affairs Bureau. The foreign ministry may also negotiate certain personnel trade-offs with another ministry to accomplish needed additions to the work force.

In 1980, to handle its increased work load, the foreign ministry proposed adding 200 employees in 1981. Long negotiations were held with the AMA and the finance ministry to devise an amendment to the personnel ceiling law of 1970 that would allow for the necessary increase. When agreement was finally reached, the government submitted it to the Diet for approval. The ministry, with the help of its supporters in the Liberal Democratic Party and the unexpected backing of the opposition Japanese Socialist Party, was able to get the amendment approved.[2] Under the manpower expansion program, the ministry must add nearly 300 employees annually to meet its goal of 5,000 personnel by 1985, which it is not likely to do given the government's difficult fiscal situation. Remembering the experience of the 1980 negotiations, the chief of the Financial Affairs Division has said that the transition to the second phase of the program will require essentially the same cumbersome process.[3]

Table 10

Annual Increase in Japanese Foreign Ministry Personnel, 1974–1980

Year	Increase	Total
1974	55	2,926
1975	124	3,050
1976	89	3,139
1977	86	3,225
1978	86	3,311
1979	89	3,400
1980	80	3,480

SOURCE: Foreign ministry statistics, November 1980.

The number of personnel increased by 430 from 1974 to 1980; in 1980 there were 3,480 foreign ministry employees: 1,558 in Tokyo and 1,922 overseas. Table 10 and Figure 11 give statistics on personnel increases since 1974.

Figures 12, 13, and 14 illustrate three aspects of the manpower problem. Figure 12 shows the disparity in size between the Japanese Foreign Office and the Foreign Offices of six other major countries. Figure 13 shows the number of employees staffing Japanese overseas posts; 54 missions have fewer than five employees. Fifty-two percent of total overseas establishments have fewer than seven employees. An eight-member staff is generally considered the minimum necessary to carry out essential duties at an overseas post. Such a staff consists of the ambassador, the counselor for administration, the counselor for economic and economic cooperation affairs, the counselor for public information and cultural affairs, the consul, a telecommunications officer, a financial clerk, and a guard. Figure 14 gives statistics on the increasing work load, which is affecting health and morale.

Cable traffic has increased and support activities at embassies and consulates general are on the rise. Moreover, the crisis situations that Japan and the Western world have had to confront (such as the oil embargo of 1973, the overthrow of the shah, the Polish problem, and the Soviet invasion of Afghanistan), as well as the trade and defense issues between Japan and the United States, have placed a constant strain on the foreign ministry.

Japan's economic strength has given it a major voice in world affairs but has also placed heavier demands on it for more active participation in solving international problems. This is a new role for Japan. Heretofore it has been content to play a rather passive role, and the diplomatic resources

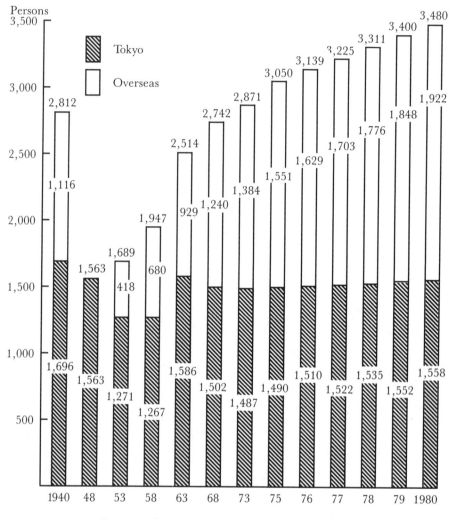

Figure 11
Japanese Foreign Ministry Manpower Capacity:
Tokyo and Overseas

(Japanese foreign ministry statistics, November 1980.)

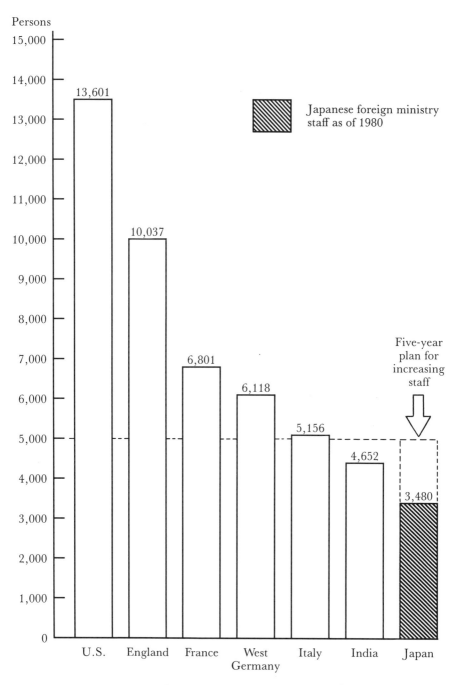

Figure 12
Size Comparison of Foreign Offices in Seven Major Countries

Persons

Japanese foreign ministry staff as of 1980

Five-year plan for increasing staff

13,601

10,037

6,801

6,118

5,156

4,652

3,480

U.S.   England   France   West Germany   Italy   India   Japan

(Japanese foreign ministry statistics, November 1980.)

Figure 13
Staff Complement at Japanese Overseas Posts

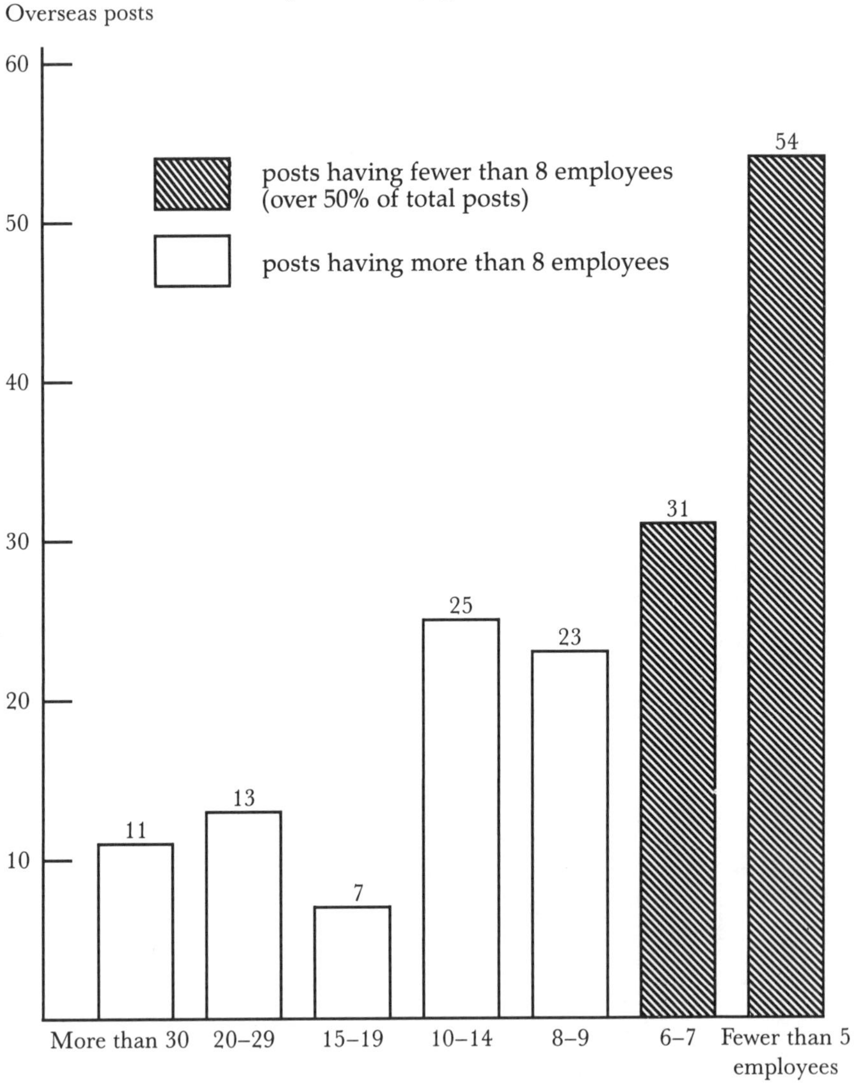

Overseas posts

(Japanese foreign ministry statistics, November 1980.)

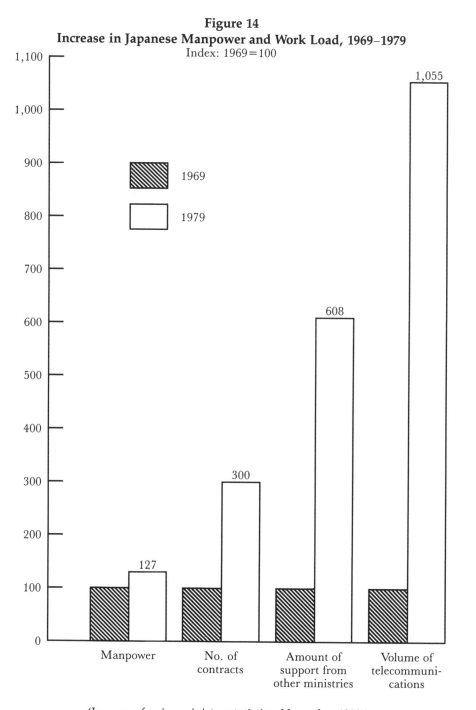

Figure 14
Increase in Japanese Manpower and Work Load, 1969–1979
Index: 1969=100

1969

1979

1,055

608

300

127

Manpower

No. of
contracts

Amount of
support from
other ministries

Volume of
telecommuni-
cations

(Japanese foreign ministry statistics, November 1980.)

it has developed reflect a national reticence to engage fully in international intercourse.

Top management is concerned about the long hours and physical hardships resulting from the lack of adequate manpower. New crises will have to be dealt with as they arise, using the resources at hand. Frustrations resulting from solutions blocked or delayed by tradition add complications. One unfortunate side effect of the government's policy for administrative reform, which contemplates reductions in government employment, is that bureau directors, because of increasing work pressure, cannot devote as much time to overseeing and guiding young career diplomats. (Several senior diplomats have attributed whatever success they have achieved in their careers to just this kind of supervision.)

Many observers of Japanese diplomacy marvel that Japan has been able to deal with problems as skillfully as it has, given insufficient numbers of personnel. The successes achieved have resulted in part from the hard work and dedication of the ministry staff. More could have been achieved if greater attention had been paid in the past to developing a varied group of language and area specialists. Fortunately, this is happening, but the program is being resisted by career officers who subscribe to the generalist philosophy.

The ministry is not without supporters in the Diet and the press. Diet members sympathetic to the ministry's plight have banded together to assist it in achieving the manpower goals of the five-year plan, and newspaper commentators have written sympathetic articles about what should be done. Typical is an article in the *Sankei Shimbun* (September 4, 1979) that pointed out the need for personnel increases and noted that the continued understaffing of overseas posts hampers the efforts of Japanese diplomats to gather and evaluate the information needed in Tokyo and undercuts efforts to promote a better understanding of Japan's foreign policies by other nations. Inasmuch as Japan has forsworn the use of military power as an instrument of foreign policy, effective conduct of diplomacy by a highly skilled corps of diplomats is imperative to protect Japanese interests.

Tied closely to the whole question of a manpower increase is the possible effect such increase would have on a time-honored personnel policy: keeping the system in equilibrium. I detected the potential for some small concessions to balance—namely, the opinion voiced by several senior officials that greater competition with more emphasis on merit and less on seniority was probable as recruitment rates were stepped up.

The ministry leadership will have to persuade FSOs that a personnel increase will not adversely affect their careers. A senior officer told me that he thought such persuasion would be easier because greater opportunities for ambassadorial appointments were expected in 1980. He explained that the ambassadors of the 1980s come largely from the classes of 1943, 1944, and 1945, a period when the foreign ministry had to absorb officers from the Greater East Asia Ministry. Their ranks are beginning to thin; consequently, in the late 1980s ambassadorial openings should be more numerous.

Other officers have alluded to the dwindling number of ambassadors from the classes of 1943, 1944, and 1945 as an important reason for the concern of management for stability. This stability will also be affected by changes in the structure and operation of the key bureaus in the ministry and by international pressures that continually test the viability and resources of these bureaus.

Specific Problem Areas

The Division

The manner in which personnel resources are allocated in a typical division in a geographic bureau illustrates the manpower problem faced by the foreign ministry.

A typical division has three units: a research section, a general affairs section, and an administrative section. The division chief has a principal deputy who is also a career officer. In addition, there are generally two FSOs in the general affairs section who coordinate the work of all three sections. Figure 15 shows the organization of the First North American Affairs Division in the North American Affairs Bureau. One or two career officers in training are assigned to the general affairs section at any given time. Of the approximately fifteen officers assigned to the First North American Affairs Division, four are FSOs and the remainder are noncareer personnel.

The ambience within the division is not always conducive to change because the chief and his career subordinates share common interests, a sense of career destiny, and a belief that they hold a heavy responsibility for Japan's foreign policy. This camaraderie does not usually extend to non-career officers, who are considered specialists, not generalists. They are not usually consulted on matters of policy coordination, recommendation, or implementation.

The counterpart of this division was the Japanese Imperial Navy, where careerists (who were graduates of the Naval College) were distinct from noncareerists; the lines of authority were rigid. The system was described in a *Chūo Koron* article in July 1978 as one in which all important work was done by the chief and his senior deputy, both of whom were career officials. The "gray-haired" assistant director, who was not a member of the career

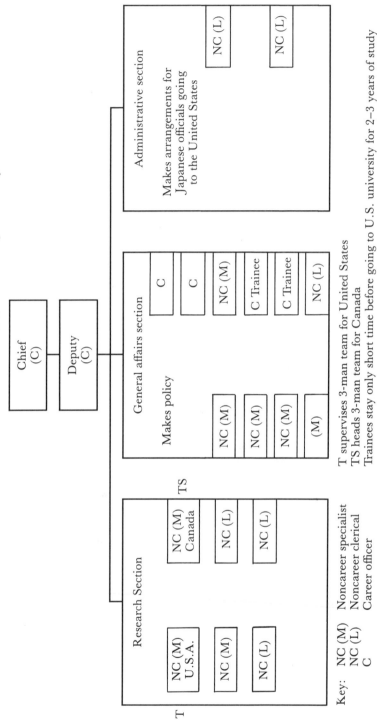

Figure 15
Organization of First North American Division,
North American Affairs Bureau of Japanese Foreign Ministry

Chief (C)

Deputy (C)

Research Section

T

NC (M) U.S.A.

NC (M)

NC (L)

NC (M) Canada   TS

NC (L)

NC (L)

General affairs section

Makes policy

C

C

NC (M)

C Trainee

C Trainee

NC (L)

NC (M)

NC (M)

NC (M)

(M)

Administrative section

Makes arrangements for Japanese officials going to the United States

NC (L)

NC (L)

Key:

NC (M)   Noncareer specialist
NC (L)   Noncareer clerical
C   Career officer

T supervises 3-man team for United States
TS heads 3-man team for Canada
Trainees stay only short time before going to U.S. university for 2–3 years of study

group, played only a secondary role. Career officers took charge of negotiations with other ministries and participated in intraministerial conferences. They socialized only when the division as a whole met for some social activity (for example, a weekend excursion to Hakone).

During normal office operations, noncareer officials treat their career superiors with respect, which is usually reciprocated. One noncareer officer explained that before World War II, there was a great deal of class consciousness, and young career officers were often blunt and impolite to noncareer personnel. But he thought that attitudes have begun to change and that the noncareer officer of the 1980s is being treated with more consideration.

In setting the tone of personal relationships, much, of course, depends on the leadership of the division chief. All division chiefs must observe tradition in the operation of their divisions, but some are more skilled than others in giving the noncareer officer a sense of belonging and in encouraging him to participate in important division activities. There are some divisions, such as the Russian Division in the European and Oceanic Affairs Bureau, where a knowledge of the language, politics, and history of a country (usually the noncareer officer is the specialist in these fields) is important to the successful conduct of the division's business. Solution of the fisheries problem, for example, requires someone with a good deal of background and expertise in that area, and the division chief therefore leans heavily on the knowledgeable noncareer officer.

The Russian Division chief explained that the career officers in his division were in the general affairs section and handled policy coordination and recommendations, whereas noncareer officers dealt with functional issues, such as fisheries and special economic problems, and provided information on and analysis of Soviet domestic politics. The career officers used information provided by noncareer specialists for policy coordination and recommendations, he said, whereas the noncareer officer furnished information on his specialty that was used in the decision-making process.

This division chief indicated that his principal deputy was a career officer but not a Russian expert. He was deliberately chosen for that position in order to provide a non-Russian perspective on policy problems. The chief said the arrangement was working well, due mainly to the support given the deputy and other career officers by the noncareer specialists.

Despite the efficiency and teamwork in the Russian Division and despite whatever "democratizing" may have taken place, the traditional gulf separating the career and noncareer groups, both substantively and psychologically, is still discernible in the division of labor in the office and to some extent in personal relationships. There is little indication that it will soon disappear.

Much division work is routine, originating in the embassy or consulate general concerned, other divisions in the ministry, or other ministries in the Japanese government needing foreign ministry guidance and recommendations. The clearance procedure is time-consuming, for it often requires officers to engage in long discussions over procedural and substantive issues. The inevitable meetings that generally concern mundane activities also consume many working hours and place a heavy burden on the career officer. *Ringisei*, or the procedure for gaining consensus, is the traditional Japanese method of problem solving, both in the bureaucracy and in society, and is faithfully followed by the bureaucrats.

All division chiefs with whom I talked complained about the lack of career officers. Yet, when I suggested that it might be helpful to allow the brighter noncareer officers to take over some of the substantive responsibilities to alleviate the manpower problem, the response was always the same—that noncareer officers were specialists, not generalists, and had not been trained to handle substantive matters. These division chiefs seemed to have little disposition to initiate change.

One particularly frank division chief said that division operations could be adversely affected by the low morale of noncareer specialists. He explained that when serving overseas, these officers had important responsibilities because of their area expertise. They were looked to for information and advice, but when they returned to Tokyo, they were often shunted aside. They had to obey the orders of young career officers with less experience and had to submit papers and reports to the division chief through them; in addition, they were often excluded from official meetings. They often wondered why they had to submit to such petty bureaucratic practices when they were older and more experienced. One reason, he explained, was that the foreign ministry desired to train young career officers in all facets of the diplomatic system—to make them good generalists. He said he often included noncareer officers in division consultations but abided by time-honored tradition in reserving decisions on policy for the career group.

The Career-Noncareer Service

The problem of the career-noncareer officer is not unique to the foreign ministry but prevails throughout the Japanese government. Opinions vary on its seriousness, but there is grudging admission by junior as well as senior officers that some change is necessary.

In explaining the problem, one senior officer told me that both career and noncareer officers are divisible into three classes: above average, average, and below average. The middle and lower levels of the noncareer group have relatively few complaints; they know their place in the system, their qualifications, and their capabilities. But when the members of the highest level of this group begin to compare themselves with the lowest level of the career group, frustration, envy, low morale, and friction become apparent. Most officers in the high noncareer group who resign from the ministry do so out of a sense of frustration because they cannot "cross the career line." In 1979, for example, 28 officers from this group left to take positions in private industry or to retire. Early indications of unhappiness and a desire to leave were the principal reasons the ministry inaugurated its *tōyō seido* (integration program) in the 1970s to offer limited opportunities to noncareer officers to enter the career service. About two officers enter each year. The program has given a small lift to morale but has done little to relieve the work pressures on the career service.

Not all noncareer officers feel a lack of professional fulfillment. Language and area experts specializing in the Middle East, China, and the Soviet Union, for example, seem to have self-confidence, a special sense of mission, and relatively high morale; they do not feel challenged by others. The letdown comes when they return to Tokyo and once again become immersed in the rigid bureaucracy.

A special irritant for the noncareer officer is the seating arrangement in the division. He feels demeaned because he must sit in a corner while the young career officer has a seat in a more favorable section of the office. When I visited several divisions in the ministry, I noted that older officers (later identified as noncareer personnel by the division chief) were indeed seated in less conspicuous parts of the office. To attach importance to such petty considerations might seem foolish, but the noncareer man interprets the seating arrangement as reflecting his position in the office.

A *Tokyo Shimbun* reporter who has covered the foreign ministry for many years told of several members of the same university graduating class who had taken the career and noncareer examinations and had entered the ministry. Some of the noncareer officers felt so uncomfortable working with friends who had graduated in the same class with them but had gone on to become career officers that they resigned. He said that this demonstrated the extreme status consciousness of noncareer officers.

Senior officials recently changed the title of the noncareer examination from *chūkyū* (midlevel) to *senmon-shoku* (specialist). This trivial act lessened somewhat the psychological pain experienced by noncareer officers, but it did little to remove the distinction between the two groups.

Another problem is that little, if any, interchange exists between career and noncareer groups in the assignment process, and this limits the flexibility of the division in allocating resources at critical times. Noncareer officers can generally expect to rise no higher than consul general or deputy division chief in the foreign ministry in Tokyo. The latter position is usually always earmarked for a noncareer officer. The same situation obtains for career officials. They seldom if ever occupy a position formerly held by a noncareer employee.

A former high official, like many other officials with whom I talked, believed there was an "ability difference" between the career and noncareer officer, but she qualified the remark by explaining that of 25 career officers recruited, 20 were outstanding and 5 were about average. She also conceded that top noncareer officers compared favorably with some of the best in the career group. Some formula must be found to reward the bright noncareer officers, she admitted, but she was unsure about what could be done.

Despite the gulf between the two groups, career officers and top managers expressed considerable sympathy for the noncareer officer. "We are doing all we can to correct the situation," said one personnel officer, "but there is only so much that can be done without creating disharmony and instability." Similar expressions of concern came from division chiefs and bureau directors general, but when I pressed these officers for specific recommendations as to how to improve career opportunities for noncareer officers so they could better use their talents to relieve the heavy burdens borne by the career staff, few suggestions were forthcoming. I was repeatedly reminded that career officers were educated and trained to assume the duties of career men, whereas noncareer officers were not. When a noncareer officer is integrated into the career corps, he is generally happy and satisfied with his good fortune, but those who are not selected become more unhappy and frustrated. The noncareer officer theoretically can take the career examination even after he enters the foreign ministry; in actuality this is most difficult because there is little time for preparation. However, if a division chief spots a bright young noncareer officer, he sometimes gives that officer time off to study for the examination. Noncareer officers continue to identify with their colleagues in the noncareer service after they enter the career ranks. As one deputy vice-minister for administration mused, "Once a noncareer man, always a noncareer man."

One former ambassador was concerned about the slow progress being made in solving the problem of the noncareer officer's role. He said the integration of two or three officers a year into the career service was having little impact on the manpower problem and doing little to raise the morale of noncareer officers. At that rate, he estimated, it would take over twenty years for the noncareer officer to be put on a more equal footing with his career colleagues for assignments and promotions. Like other former active and retired senior officials, this ex-ambassador stressed that some of the noncareer officers are bright and very capable but their salaries are low and they often find their futures limited. They become discouraged and because their sense of commitment is not as deep as that of the career officer, they are not as reluctant to leave for business careers. With their language skills and geographic area knowledge, they are welcomed by companies that find them a great asset in overseas operations.

Discrimination against the noncareer officer exists in all ministries of the Japanese government, but noncareer officers in other ministries are generally more satisfied because there is a greater number of positions to which they can be assigned.

Statistics for 1981 illustrate the difficulties experienced by noncareer personnel in gaining top positions in the foreign ministry and at overseas posts. It took a noncareer officer almost twice as long as a career officer to reach a senior position; out a total of 59 deputy division chiefs in the ministry, 57 were career officers with an average age of 36 and 2 were noncareer officers, both age 54. It took the two officers 27 years and 39 years, respectively, to reach the deputy division chief level, whereas career officers were promoted to the position in about 12 years. In 1982, no noncareer officers held the position of division chief. Since 1970, no noncareer officer has been appointed a director general of a bureau in the foreign ministry. However, two noncareer officers were appointed ambassadors to Bolivia, three to Honduras, two to Nicaragua, two to Gabon, one to Liberia, and one to Ghana. Noncareer officers are also assigned as consuls general, but the trend is away from assigning them to more desirable posts. Noncareer officers have been posted to Japanese Consulates General in Leningrad and Nahodka, but these officers were Russian language and area experts.

It is perhaps too much to expect career officers to share their prestige and decision-making role with noncareer personnel. They claim, perhaps rightly so, that they are better educated, have taken a more difficult examination, and are thus entitled to join the exclusive club of careerists in which tradition, elitism, and hierarchy are the standards set for the whole career service. Even if the two groups were joined, it would only be a matter of time, said one careerist, before the better educated would emerge in leadership roles, and there would then be "leaders and followers," a situation that is the norm in any organization.

The noncareerist, although restless, unhappy, and frustrated, continues to consider ways to improve his position. On July 10, 1981, a group of 30 noncareer officers drew up a petition to the foreign minister asking consideration of the following points:

1. A unified entrance examination should be established.
2. There should be more equitable pay and allowances at overseas posts.

3. There should be shorter promotion time between classes. (The petition explained that it takes a career officer six years and a noncareer officer ten years to reach class 4.)

4. Noncareer officers should be assigned to more challenging work— to line work in a division rather than to staff work.

Although there is precedent for reformist movements in the Japanese bureaucracy, it is still rather unusual for a group of noncareer officers to protest in this way. A senior management official said that it is very unlikely that such action would gain the desired ends.

The strong reform advocates in the noncareer group are in classes 3, 4, and 5. Young senmon-shokū officers have not been in the service long enough to become frustrated, and the older ones, in classes 2 and 1, have become resigned to their role and do not believe seeking redress of grievances is worth the effort.

Some senmon-shokū officers admitted that they would feel uncomfortable if assigned as a division chief or an ambassador, for they would always be conscious of the difference in status between themselves and the career group. They believed they were not trained to assume such heavy responsibilities and were therefore not particularly eager to be placed in such positions. After all, as one senmon-shokū officer put it, the traditions and practices of the foreign ministry relegate the noncareer officer to a less prestigious position, and so *shikata ga nai* ("it cannot be helped").

The distinction between the two groups sometimes has unfortunate consequences for these officers and their families. Several former ambassadors told me that noncareer officers scheduled for overseas assignment are sometimes given career or diplomatic titles (such as first secretary and counselor) in an attempt to ease their frustration. Often such concessions are resented by the careerists, to the detriment of harmony and unity at the post. One former ambassador said that if the principal officer or ambassador is skilled in staff management, such unfortunate consequences can often be minimized or eliminated. But discrimination does exist, and sometimes extends to the wives. One former noncareer officer who holds an important position in the energy field told me that when he was assigned to a Japanese Embassy in Asia in the early 1960s, his wife was treated rather badly by career officers' wives; it so disturbed him that he never forgave the foreign ministry or its career service. There is no particular pattern of discrimination against families of noncareer officers, but enough incidents were mentioned to me to suggest that it is a matter requiring the attention of senior officials.

The Generalist-Specialist Question

I define a generalist officer as one who has been assigned to several geographic and functional bureaus, has served in several countries, has some proficiency in one or more of the Western languages, and has been given increasingly important assignments involving policy coordination, decision-making, and the management of people and programs. He has a superficial familiarity with several functions and areas but is a specialist in none.

The specialist is defined as an officer, usually noncareer, who has had extensive geographic area and language training and has become a leading authority on a specific country's history, culture, politics, and economics. He is expected to use his skills to provide necessary information and advice to career officer superiors and to his ambassador. He is also expected to develop certain functional skills in order to lessen the foreign ministry's dependence on such ministries as MITI.

The lack of emphasis on specialization in the officer corps, especially in the career category, weakens the foreign ministry's ability to represent Japan's interests effectively at conferences and meetings dealing with transportation, communication, nuclear energy, fisheries, trade, and economic matters, for example. The ministry's emphasis on the generalist orientation of its career officers means that personnel have to be borrowed from other ministries such as MITI and the Ministries of Finance and Agriculture, Forestry, and Fisheries to deal with technical issues. The assignment of officers from these ministries to overseas posts, in turn, increases the support responsibilities of the regular foreign ministry staff, a burden already heavy because of lack of adequate personnel. Reliance on other ministries also lessens the foreign ministry's influence as the chief formulator, implementer, and enunciator of Japanese foreign policy. A former vice-minister deplored the competition that has long existed between the foreign ministry and MITI, which he attributed to a lack of special skills on the part of the career corps of the Ministry of Foreign Affairs and the hesitation of the members of that ministry to speak out authoritatively on economic issues.

From his entrance on duty, the young jōkyū (career officer) is trained to be a generalist. His assignments are based on the beliefs that an officer must be able to analyze, interpret, evaluate, and coordinate broad policy problems, and that he must have the proper training and background for the assumption of a policymaking role and the management of divisions, bureaus, and overseas posts. Every career officer I talked with during the one year of my research expressed unqualified support for the generalist approach to career development. Specialization would not have led to the rewards they expected.

Assignments to different geographic areas and functions give a career officer the broad background necessary to move ahead. His generalist training does not equip him to deal with specialized problems in such fields as transportation, communications, and nuclear energy, but his ability to understand quickly the essentials of a problem often helps him contribute to its solution.

A career officer often attains a limited specialization in a language and geographic area or function. For example, he might be assigned to several posts where he is responsible for economic affairs; or to the Organization for Economic Cooperation and Development (OECD), for specific economic reporting and analysis; or to countries in South Asia or Europe where he deals with political or information work; or to the ministry in Tokyo where he may have policy planning responsibilities or be assigned to the prime minister's office. Diplomats must deal with all kinds of problems that concern Japan's relations with foreign countries, and the generalist is the only one who can do this. "When you are the chief negotiator," one senior official said, "you do not need to know too much detail; if necessary you can borrow the expertise from another ministry or rely on your own noncareer specialists."

Several former vice-ministers strongly defended the policy of emphasizing a generalist orientation for career officers. One explained that the senior officers have either a legal or an economic background, which allows them to handle a broad spectrum of problems while relying on experts for details. Another former vice-minister said that the foreign ministry needs career officers with a wide knowledge of diplomacy. Specialists cannot understand broad aspects of foreign affairs because they do not have this type of training.

Despite the strong contention of present and former high ministry officials that the generalist approach to career development is in the best interests of Japan's foreign policy and the careers of the country's diplomats, there seems to be growing recognition that some reconciliation is necessary between this approach and an approach that recognizes the need for greater language, area, and functional specialization by both career and noncareer officers. The emphasis seems to be on increasing the number of noncareer specialists. But there is also some support for the notion of giving the career officer a greater exposure to geographic or functional specialization. One division chief told me that during the late 1980s, there will be a greater need for specialists in the fields of energy, transportation, and communications, but if the career officer is to be induced to opt for such specialization, he must be convinced of appropriate rewards—essentially, equity in the distribution of coveted assignments.

It was this division chief's opinion that traditions are changing in the foreign ministry; that there are stirrings for innovative policies in personnel management; and that Japan is becoming, in effect, a society of specialists and this will be reflected in the foreign ministry's personnel policies. He believed that the transition from generalist to specialist should be accomplished gradually. The new emphasis on specialization for the career corps would have to be evaluated after the initial three to five years to determine whether career officers accepting training and assignments as specialists were, in fact, obtaining ambassadorships and other top positions to the same extent as their generalist-oriented colleagues. Such evidence would convince skeptics and give a needed boost to the new policy. He thought that a majority of the career officers could support such a policy if their doubts were resolved.

A former ambassador commented that it would probably take over ten years for sufficient evidence to develop to convince the career officer to become a specialist. He said the attractions were not yet sufficient to induce a sizable number of career officers to opt for specialization.

A former vice-minister observed that in any event, the functional needs of the foreign ministry are better handled by the Ministries of Finance, International Trade and Industry, Transportation, and Agriculture, Forestry, and Fisheries, which have the specialists to deal effectively with special problems. The foreign ministry career diplomats should understand the general nature of problems and how to present them to officials of foreign governments; they should not attempt to become specialists.

A newspaperman who has covered the foreign ministry for a long time told me that in recruiting new career officers, the ministry accepts candidates who have majored in fields other than law (the traditional route to appointment), such as economics and science, but that in general, these officers cannot expect to become ambassadors to a major post, bureau directors general, or division chiefs in important geographic bureaus; such posts continue to be reserved for the successful generalists.

Finally, a former ambassador to the United States who is an adviser to one of Japan's largest banks told me that tradition, very strong in the ministry, has shown that the surest way to reach the summit of the Foreign Service is still to be a career generalist. He conceded that continued foreign ministry reliance on other government departments for assistance in special fields has weakened the influence of the ministry.

These are the major arguments for and against developing a corps of specialists. However, the problem is more complex than the arguments suggest. It seems unlikely that the generalist orientation of the career officer will be changed substantially as long as the system uses the traditional career examination for recruitment. Moreover, as long as the career officer's assignments in the ministry and overseas call for policy coordination and decision-making, and as long as he continues to be conditioned by education and training to think of himself as a member of a small, exclusive group of generalists who are the "shapers and shakers" of Japanese foreign policy, there seems little likelihood of substantial change.

How far senior managers wish to veer from the traditional path of career development is unclear. Area and language specialization, especially a concentration on the more exotic languages of the Middle East, Africa, and South Asia, will continue to be the preserve of the senmon-shokū officer. Career officers who are asked to move into these specialities must expect appropriate rewards and be convinced that if they do so, their careers will not be jeopardized. A new system will probably be instituted in which both career and noncareer officers will gradually transfer to specialties identified by management as vital to the conduct of foreign policy. One senior officer said that if a successful transition is to be made to a system that more clearly serves the interests of Japan, the "education for change" process will have to begin in the classroom.

Staffing of Overseas Posts

Another area where Japanese tradition has proved inadequate to deal with modern personnel difficulties is in the staffing of overseas posts. This is a difficult problem for managers and is becoming more tedious and vexing. In 1981, of a total of 3,446 foreign ministry personnel, only about 690, or less than 20 percent, were career officers. These officers must be distributed among more than 100 posts. Statistically, on the average about 5 officers, career and noncareer, are assigned to a post. The ministry wishes to increase this figure to 7. At the average embassy, there are only 2 FSOs, excluding the ambassador. The disproportion between career and non-career officers is best illustrated by the example of the Japanese embassies in Brazil and Mexico. In the former, there are 2 career officers and 15–20 noncareer officers, whereas in the latter the ratio is 3 to 20.

One former ambassador said that a Japanese Embassy often resembles the government of Japan in microcosm. There are representatives of the Ministries of International Trade and Industry, Finance, and Justice, as well as the Defense Agency and other government departments. The small embassy staff must administratively support these agency representatives, performing such duties as handling cables, filing, and coding.

The personnel shortage in some embassies is so acute and the burden of work so heavy that efficiency is reduced. As a result, said one deputy director general of a major geographic bureau, the quality of work produced in embassies and consulates general frequently suffers. Embassy officers sometimes get so weary that they merely go through the motions and accomplish little. If an officer becomes ill, the ambassador himself often must do the administrative work. Home leaves are postponed or relinquished if there is sickness at the post or if the work load gets too heavy.

The most severe shortage is in support staff—the clerks and administrators. This deputy director general said that of the 80 persons in the Japanese Embassy in Washington where he served, 20 were career officers, 40 were noncareer and clerical personnel, and 20 were representatives from other government ministries and agencies.

A major problem facing the foreign ministry is the recruitment of clerks and secretaries willing to serve abroad. Once these employees enter the ministry and find they have to work long hours and may be assigned to hardship posts, they sometimes resign and accept positions in private companies, where work schedules are more predictable and life is more comfortable. If they stay in the foreign ministry, it is often on the condition that they not be sent abroad. Another inhibiting factor is the requirement that they learn a foreign language—many do not wish to undertake what they regard as an onerous task. The ministry consequently must recruit a support staff not fully committed to it, a staff that may not stay long.

My source explained that one way the ministry deals with this problem is by using the services of the *Kokusai Koryu Kyokai* (International Cooperation Committee), an organization that assists in filling support staff positions. University students are employed on a temporary (two-year) contract basis to work at missions abroad. The students may go to countries whose language they are studying at the university or whose culture, politics, economics, and history are a part of their university curriculum. After the assignment, they return to the university to complete their academic work. Because of their ministry training, they usually can obtain attractive positions with private companies after graduation. These companies are eager to recruit such people because they do not have to go to the expense of training them. The source said that in the Japanese Embassy in Peking, there were five such students who not only performed clerical duties but went to the airport to meet visiting delegations. This, he said, is not a permanent solution, but it is the best that can be devised under the strict government economy measures in effect.

One former high official in the Japanese United Nations delegation told me she thought turnover at Japanese overseas posts was too rapid. The general policy, she said, is to transfer an officer after two years. In an important post like the United States, it takes several years to develop the kinds of contacts useful to the embassy, especially since U.S. foreign policy is a concern of so many different groups—the White House, State Department, Pentagon, congressmen and senators, government bureaucrats, the media, businessmen, scholars, and lawyers.

An officer in the Personnel Division told me that the foreign ministry is considering extending the tour of duty of several key officers in important posts such as the United States, Great Britain, and the Soviet Union from two to three years but that this proposal has encountered objections from career officers anxious to develop their own careers through assignments to these posts. (The longer an officer stays in the United States, for example, the longer another officer must wait for the coveted assignment.) In addition, some posts are not challenging, and officers wish to move on to more stimulating work. Other posts are located in hardship areas and officers, for health and family reasons, wish to be reassigned after two years. As the personnel officer explained, reassignment of one officer sets in motion a series of other moves affecting the assignments of officers both overseas and in Tokyo.

I received mixed reactions from career officers with whom I talked about the staffing problem. One young deputy division chief in an important geographic bureau said that the rotation policy has its good and bad points. In a country like India, it is relatively easy to learn job responsibilities, make contacts, and conduct daily work. A two-year assignment, therefore, is appropriate. But in Washington, it takes considerably longer to "get on top of things," so an assignment there should be extended to three or four years. It is obvious, he said, that a Washington assignment is prestigious and contributes importantly to an officer's career development. Hence, a longer tour there can only redound to an officer's advantage.

One former Japanese ambassador to Washington said that key officers should remain there at least four years. He indicated that many congressmen and other U.S. officials complained that turnover of embassy personnel, including the ambassador, was too rapid. He said the Japanese managers are aware of this situation but do not appear to be doing much about it—they are too concerned with meeting the needs of career officers and too preoccupied with preserving the generalist policy of career development. In the opinion of this ambassador, they should not be so concerned because many of the officers they worry about lack the potential for becoming ambassadors at major posts.

Representatives of other ministries who are assigned to missions abroad are another source of difficulty. Not only do they create additional work for the regular foreign ministry staff but, as pointed out by a former *Asahi*

Shimbun reporter, they sometimes create tensions in the mission by communicating directly with their home ministries, using the communication facilities of the local Mitsui or Mitsubishi trading company branch offices, for example. The reporter explained that the interministerial rivalries that exist at overseas posts are often present in Tokyo as well. Rivalries (or perhaps more accurately, differences over policy) often exist between the Ministry of Foreign Affairs (for compromise) and the Ministry of International Trade and Industry or the Ministry of Agriculture, Forestry, and Fisheries (for protectionism). He said that the foreign ministry is increasingly concerned over the erosion of its power vis-à-vis other ministries.

The foreign ministry has resolved to be the coordinator of Japanese foreign policy. Some senior officers still remember difficulties experienced by the ministry before World War II when there were dual lines of communication between the military representatives at Japanese embassies and the War Department in Tokyo, on the one hand, and the embassies and the Foreign Office, on the other. The ministry is determined to see that this does not happen again.

Another problem is information gathering at embassies and consulates general. Since the late 1970s, senior officials have been dissatisfied with the way overseas posts monitor and report on events of importance to Japan, especially developments in the Middle East and Eastern Europe. Efforts are under way to strengthen the capabilities of overseas posts in these areas—in particular, to enable them to keep up with fast-breaking international developments. Under consideration is a 24-hour watch officer system, similar to the Department of State's Operations Center. *Nihon Keizai Shimbun* of December 22, 1980, reported that the foreign ministry was considering a plan to request the cooperation of private Japanese companies (especially large trading companies with branches abroad) that in the past have provided valuable intelligence to the Japanese government. The article pointed out that because of their competitive nature, use of the information supplied by such companies often created a difficult situation for the Japanese ambassador. To avoid this awkward problem, consideration is being given to sharing embassy information with Japanese trading companies in the hope of fostering a reciprocal exchange of mutually beneficial information.

The ministry also hopes to deal more effectively with crisis situations by inventorying the skills of specialists and generalists and by bringing different individuals together to share their expertise. The article just mentioned indicated that the ministry contemplates forming "country panels" in Tokyo, to include not only ministry personnel but concerned businessmen, scholars, and journalists. Thus, both career and noncareer officers in Japanese embassies would be less isolated from important sources of information and would be better able to report significant developments to Tokyo on a timely basis.

Generational Differences

Perhaps a less significant aspect of the manpower problem is the generational differences that exist between the prewar and postwar generations of career officers and those who entered the foreign ministry during World War II.[4] In general, the officers belonging to the war generation group (those who entered in 1941–1945) who were assigned to important ambassadorships have not measured up to the prewar and postwar officers in terms of performance. Because there was little diplomatic activity between Japan and other nations during the war, there was little opportunity to accumulate professional experience or to gain proficiency in foreign languages.

A number of officers of the 1941–1945 generation had been inducted into the military service and had seen combat for varying lengths of time before becoming diplomats; the experience had a strong effect on them. One career officer (now deceased), with whom I developed a warm friendship, told me his service in the Japanese army in Singapore made him much more sensitive to the military implications of foreign policy and the dangers inherent in chauvinistic and jingoistic pronouncements concerning foreign affairs. His military exposure made him cautious and conservative, not given to advocating policies that departed substantially from the main currents of postwar Japanese foreign policy. He said a number of his colleagues who had been drafted into the military during the war years shared his conservatism and were sometimes pressed, albeit diplomatically, by younger colleagues to formulate more energetic policies for Japan.

A reporter knowledgeable about the foreign ministry wrote an article that was published in *Zaikai Tembo* (April 1979) concerning the problems facing the war generation Foreign Service officer. He concluded that despite the experiences these officers had had in the military, despite the lack of opportunities for gaining diplomatic experience during the war years, and despite their frustrations over their professional careers, a few succeeded in gaining prominence. Takashima Masao (who resigned as vice-minister in 1981), Okawara Yoshio (the ambassador to the United States), and Katori Yasue (the former deputy vice-minister who was appointed ambassador to China in 1982) are some members of the war generation who have risen to the top. The reporter discussed the differences in ability between the prewar generation of officers and the war generation and said that in fairness to the latter, it should be noted that the Japanese government eliminated language training for diplomats from 1941 to 1950. After 1944, the government even eliminated the General High Civil Service Examination (the examination was resumed in 1948 but was renamed the Foreign Service Career Examination), and special regulations governed the recruitment of ministry officers. It was therefore difficult for the ministry to "find the right man for the right job." According to this reporter, war generation officers had little economic expertise because they did not participate in international economic conferences, and most of them were unable to speak good English or French. It was a frustrating period for most Japanese diplomats.

In my discussions of personnel policies with senior officers, some of whom were from the war generation, I noted an excessive prudence (*koto nakare shugi*) on the few occasions when we digressed and spoke about Japan's relations with the United States, the Soviet Union, and China. Few would discuss their careers in the Foreign Service (especially those who entered during the war), and it was therefore hard to assess the psychological impact of the early professional years on their current state of mind.

I noted that some younger career officers showed impatience with the cautious approach of their seniors, which is to be expected. One officer in the North American Affairs Bureau believed that it was important for Japan to speak out more forcefully to the United States on security matters and that some of the U.S. pressure being exerted on Japan to increase its defense buildup resulted from Japan's passive acceptance of U.S. leadership and a feeling of dependency on the United States. Another young officer in the Asian Affairs Bureau, although he acknowledged the need for an empirical approach to foreign policy decision-making and the need to give due attention to past traditions in personnel planning, said that the time had come for more imagination and forcefulness in the bureaucratic process.

These are admittedly only random samplings of opinion, but the fact that young officers imply criticism of their superiors for being too cautious indicates that a generation gap does exist and is having an impact, albeit one that is difficult to measure, on the thinking of older and younger officers alike.

In personnel matters, the gap is manifested in differences regarding the method of selecting individuals for assignment to top-level positions. With some exceptions, older officers believed it important to follow tradition in selecting division chiefs, bureau directors general, and ambassadors, for they saw no compelling reasons to change. The exceptions among senior officials, both active and retired, were officers who had held top administrative and policy positions and had confronted some of the problems that arose when unqualified officers were assigned to important posts. As one such officer explained, this situation does not happen very often, but when it does, it can prove embarrassing; stiffer competition for top positions would provide reasonable assurance that the best men fill them.

Younger officers also seemed more willing to trust to competition in the selection for senior posts. One junior officer told me he had spent all of his university life preparing for a diplomatic career; he had studied English since high school, had undergone training in the ministry's Foreign Service Training Institute, and had studied abroad for several years. He thought he had a good background for the Foreign Service. Although he appreciated the importance of tradition, he thought the time was approaching when less attention should be paid to it and more to merit. When I asked him how his own career would be affected when more career officers were recruited, he replied that he knew all career officers could not eventually become division chiefs, directors general, or ambassadors, but that the imposition of the merit principle in the selection of these officers would, in the end, have a salutary effect on the foreign ministry. The best men would get to the top and this would benefit Japan.

Older officers, when commenting on the behavior and attitudes of younger careerists, were generally complimentary. One former high official said that young officers were well educated, well trained, and had the proper attitude. They entered the ministry because they wanted to serve Japan and to work for peace. They worked hard, expected rewards and generally received them, and usually lived a comfortable and challenging life. They complained, as everyone does from time to time, but their loyalty was unquestioned and their dedication exemplary.

The differences that do exist between young and older officers can be traced to dissimilarities in values. In prewar days, discipline, loyalty, morality, and hard work were emphasized. The family influence was strong. In the postwar years, there has been less academic discipline, less emphasis on patriotism, and a decrease in family authority. However, the senior and junior officers share an emphasis on service and dedication, and the bond thus created will prevail over any differences.

Solutions: Difficult Choices for the Foreign Ministry

The specific problem areas just discussed are apparent to the outside analyst and are also a major source of concern to those responsible for the management of diplomacy. Various solutions have been considered, some thoughtful and others rather bizarre. In the latter category would undoubtedly be the intriguing possibility of solving the manpower problem through a readjustment of the work load. According to an official in a major geographic bureau, some officers advocate apportioning the work load to other ministries or to the private sector to relieve the pressure. However, this could create serious problems for the foreign ministry, he thought, because it would be hard to distinguish between important and unimportant work for allotment to other government departments.

Several officers offered another solution: increase the number of positions to keep the system in balance. A deputy director of a major geographic bureau stressed that more division chief positions must be added to the present (1982) complement of 63, and he thought an increase of 10 to 15 might be appropriate. He conceded, however, that this would be difficult to achieve in light of the government's personnel retrenchment program.

One other possibility might be to increase the number of division chief positions in other ministries and prefectural and local governments earmarked for foreign ministry career officers. The deputy director noted that personnel from other ministries are assigned to embassies and consulates general, and that it might logically follow that these ministries should designate division chief positions for career diplomats. This was happening on a small scale (about 10 positions had been so designated), he said, but more such assignments should be made. He cited the example of a young career officer who was assigned to head a prefectural police policy division, supervising more than 100 personnel, and stressed that this was valuable experience for that officer. When I asked the deputy director if he would have accepted such an assignment at a similar stage in his career, he demurred, implying it would not have been good for him.

Senior managers have considered these and other solutions, such as limiting the assignment of each ambassador to one or two posts, stepping up efforts to induce ambassadors to retire by providing opportunities through cooperation with the private sector for employment (in 1981 the number of senior officers who were qualified for division chief positions and ambassadorships exceeded the number of positions), and convincing young career officers, through education and persuasion, that the gradual introduction of the merit system to the assignment process is in their interest as well as the interest of Japanese diplomacy.

In reaction, the young recruit may very likely compare his career status with that of his colleagues in other government ministries such as the Ministry of Finance and MITI and conclude that his career prospects are not as bright as theirs. Whatever his feelings, he is an FSO by choice and will make the best career for himself that he can. He will assume, and rightly, that at some point old traditions will have to give way to progress. When I visited young recruits undergoing their initial training in the Foreign Service Training Institute, it was clear to me that they had joined the foreign ministry out of a conviction that foreign affairs was to be the challenge of their life. Although all wanted to become top officials in the service, a feeling that would probably grow stronger as they progressed in their careers, they were realistic enough to recognize that with an increase in the number of career officers recruited, there would probably be more officers reaching eligibility for promotion to division chief (age 43) and ambassador (age 53) than there were available positions. Nevertheless, they indicated their resolve to work hard for their class and to achieve their professional goals. This collective attitude on the part of new career recruits is a good omen. If such feelings are shared by subsequent career recruits, the ministry may be able to accomplish the necessary change and maintain the system in balance.

Toyo Seido

One method already noted to give some relief to the hard-pressed career officer is to allow the integration of a certain number of noncareer specialists into the career corps—known as the *tōyō seido* program or the Pickup Program. Since it was inaugurated in the early 1970s, sixteen senmon-shokū officers have been integrated. The program originated as a result of the concerns of senior officials that the noncareer group was becoming disillusioned because of the lack of opportunity to advance to senior positions in the service. It was also intended to defuse some of the tension that exists between the career and noncareer corps. Tōyō seido has not had a significant effect on the manpower problem because an average of only about 1.6 noncareer officers have been integrated annually. The number is kept small because managers of the system do not want to cause apprehension in the career corps ranks that an influx of noncareer officers will jeopardize their opportunities to obtain positions as division chief, director general, or ambassador.

A reporter knowledgeable about foreign ministry affairs indicated that the tōyō seido program was established merely to improve the morale of the noncareer group; it was not intended as a serious effort to solve the manpower problem. In this regard it appears to have been a modest success, mainly because of the high quality of the noncareer officers selected by means of a comprehensive selection process. One senior officer who has participated in the process for several years explained that the selection committee usually has ten members, none with a direct relationship to the office of deputy vice-minister for administration. The names of committee members (all senior career officers) are kept secret to avoid unnecessary pressures on them. To provide desirable continuity, some members serve for several consecutive terms.

The first step in the selection process is for the administrative office to circulate memorandums to all division chiefs in the foreign ministry and to embassies and consulates general requesting recommendations of outstanding noncareer officers (usually 20 to 30) to be considered for integration into the career corps. When these officers' recommendations and official records are received, the committee begins its deliberations, meeting in approximately five separate sessions; initially it seeks to eliminate all but 10 candidates. Committee members talk with the candidates' noncareer peers, the career officers with whom they have worked, and any other officers who know them, check carefully as to the credibility of the officers recommending the candidates, and give special weight to their "corridor reputations." After careful consideration of the strengths and weaknesses of each candidate and personal interviews, recommendations are prepared and sent to the deputy vice-minister for administration. Generally the top two candidates are selected for integration and are usually approved at a level commensurate with salary grade, experience, and age.

The Pickup Program also operates on another level. Candidates from the administrative and clerical staff are selected by a similar process for integration into the senmon-shokū group. Since the procedure began in 1975, about 48 clerical personnel have been integrated.

One officer in the Minister's Secretariat described the tōyō seido program as a token gesture by management to assuage the feelings of noncareerists and to deal with their frustrations. He said that because the best noncareer officers are selected for integration, little harm is done to the elitist reputation of the career corps. Few are selected because few are capable of "filling career shoes."

However, the program leaves a residue of frustration and bad feeling on both sides. The noncareer officer knows that he can never erase his mark as a noncareerist, even when integrated into the career corps. And the career officer silently resents this intrusion into his elite world.

A Unified or Joint Examination

The examination system is another area being analyzed by senior managers seeking a solution to the manpower problem. A proposal under consideration to substitute one examination for the two-tiered examination was first mentioned to me by the deputy vice-minister for administration. The net effect of the unified examination would be to merge the career and noncareer groups into one service, leaving the clerical and administrative group as the other personnel category.

The proposal has not made much headway. The sponsors admit it is a radical departure from the traditional examination system and will require a good deal of employee support to become a reality. The present system is governmentwide and has been in place for generations; therefore, it would be very difficult for the foreign ministry to depart singlehandedly from tradition. Noncareer officers would probably vote against the proposal because they would probably feel uncomfortable competing with colleagues who had gone to more prestigious universities and had more confidence in their ability to be successful diplomats.

One personnel officer said that regardless of its merits, if the unified examination were adopted, there would be confusion for several years until things "shook down." It should probably be introduced gradually to allow the personnel concerned to become adjusted to the idea and to be educated regarding its implications for career development. He thought opposition would come from the career group, apprehensive that such a radical departure from traditional personnel practices would diminish its prestige.

A senior officer in the Minister's Secretariat, although admitting he favored a unified examination, expressed concern about its effect on recruitment. He opined that top graduates of the Universities of Tokyo and Kyoto and other schools in Japan might choose to go to other ministries. Merging the two classes would run the risk of lowering the quality of recruits, he said, and this would not be desirable, particularly when new foreign policy challenges are testing the capabilities of the career corps.

He noted that the career examination being used is unique in the government bureaucracy and is the cornerstone of the entire career system. It has been endowed with the prestige of generations of Japanese diplomats who have passed it; passing it has been and is the goal of countless Japanese undergraduates. It is the basis for the elitist mystique that provides the psychological underpinnings of the career system.

This was an eloquent defense of the status quo and I heard it often. Some officers were forthright in their opposition, others tempered their remarks, especially if they happened to be assigned to the Personnel Division; some were frankly puzzled by the proposal and wondered how it would work in practice—how the two groups, career and noncareer, could merge without disruption and schisms. One division chief questioned whether top graduates of the University of Tokyo, who heretofore had chosen to take the career examination because the small career corps exemplified elitism, would elect to take an examination for the purpose of recruiting 50 or 60 officers rather than the traditional 25–27. "We might find, under the unified examination system, a decline in quality," he said.

A noncareer officer also expressed some misgivings about the joint examination. He conceded that one of the objectives was to improve the career position of the senmon-shokū officers but thought that many of his colleagues would feel uncomfortable merging with career officers. He wondered how many graduates of lesser universities and colleges who were planning to take the senmon-shokū examination and would feel relatively comfortable in doing so, would take the new unified examination in competition with University of Tokyo graduates. These important considerations would very likely trouble many other noncareerists or prospective candidates for the unified examination who had graduated from less prestigious universities.

Most of my retired ambassadorial contacts could see little good in the unified examination proposal. Some wondered how it would work in practice and what length of time would be required before a truly merged and settled system was in place. Others were concerned about image—Would the ministry lose its reputation for career excellence? Would the quality of personnel recruited under the new system measure up favorably with those recruited under the old system? How would training be affected? What would happen to the generalist philosophy of career development? Would there be much change in the method of selecting top officers? Would more able officers emerge as a distinct group even under the new system? These questions and concerns troubled the career and noncareer officers as well.[5]

Some time will pass before a consensus emerges regarding the joint examination proposal. What is more likely is some modification that will allow for a gradual merger of the career and noncareer groups, with limited changes in the examination structure. Whatever solution is adopted is unlikely to have much immediate impact on the critical manpower shortage.

Outside Specialists

As foreign affairs become more complex and the need for specialists in such fields as energy, communications, nuclear energy, and transportation becomes more pressing, the foreign ministry is becoming increasingly dependent on experts from other government ministries. After receiving a temporary appointment, such officials are generally given a brief orientation in the foreign ministry's Foreign Service Training Institute and some are then sent abroad on a two- to three-year assignment. Others are assigned to the ministry in Tokyo, especially to functional bureaus such as the Bureau of Economic Affairs and the Bureau of Economic Cooperation. These bureaus also recruit temporary employees from the private sector (who are paid salaries by their companies) to assist in the solution of difficult economic and trade problems. By giving temporary employment to these individuals, the ministry hopes to enhance its reputation and to give the public a better idea of how the foreign ministry functions.

The idea of borrowing employees from other ministries is not meeting with much enthusiasm from top management, which is concerned that reliance on outside help will reduce the influence of the foreign ministry. Senior career officers were quick to respond concerning this problem of diminishing influence, stating that the ministry's role is one of policy coordination, which is quite compatible with dependence on outside experts for assistance. Several said they hoped that the ministry could eventually develop experts in such fields as energy, transportation, and communication in both the career and noncareer corps to lessen ministry dependence on other government departments. They acknowledged it might be difficult to train career officers for such duties; however, some thought a superficial knowledge of a particular energy problem, for example, would suffice to keep the career officer in control of negotiations if he were the policy coordinator on an energy issue. As one former senior official of a major geographic bureau put it, "We can reach a level of expertise that will make it possible for us to supervise negotiations and discussions that include experts from other ministries. But we still have to do more to build up a corps of functional experts."

Even if the foreign ministry had its own experts, it is highly probable that ministries such as MITI and the Ministry of Finance would insist upon a role for themselves in negotiations in which they had a special interest. One high official asserted that media reporting of interministry tensions was exaggerated. Despite such disclaimers, tensions do exist and are inherent in the bureaucratic process. This became increasingly clear in my discussions with officials of other ministries. They believed they had a right to participate in and direct the course of negotiations with other governments on issues over which their ministry had domestic jurisdiction—such as the question of limiting the number of Japanese-made automobiles imported into the United States. There was an intense struggle between the foreign ministry and MITI over which one was to deal with the basic policy issue involved. The jurisdictional problem was finally resolved through compromise, but both ministries were less than happy with it.

During the period 1975–1980, the foreign ministry recruited 58 individuals from private enterprise—3 from academic circles and 7 from the media. Over one-half of them were posted abroad as general officers after ministry orientation. A breakdown by year, source, and position is given in Table 11.

The most ambitious and realistic approach to a solution of the manpower problem is the effort to increase the size of the foreign ministry to a total of 5,000 employees by 1985. Protracted annual negotiations can be expected, even though this approach is one that is perhaps most acceptable to all parties in the ministry. Strong efforts will be made to maintain a semblance of the status quo, for career officers are not in a mood to sacrifice their career expectations for untried solutions, especially those that seem to undermine cherished traditions and customs. These expectations are firmly embedded in the psyche of each new recruit and it will be difficult to dislodge them. Any changes that do occur will undoubtedly be preceded by an educational program to persuade careerists of the necessity for change.

Table 11

Personnel Recruitment Outside the Japanese Foreign Ministry, 1975–1980

Source	Number Recruited							Position When Recruited			
								Foreign Ministry		Overseas	
	1975	1976	1977	1978	1979	1980	Total	General officer	Ambassador	Minister counselor	General office staff
Private corporations	14	4	10	9	13	8	58	52	1	—	5
Academic circles	—	2	—	—	—	1	3	—	—	3	—
Press	4	—	1	—	—	2	7	6	—	—	1
Total	18	6	11	9	13	11	68	58	1	3	6

SOURCE: Foreign ministry figures, November 1980.

Implementation of any change will have to be gradual to avoid upsetting the equilibrium of the system.

Increasing the size of the career corps, introducing more merit into the selection of ambassadors and key ministry officials, placing greater emphasis on language, area, and functional specialization in the training of career officers, and restructuring bureaus are changes that many officers consider radical. One former ambassador questioned whether such changes could actually be carried out. After all, he pointed out, career officers consider themselves elitist, and it is not in their nature to propose or accept radical reform—to do so would reflect on their judgment and ability. The older career officers, especially, are proud of the present system, a system through which they advanced to high positions as a result of their ability and hard work. Many of them will logically defend the status quo.

Although there will be resistance to change, important modifications of the personnel system appear to be inevitable; some mutations are already discernible. The stress on greater specialization is a trend that seems bound to continue. It will gain momentum as career officers realize that it does not counter the basic philosophy of the generalist and that it will further rather than hinder career advancement. The deputy vice-minister for administration told me in our closing interview that candidates for top positions must in the future be not only good generalists but good specialists in such areas as fisheries, nuclear energy, security, transportation, and labor. Without this knowledge, it is unlikely that they will be promoted to senior positions. This will be one aspect of personnel policy that his successor will be no less dedicated that he to implementing.

Another discernible change is a greater emphasis on merit in selecting top career officials for the ministry and for key ambassadorships. There is considerable resistance to changing what has become an institutionalized practice—the almost automatic promotion of career officers to ambassadorships and to the positions of director general and division chief. If the ministry eventually reaches an annual recruitment level of 30–35 career officers, it will be obvious, said one senior official, that all officers will not reach the top. There will be more competition for choice assignments, he pointed out, and career officers will have to accept that fact. In the future, merely passing the career entrance examination will not guarantee promotion to senior positions. Specialization, as well as evidence of a "generalist" capability, and a sustained high level of performance will be the criteria for selection.

One young career officer who seemingly reflected the mood of his colleagues told me in our concluding interview that more stress must be placed on the political and military aspects of Japanese diplomacy. Heretofore, the main focus has been on promoting Japanese economic interests abroad, and this program has been quite successful. But times are changing, he said. Japan must recognize the increasing importance of political and military affairs and develop a group of career officers who are experts in this field. They should be given the opportunity to participate fully in the decision-making process and to compete with their colleagues on an equal basis for top positions.

These are the main elements in the manpower picture. Some may be easier to change than others, but in the next few decades, modifications of the personnel structure will undoubtedly be necessary to enable Japan to manage diplomacy more effectively.

7

PROBLEMS IN DIPLOMATIC MANAGEMENT: UNITED STATES

Although the Department of State does not have the career-noncareer division and the attendant organizational and functional problems of the Japanese foreign ministry, it is facing personnel challenges that will necessitate changes in the way personnel matters are administered. The Foreign Service Act of 1980 will provide the blueprint for many of the new policies.

Conditions of Service

Personnel problems that plagued the State Department and the career Foreign Service in the 1970s included a single personnel system, senior officer glut, mistakes by management, inordinate interpersonal competition that threatened to prevent the department from carrying out its larger mission, a fledgling union movement that initially sowed more discord than unity, a promotion system that tended to spread rewards somewhat unevenly, a paucity of language and geographic area experts knowledgeable about regions important to U.S. foreign policy, and the generalist versus specialist controversy.

Hardship Posts

The Foreign Service must deal with these problems and also be willing to accept burdens and risks unknown some years ago. Its officers must routinely confront problems of inadequate housing caused not only by scarce resources, but also by an inflation rate that is often higher abroad than in the United States. Hardship conditions (caused by climate, isolation or confinement, danger, and lack of educational, cultural, and recreational facilities) exist at some 125 overseas posts.

In Africa, 46 of the 48 posts are designated hardship posts, thereby entitling individuals serving there to a hardship differential of up to 25 percent of base salary. They may be confronted by high heat and humidity, a hostile environment, unsanitary conditions, and the threat of tropical diseases such as malaria, hepatitis, cholera, and meningitis. Hospitals may have inadequate staff and/or facilities, and there may be few flights in and out of the capital city, which are necessary in medical emergencies. The isolation is compounded by a lack of indigenous cultural attractions. Often, because of government import restrictions, production shortages, or the lack of foreign exchange, food is scarce and luxury goods are nonexistent. Schools are frequently inadequate. The result in some situations is the breakup of the family, with the spouse and children staying in the United States.

Many of the cities in Eastern Europe are drab and isolated geographically from centers of Western culture. It is difficult to make informal contacts with the citizenry because of restrictions imposed by the strict authoritarian governments and the atmosphere of oppression, suspicion, and fear. Somewhat similar conditions are found at many posts in the Middle East, Latin America, and Asia. Conditions that may be novel, instructive, or only mildly irritating to the casual tourist can become overwhelming obstacles to those serving for several years at such posts.

Added to these environmental burdens is a relatively new fact of Foreign Service life—terrorist activity in the form of kidnapping, assassinations, and bombing of embassy buildings. Between 1970 and 1982, five U.S. ambassadors and five FSOs were killed by terrorists.

Fortunately, this rather forbidding picture has another aspect. Many FSOs willingly accept challenge and hardships. Interest in a country's culture, especially if it is primitive, can provide an antidote for the imaginative and curious FSO. In fact, morale at some small African posts is high.

Leadership, Morale, and Attitudinal Problems

Other considerations that are closer to home also have a strong influence on Foreign Service officers and State Department civil service employees. Because of the institutionalization of the executive turnover process, continuity in the administration of U.S. foreign policy often suffers, despite the officially apolitical nature of the State Department's operations, including the Foreign Service. The existence of a new team of executives at the policymaking level of the department (that may or may not include senior Foreign Service officers and new ambassadors at posts abroad) tends to destabilize the making of foreign policy. There is little, if anything, that can be done to remedy this situation. However, the harm done to U.S. foreign policy because of the inordinate politicizing of the policymaking process is considerable.

Any new foreign policy team led by a new secretary of state is generally anxious to select the assistant secretaries and deputy assistant secretaries of key geographic bureaus in order to put its imprint on the State Department and the career service. The new team also brings with it lingering suspicions about the loyalties of the "old career team" and is not reluctant to purge career officers thought to be too closely associated with the policies of the previous administration. Several years are usually required for the process to shake down so that there is again business as usual.

These conditions tend to produce a stereotypical Foreign Service officer. Beginning with the induction process, new appointees are exposed to an acculturation process during the period of orientation and their first few years in the service. At some point during this initial period, the officer either adopts the subcultural norms and values and reflects them in his own behavior, or he rejects them, thus jeopardizing his career. Dissent can result in a poor corridor reputation, average efficiency reports, a slow rate of promotion, and mediocre assignments. A key element in policy dissent is the matter of style—knowing how, when, and to whom to express one's opinion. Awareness of the risk of dissenting improperly tends to produce an officer who is cautious and conformist. As long as the service puts a premium on these characteristics and dispenses rewards to officers who have them, it is unlikely that the typical FSO will step out of this mold. In this respect he shares some of the behavioral traits of his Japanese counterparts.

There is evidence that younger FSOs are disgruntled with the old stereotype, impatient with the conservative style of their elders, and less reticent about expressing dissent. But there is also a high probability that, as their commitment to the Foreign Service and its values deepens with longevity of service, they will adopt many of the career traits they found objectionable in their earlier years.

An FSO will always be rank oriented; his thoughts center on obtaining a promotion. The traditional success pattern—that of the political officer with a language and area specialization and a "home" in an important geographic bureau—will probably continue to prevail. Elitism also increases as FSOs develop a sense of commitment to the Foreign Service. Junior officers are less concerned with it than their senior colleagues.

Some FSOs express annoyance with the traditional image of an elitist corps. Even though the subcultural norms associated with the traditional image have changed, the stigma lingers on. However, despite this annoyance, FSOs as a professional group are considered by a number of Washington observers to represent an elite because of their education and superior intelligence (indicated by passing a difficult entrance examination). This and other differences in perception between junior and senior officers are some of the problems facing the Foreign Service in its efforts to change with the times.

The senior Foreign Service officers of the 1980s have known the Depression, World War II, the rebuilding of Western Europe, the Korean War, McCarthyism, the cold war, Wristonization (integration of State Department civil service personnel and Foreign Service staff into the career Foreign Service), and the polarization of attitudes in an increasingly militarized, technologically advanced, international environment. Upon entering the Foreign Service, these men were essentially conservative, disciplined, and elite oriented in the traditional sense. Consequently, they accepted the established values and norms without seriously challenging them.

The junior Foreign Service officers, on the other hand, may or may not remember World War II, but in general, their intellectual development and philosophical orientation had their roots in the time of President John Kennedy and matured with the problems of Vietnam, ecology, civil rights, and the drug counterculture. This particular outlook seeks change at a rate that may appear threatening to an established order such as the traditional Foreign Service. Until they have developed a real sense of commitment, junior FSOs have no personal stake in the system that they wish to protect other than immediate job security. (An officer's sense of commitment must be developed by the time he reaches the level of FS-2; otherwise he is trapped due to age, increasing economic responsibilities, and skills that are not easily marketable.)

Morale in the Foreign Service can be analyzed from two perspectives. One is the extent to which an officer can participate in the resolution of a problem. He may try to resolve, informally, any problem concerning assignments, training, promotion, or involuntary retirement, or any personal grievance; or he may initiate a formal grievance after attempting to resolve the matter informally. The knowledge that he has some recourse makes him less deferential to management, more prone to dissent, and less conformist in his approach to his responsibilities.

The second perspective concerns the relationship between the senior managers and policymakers on the seventh floor and the Foreign Service. For some time, members of the service have sensed a lack of direction from the top. From time to time, secretaries of state have been profuse in their praise of the Foreign Service, but these accolades have not lessened the suspicion held by many FSOs that the officials on the seventh floor are unconcerned about them.[1]

Although, as I have noted, the apex of the department is politically oriented and reflects presidential policies (as it should, since it is part of the executive branch), effective leadership is still, in part, a function of individual personality and style. Preoccupation with crises and the politics of foreign policy issues sometimes makes it difficult for secretaries of state to appear concerned with and appreciative of the work of the Foreign Service. FSOs have come to expect this, but they do not like it.

These are some of the considerations that affect the conditions of the Foreign Service and the behavior and attitudes of its officers. They are complex, subtle, and elusive; they tend to ebb and flow with the tides of time yet to have a historical continuity. Even though each new generation of FSOs has its own particular characteristics, mores, and values, its ways of thinking tend to mesh with the historically established role of the FSO in the foreign policy process so that the public's perception of the FSO remains essentially unchanged. However, more women and minority members are entering the service, more tandem assignments are being made, and the service in other ways continues to become "democratized." Therefore, it is very possible that the sometimes negative image of the FSO in the public mind will be replaced by a more positive view.

Will the Foreign Service Act of 1980 really mark the beginning of a new era for the Foreign Service by correcting the problems that have threatened efficient management for so long? Already there is evidence that major changes are occurring, some as a result of the act. For example, unionism is in and arbitrary management is out; litigation and grievances are in and the noncomplaining, nonlitigious FSO is out; management accountability is in and freewheeling by management is out.

A new era has begun for the FSO, but not without advance notice. Executive orders have been passed establishing new union-management guidelines and warnings have been issued that the senior officer surplus, the sometimes flagrant use of the Foreign Service reserve officer system to obtain career status for favorite reserve officers (in which officers who receive temporary appointments for a specific period of time are later converted to permanent status), and the promotion system were all potential problems.

Returning to the State Department in the early 1980s after a number of years' absence, I was struck, on the one hand, by the new mood that pervades the corridors, and on the other by the timelessness of things—the assignment process still has many of the characteristics of an "old boy network," the promotion system is still characterized by intense competition, and the Selection Board retains a reputation for being more equitable than any other personnel evaluative body or process in the federal bureaucracy. There is some irony in the fact that earlier efforts to reform and modernize the system had the same goals, but it was the Foreign Service Act of 1980, shaped and supported by a small band of enlightened personnel managers in the State Department and by a group of senators and congressmen who were genuinely concerned about the effectiveness of the management structure, that has provided the basis for the changes that have been made in the Foreign Service.

The prospects for change in the way the service is managed in such important areas as recruitment, training, assignment, and promotion will depend, to a considerable extent, on how successful management and AFSA are in drawing up the administrative regulations to implement the act. The State Department's annual report to Congress on progress in implementing the act revealed some of the divergent views held by management and AFSA. Management tended to have an optimistic and long-range view, explaining what actions had been taken and what remained to be done. AFSA, on the other hand, expressed disappointment regarding the pace of implementation. It accused management of being too slow in presenting draft regulations for the union's consideration and of further trying to cut costs by attempting to negotiate restrictive regulations covering incentives. In 1982, the union judged the negotiations to date as being characterized in many cases by "a sort of lowest common denominator blandness that offends no one, changes little, and is principally cosmetic in nature."[2] Clearly, more earnest attempts need to be made by both sides.

A senior manager in the Foreign Service described the general problems facing it and the State Department rather cogently when he said that the role of the department in the foreign policy process is determined less by administrative manifestos and regulations than by the strength, decisiveness, and political clout of the major personalities, as well as their working styles and the nature of the issues. He opined that FSOs complain too much and spend too much time worrying about the wrong issues (prerogatives, deference, efficiency reports, promotions, and elite status); they are more concerned with their own careers than with furthering U.S. foreign policy interests—an image that has been reinforced by their increasing tendency to resort to litigation. The way to obtain and exercise influence in Washington, he said, is by being useful to the top managers of government and to important politicians in Congress.

According to this official, the State Department is the only place in government where one can get a comprehensive view concerning an important foreign policy issue. Other bureaucracies in Washington tend to focus on one segment of the problem, and their expertise is limited to that segment. Therefore, the most important skill of the FSO in the future will be to be able to use the expertise of others and to distill what he needs from it to solve a foreign policy problem. This is the core skill in the service that is in the shortest supply and is consequently needed the most.

He noted that many aspects of a service career are changing. Wives of some FSOs are opting not to go abroad with their husbands, and those who do, want to work. This may result in a further increase in tandem assignments. It is also possible that in the future, more officers will, for family reasons, opt to leave the service and begin a second career in their late thirties or early forties. He concluded that this development could result in more lateral entry at midlevel grades, hitherto regarded as an anathema by most FSOs.

These are difficult times for the FSO, and perhaps the most arduous task confronting him is how he perceives himself. He must acknowledge and adapt to the reality that his role in the foreign policy process is shrinking; other parts of the Washington policymaking community are challenging him for primacy in the process. Management deplores, but can do little about, what it sees as a serious lapse in service discipline. The FSO of the 1980s is more aggressive, more frustrated, more concerned with bread-and-butter issues than with service ethics, more uncertain about the direction his career will take, and above all, deeply worried that the Foreign Service is losing its professionalism and evolving into merely an occupational group. As a result of these concerns, morale and comradeship, which hold the Foreign Service together, have declined.

There has always been a good deal of frustration associated with a career in the Foreign Service. Highly educated and talented men and women have their own conceptions about what the pace of their career development should be, are often intellectually independent, and feel the need for rewards commensurate with their self-perceived abilities. They perpetually sift and evaluate relative talents and abilities, while continuing to experience the joys and disappointments of the competitive race. This is all part of a career in the Foreign Service, and there are few signs that these characteristics are changing.

If the FSO is to play an important and effective role in foreign policy, he will have to master a new set of core skills, which includes an ability to integrate the diverse segments of a foreign policy issue and to distill the expertise of others in attempting to solve foreign policy problems. He must learn to live and work in a Washington bureaucratic environment that is so fragmented and compartmentalized that it is frequently difficult to determine what the U.S. position is regarding certain foreign policy issues. He must strive to maintain the primacy of the State Department in foreign affairs, a primacy that is being seriously challenged by the National Security Council and the Pentagon. These challenges are having an impact on his role as an FSO. One Japanese diplomat told me, "I really wonder at times who is in charge in Washington. Whom I should talk to about a problem in United States–Japan relations? Who has the clout to respond to my request?"[3]

The first part of this chapter has been a summary of the more important issues and conditions that the Foreign Service will confront in the years ahead. I am not certain that the managers are fully prepared to make the adjustments in policies regarding assignment, promotion, and training that will be required to meet the new challenges. Whether it will be business as usual or whether the process will be revitalized to give the FSO the tools necessary to meet new foreign policy challenges will depend on several factors: the willingness of the president to give more responsibility to and rely more heavily on the Foreign Service; the determination of the secretary of state to demonstrate departmental leadership by marshaling existing service talents, developing new talents, and using these talents skillfully in a charged political environment; and most significantly, the recognition by the FSO that his ability to play the role he wishes to play as an influential member of the foreign policy team will depend in the last analysis on his own willingness to disregard some of the traditional paths to the top and rather focus on new career directions that will demonstrate his possession of or willingness to master the skills necessary to participate in the formulation and execution of U.S. foreign policy. The ability of the State Department and the Foreign Service to carry out their responsibilities in these crucial areas in the future will determine their destiny.

Specific Problem Areas

The Generalist Versus the Specialist

Like his Japanese counterpart, the U.S. Foreign Service officer feels strongly that to be a real diplomat, one must be a generalist and that this is the fastest and surest path to the top. Like his Japanese counterpart, he is becoming aware of the growing importance of specialization, but he is still unconvinced that this could ever be the best route for him.

There has long been a controversy about whether the Foreign Service should be generalist oriented or dominated by specialists. The need for greater technical expertise in such areas as economics, finance, science, transportation, and communications has given the controversy an anachronistic ring and has persuaded management to take a new look at the problem.

What should be done? First of all, recognition must be given to the fact that the responsibilities of positions in Washington and overseas call for somewhat different skills and interests. Foreign Service officers are overseas oriented, and when they do return to Washington for assignment it is usually for a relatively short period. They must deal with a foreign affairs bureaucracy whose members are permanently assigned to their agencies and have, over the years, mastered the complexities of doing business in the nation's capital. As a result, the Department of State is sometimes at a disadvantage in its relations with other governmental agencies and departments.[4]

Another attitude in need of change if progress is to be made toward resolution of the generalist-specialist problem is the belief of many FSOs that the ideal FSO should possess management and negotiating skills, including persuasiveness, and not be overly concerned about gaining technical expertise. (This suggests that the generalist mentality is reinforced by an increasing concern with program direction at a time when the need to manage large-scale programs overseas is diminishing.) As long as the FSO corps believes that these skills are the key to success, the service is not likely to be able to recruit or train individuals who have the expertise or the combative style needed to survive in the Washington arena.

No change in recruitment policies to reflect a greater need for experts in the service seems likely. Entry into the service at the bottom of the career ladder is considered the only acceptable way of becoming an FSO. Foreign Service officers have long resisted lateral entry of "outsiders" at the middle or senior levels, regardless of their skills, because lateral entry means a reduction in promotion opportunities for career officers. Regardless of departmental needs, FSOs want no personnel actions taken that might adversely impact on the existing service structure or the mores of the FSO culture.

That generalists are still preferred is reflected again by the recruitment process. Broad formal education with concentration in the social sciences and humanities is still the best preparation for passing the written examination. Yet in midlevel jobs, specialized knowledge is becoming increasingly necessary. Without employees who possess it, the Department of State is finding it more difficult to fulfill its role as an integrator of policy. Unfortunately, the incentive for FSOs to acquire specialized knowledge is lacking, mainly because the policy regarding promotion to senior ranks emphasizes evaluation of an officer as a generalist.[5]

The generalist-specialist problem comes down to the question of the appropriate role for the Foreign Service and the Department of State, especially at a time when the major foreign policy issues increasingly concern such areas as arms control, nuclear proliferation, environmental degradation, energy conservation, narcotics, and refugees, all of which require substantive and technical knowledge outside the framework of the traditional disciplinary backgrounds and conal specializations of FSOs.

Are the State Department and the Foreign Service attempting to develop the skills necessary to meet these new challenges? Yes, but slowly and with a palpable lack of enthusiasm. Until FSOs are able to convince themselves that they can be promoted as fast on the specialist track as on the generalist track and that they can become ambassadors, assistant secretaries, and special assistants with offices on the seventh floor as easily by being a specialist as a generalist, there will be resistance to policies that stress the need for specialists.

The FSOs who occupy senior State Department positions and who fill important ambassadorships are the product of the generalist school, and this is not lost on younger FSOs. These young officers see a system that rewards the generalist and places a career ceiling on the specialist. They are aware that, throughout the processes of recruitment, evaluation, promotion, and assignment, greater attention is paid to the career aspirations of generalists than to those of specialists, and that although the importance of such issues as arms control, nuclear energy, and refugees is recognized, FSOs are given few substantive incentives to specialize in these fields. The Foreign Service Act of 1980 does provide that both specialist and generalist officers may become members of the Senior Foreign Service. But unless management concentrates on matching people's skills with their responsibilities, and on allowing specialists and generalists to compete on an equal basis (a very difficult process), there is little likelihood that efforts to restructure the system under the 1980 act will be any more successful than previous efforts have been. Management continues to emphasize the need for those qualities that senior officers require to be ambassadors and deputy chiefs of mission, rather than stressing the qualifications and training required to fill technical and specialized positions, both in Washington and overseas.

Education and Training

Factual and linguistic knowledge are fundamental tools of the diplomat's trade. What we readily assume with respect to the law or medicine or business or the military—that its practitioners must be knowledgeable to be effective—we thus far seem to have failed to establish with respect to foreign policy. Before 1981, the Foreign Service Institute paid little attention to training officers in the art of negotiation. Until the Foreign Service Act of 1980, too little effort was given to providing language training for diplomats assigned abroad, aside from those officers destined for language-designated positions. President Carter established a National Commission on Foreign Language and International Studies but was apparently too busy to receive the commission's report when it was completed, and neither the Reagan administration nor the Congress has taken any action on the commission's recommendations.

It is difficult to move the managers of our public school system, with its roots in the nineteenth century, to analyze the problems of the twenty-first century. As the international interests and obligations of the United States grow at a rate that is almost geometric, the percentage of U.S. colleges and universities requiring even minimal foreign language competence has declined from 85 percent in 1951 to 34 percent in 1966 to 8 percent in 1980. To illustrate the problem another way, in 1980 there were several thousand English-speaking Japanese businessmen in New York City alone, but there were fewer than 100 Japanese-speaking U.S. businessmen in Tokyo. During the decade ending in 1977, a period when 2 million additional U.S. jobs became dependent upon U.S. exports, enrollment in college-level language courses declined by 21 percent. Fewer than one in twenty college students takes even one course dealing with foreign peoples or cultures. A scant 5 percent of all the teachers in the United States have had any exposure to international studies. Yet one of every six manufacturing jobs in the United States produces for export, and nearly $1.00 of every $3.00 of U.S. corporate profits derives from international activity, such as exports and foreign investments.[6]

The United States is not preparing its diplomats to function in an international environment that demands a much greater knowledge and understanding of at least the major foreign cultures; rather Americans are inclined to think in terms of inaccurate, misleading stereotypes and to live more by their wits, now that the United States is no longer wealthy enough to throw dollars at its foreign problems. The educational system is producing a sense of insularity and parochialism that makes difficult the conduct of an informed foreign policy.

What is needed is a national sense of the importance of education in the preparation of young men and women for careers in the Foreign Service. Candidates must be recruited with care; their training should include foreign languages, area study, and the core skills (management and negotiation) so necessary for today's diplomat. It is encouraging to note that the Foreign Service Institute has already begun this effort.

Consular and Administrative Cones— A Challenge for Management

It has always been difficult to keep consular and administrative positions appropriately filled, especially at the senior levels. One does not have to look far for the reason: the State Department has not developed satisfactory career ladders (that is, sufficient career incentives and rewards) for consular and administrative personnel.

These officers cannot aspire to ambassadorships or to most senior executive positions because they have not had the substantive training necessary to take on such responsibilities. When an outstanding consular or administrative officer is proposed for an ambassadorship, for example, the assistant secretary concerned usually vetoes the proposal on the grounds that the candidate is not qualified. Only one senior consular officer who was on active service in 1981 became an ambassador, and this appointment was made only after long and arduous negotiations between the Bureau of Personnel and the Inter-American Affairs Bureau. Senior administrative officers become discouraged and leave the service, and this creates serious shortages in administrative (and, to a lesser degree, consular) ranks.

Administrative and consular officers are often considered the step-children of the Foreign Service. They do not have the prestige or status of their economic and political officer colleagues, they do not get the best posts, their rate of promotion is generally slower, and their work focuses on the less challenging aspects of foreign policy; yet a post cannot survive without them. The consular officer is the Foreign Service's liaison with the public, and the administrative officer provides the critical support for the basic mission of the post. Why, then, is there a problem?

In 1981, an ad hoc committee was established in the Bureau of Personnel to find out. It is not the first committee to be so organized, and it probably will not be the last. When I served in that bureau, I talked with many consular and administrative officers and frequently listened for hours to their complaints. They wanted greater recognition for their contributions to the Foreign Service, equal consideration in the promotion process, more training, and out-of-cone assignments that would prepare them for the positions of program direction officers in the State Department and chiefs of mission overseas. It will continue to be difficult for the committee to act favorably on these legitimate requests and to prepare acceptable recommendations as long as the myth persists that only political officers are qualified to be ambassadors and program and/or executive direction officers. Discrimination against the consular and administrative officer exists in the U.S. Foreign Service, similar to that prevailing against the senmon-shokū officer in the Japanese foreign ministry. For an organization that prides itself on being egalitarian, especially in its distribution of career rewards, such a practice seems inconsistent.

One senior personnel officer said that the staffing problem exists because there is a shortage of officers in the consular and administrative cones. If this is, indeed, the core of the problem (which I doubt), steps should be taken to make the two cones more attractive to young FSOs—to increase the rewards for conal service. The problem will not be solved until this is done; meanwhile, the Bureau of Personnel will continue to be harassed by shortages of these officers. If clear evidence need be shown that the problem exists, it can be found in the open assignment process. Consular and administrative positions often go begging while FSOs stand in line for the choice political and economic positions. The FSOs cannot be blamed—they seek challenging assignments that offer opportunity for promotion. They are convinced that if they accept administrative and consular positions, their colleagues in the political and economic cones will pass them by in the competitive race. This reality must be addressed openly by the ad hoc committee if the State Department and the Foreign Service are to be staffed by energetic and well-qualified consular and administrative officers.

Labor-Management Relations

With the passage of the Foreign Service Act of 1980, which codified many of the regulations concerning labor-management relations, a new era began with regard to these relations. The prognosis is for stormy as well as tranquil periods, for mutual trust and respect have not yet been established. However, both parties are negotiating on an almost continual basis and settling issues that have import for officers and their careers. As a result of the act, AFSA can negotiate with management a myriad of issues pertaining to such matters as working conditions, promotion, selection out, and assignments. Several union officials with whom I spoke seemed suspicious of the intentions of management and felt that they had to be alert to protect the interests of their members—the Foreign Service officers. "We have to keep management honest," said one young union official (who is also an FSO). "We have to force management to be good managers. It is especially important that management make the right decisions regarding competitive groups for promotion purposes—whether there will be functional competition, classwide competition, specialist against generalist competition, or specialist against specialist. It is important for AFSA to have an input to these decisions, and AFSA is demanding and getting that input."

Although he was hopeful about reform of the service, this FSO thought that there was little the union could do to lessen the politicking for the good assignments so long as the structure of the system remained unchanged.

A senior management official said he thought that AFSA, on balance, was exerting a positive influence on the personnel system but was also complicating the role of management by constantly harrassing management over policy details and by making some immature proposals. He cited as an example of the latter the union's proposal that the promotion system be two-tracked, with 20 percent of the promotions reserved for outstanding officers and 80 percent to be based on longevity. The proposal proved unworkable because a system that allowed fast promotions for some and slower promotions for others was not an equitable system. When it finally realized this, AFSA withdrew the proposal. The official felt that with growing maturity, AFSA would make increasingly sound contributions to good management. Clearly, it is a time of testing for both sides.

Grievances

Allied to the general problem of labor-management relations is the grievance process, a mechanism for administering justice, for providing relief from the pressures of the system, for institutionalizing the principle of due process in adjudication of disputes, and for giving the FSO a "square deal." The grievance process is being used increasingly because of the litigious atmosphere that exists in the State Department.

The grievance process as an instrument for correcting injustices in the personnel system had its beginning in 1976, when an amendment to the 1946 Foreign Service Act established a procedure to deal with complaints against a perceived unjust act by management. It originated under tragic circumstances—the suicide of a former FSO that some believe was prompted by unfair treatment by personnel managers. Whether they contributed to it or not, the suicide was the catalyst of a chain of events that culminated in the institutionalization of the principle of due process.

Presentation of a grievance against management is now an accepted practice and has caused management, and especially officers preparing efficiency reports on subordinates, to evaluate employee performance more carefully. Some consider it a form of intimidation—a device to keep management in line. I doubt it is having an intimidating effect, but it does provide recourse for FSOs who, for example, believe themselves to have been judged wrongly by their supervisors in an efficiency report or who think management should not have refused to approve a travel voucher.

In 1981, 93 grievances were brought before the Grievance Staff in the Bureau of Personnel. Almost two-thirds were complaints about efficiency reports. The chief of the Grievance Staff told me that individuals feel more free to bring grievances than they did in the 1970s because of the freer climate existing in the United States. As a result, he said, lawsuits have inundated the courts and his staff is overworked. Decisions of the Grievance Staff can be contested by AFSA. The union usually takes a strong position in support of the grievant, and its inordinate concern often takes the form of meddlesome actions that hinder the work of the staff. The staff negotiates almost continuously with AFSA with regard to procedures and practices. A set of principles and policies acceptable to both AFSA and the Grievance Staff is gradually emerging and should lead to smoother working relations between them and more prompt action on grievances.

An officer instituting a grievance is required to furnish the names of individuals who know him and may be able to shed some light on the nature of the grievance. The Grievance Staff then investigates the complaint, evaluates the evidence, and makes recommendations. According to the staff director, officers on the grievance staff have developed a capability to analyze and evaluate grievances, especially those concerning efficiency reports, fairly rapidly.

If an FSO is dissatisfied with the decision of the Grievance Staff, he can appeal to the Grievance Board. He has a further appeal right to the courts, but actions are rarely taken that far.

The staff director said he thought the increasing propensity of FSOs to present grievances was related to their feeling of superiority, especially to civil servants, and their dislike of criticism. The FSO rationalizes that because he is a pre-eminent figure in the federal bureaucracy, his performance is always above criticism, so there is no reason for him to be low-ranked by a Selection Board (even though he knows that the Selection Board is compelled to low-rank certain FSOs if their performance justifies it). Such action adversely affects his performance.

Time in class also disturbs FSOs—again because they feel that, as members of an elite of public servants, they should not be subject to it. Low-ranking by Selection Boards and decisions regarding TIC are often considered by the FSOs concerned as being based on unfair efficiency reports. For this reason they register grievances against the personnel system.

In the 1970s, many grievances would have been ignored, and FSOs would have suffered career damage without having recourse to remedial measures. Management, without pressure to be fair in making personnel decisions, would have continued to make unfair judgments at the expense of the Foreign Service. It is in this light that we must judge the merits and demerits of the grievance procedure: its contribution to a better understanding of the Foreign Service, the license it gives mediocre FSOs to complain about their careers and to use the procedure to compensate for substandard performance, the pressure it exerts on management to ensure that it is impartial, and the demand it makes on both employees and management to be alert to injustice and to be faithful to truth.

On balance, the grievance procedure is serving the best interests of the Foreign Service and the State Department. It is a nuisance to some, an inconvenience to others, a source of agitation to certain individuals (especially those who would prefer the old freewheeling days), a means of obtaining remedial action for FSOs with real complaints, and a testimony to the importance of due process as an inherent right of all Americans, in and out of government, to seek redress of grievances. It has become a fixture in the personnel system, codified by the Foreign Service Act of 1980 and accepted by management, the union, and the career Foreign Service as the best way to deal with complaints.

8

THE IMAGE PROBLEM

IN ADDITION TO ALL THE COMPLEXITIES OF DIPLOMATIC MANAGEMENT IN Japan and the United States, discussed in earlier chapters, both diplomatic establishments must contend with an image problem. In both countries the public feels a sense of remoteness from these agencies, and legislators are often unimpressed by their urgent requests for financial support and other assistance. (Legislators do not have to depend on the foreign ministry or the State Department for votes.) Moreover, other executive agencies, especially those with foreign economic, political, and security interests, are often in competition with the Ministry of Foreign Affairs and the Department of State for pre-eminence in the foreign affairs field.

The Ministry of Foreign Affairs

In Japan many citizens regard the foreign ministry as a rather secretive organization whose members are reserved and out of touch with the main currents of Japanese society. Others think of the ministry as the foreign arm of the Japanese government and, again, feel little or no relationship to it. Despite these rather negative opinions, I sensed that even those Japanese who are most critical respect the Japanese diplomat; they award him high marks for diligence, intelligence, and loyalty and accord him a high station in the social hierarchy.

The ministry has been criticized for not doing more to gain advocates for its cause. A senior official opined that manpower and budget problems would be eased considerably if more leaders in the business community, for example, could be persuaded to give greater support. "We have to work much harder," he said, "to win their backing for our programs and policies."

Many Japanese diplomats do not appear to be overly concerned about the public's perception of the foreign ministry. One former vice-minister, explaining this attitude, said that the FSO believes the public will respect him for his expertise and knowledge of complicated international issues. Even if there are complaints, he has the consolation of knowing that, in the end, his judgment will be proven correct.

Another former vice-minister disagreed, saying that complacency regarding public attitudes is a luxury the ministry cannot afford. His words indicate his concern about what he described as the ministry's "introverted nature": the diplomat's circle of professional and social acquaintances is too narrow; he has little knowledge of what people are thinking; and his idea of what they think of the ministry is distorted. Top ministry officials should leave Kasumigaseki (the district in Tokyo where the foreign ministry is located) from time to time and get to know business, academic, and professional leaders. The ministry, he said, has never been notably successful in selling itself—perhaps its diplomats are too smug. But the fact is that as the makers of Japan's foreign policy are confronted by greater challenges, there will be greater need for public support. The visibility of the ministry must be increased and respect for the career service must be enhanced.

One solution, according to this former vice-minister, would be to lengthen the tour of duty of the vice-minister. This would provide him an opportunity to meet business, academic, and professional leaders and to give leadership to programs within the ministry to foster better public relations. Promotion of senior officers might be slowed somewhat as a result of extending the tour of the vice-minister, but the career service must realize the importance of better relations with the public, he said.

Several senior officials in the Minister's Secretariat admitted that the ministry's public relations needed improvement, but they cautioned that with the paucity of career officers to handle the day-to-day work, sidelining the few truly outstanding officers for temporary public relations assignments could impair operations. The problem is complicated because the officers who are best suited to work on the image problem are the very ones most in demand for key assignments in the major geographic bureaus.

A different point of view, expressed by a former senior official, was that diplomacy should not be the subject of publicity, nor should officers be asked to promote a better public image. Diplomacy is a very private business. It must frequently be conducted in secret to safeguard national security interests and to inspire confidence in other countries that the information they provide will not be revealed. For these reasons, he stressed, ministry officials must be careful about what they say and do in public. When there is conflict between these public statements and actions and an image-building program, the latter must be sacrificed.

Another facet of the image problem is the perception of the foreign ministry by other ministries in the Japanese government. A Japanese professor who has studied the Japanese bureaucracy for many years told me that other ministries, especially MITI and the Ministry of Finance, are not always certain that the foreign ministry is protecting Japanese interests as forcefully as it should. He said that the foreign ministry has the reputation in a number of ministries of being too solicitous of the feelings of foreign diplomats during negotiations, of not wanting to seem impolite by disagreeing with them at conferences. For these reasons, MITI and the Ministry of Finance, especially, wish to have a stronger voice in foreign affairs to "better protect Japanese interests." This professor thought that the scope of foreign ministry activities would narrow as foreign relations became more complex and as other ministries became more insistent on playing a larger role in the foreign policy process.

I talked to several officials in MITI about these observations, and although they were not as critical of the foreign ministry, they did agree that it was not aggressive enough in protecting Japanese interests and confirmed their belief that MITI would have to become more involved in the making of Japanese foreign policy.

A newspaperman who is well informed about the foreign ministry observed that the issue was not whether that ministry is aggressive enough in protecting Japanese interests, but rather other ministries' perception of it. He felt that the ministry was carrying out its responsibilities satisfactorily and suggested that criticisms might be a ploy by other ministries to gain a greater voice in the foreign policy process. If so, such actions are unprincipled, he said, but they are symptomatic of the infighting that characterizes the Japanese bureaucracy.

A senior foreign ministry official on detail to another government agency said the ministry sends its best officers to class A posts so that these countries will be impressed and have a favorable image of Japan. The ministry is concerned about its reputation with important foreign governments but is rather indifferent concerning the image of it held by other ministries in the Japanese government. He added, rather sadly, that Japanese culture is a culture of shame—that Japan feels ashamed if it sends mediocre diplomats to Great Britain, France, China, the United States, or the Soviet Union.

A Japanese ambassador can also influence the attitudes of Japanese citizens toward both the foreign ministry and the Foreign Service. A former senior official of the ministry, presently an upper-house Diet member, told me that when a delegation of dietmen visits a particular country and requests briefings and other services from the resident Japanese ambassador, they are sometimes treated indifferently. When these dietmen return to Tokyo, they naturally express their indignation that such diplomats can be assigned as ambassadors. This same Diet member claimed that career diplomats assigned to Tokyo damage their own image by failing to mix more freely with journalists, scientists, businessmen, and scholars and said that this was primarily a matter of good public relations. He thought that special groups and forums should be organized so that the career diplomat could exchange views with these people. He was aware that some special groups do exist but said that there are not enough of them. This official expressed sympathy for overworked careerists but insisted that personnel resources should be so managed that officers can be given time occasionally to meet outside contacts.

The image of the foreign ministry and the Foreign Service is also shaped by the media, especially television and the press. (Certain offices in the foreign ministry are allocated to the press to facilitate ministry coverage; media representatives have similar offices in the State Department.) A newspaperman's sole responsibility may be to cover the ministry; some have been doing it for a long time and are experts on ministry operations and policy. These men have an important influence on the ministry's image.

Ministry officials were perhaps more interested in what I had learned about the ministry's image than in my observations about the personnel system. I believe a sensitivity to image exists, though some officers profess indifference. There also appears to be a determination by senior officers to improve that image, no matter how difficult the task.

There is a reservoir of public respect for the Japanese diplomat, but there is also a good deal of frustration and misunderstanding about Japanese foreign policy and the role of the foreign ministry in implementing that policy. As one senior official put it, what the ministry needs is a good public relations firm to improve its image. But this will be hard to accomplish, given the nature of diplomacy. What is needed more than a public relations campaign, in my view, is a greater effort by the media and by Japanese leaders to enlighten the public about Japanese foreign policy objectives.

The ministry cannot claim much success so far. Perhaps it is because of the nature of diplomacy that this is so, but there are still steps that could be taken. Ambassadors could be more attentive to Diet delegations, senior officers could try harder to arrange meetings with business and professional leaders in order that all could exchange views on matters of mutual concern, the Information and Research Bureau could be more imaginative and innovative in attempting to persuade the media to give the ministry a "better press"—solid successes on the diplomatic front could be pointed to in creating the image of power and prestige that existed, for example, when Baron Shidehara Kijuro was foreign minister (1924–1927, 1929–1931).

The Japanese Foreign Service Officer

The typical Japanese FSO projects an image of self-assurance, tactfulness, and self-confidence born of the knowledge that he is highly educated and trained to think and work as a guardian of Japanese foreign policy interests. Yet he tends to be isolated from the mainstream of Japanese life, serving as he does for considerable periods in overseas posts. Even while in Tokyo, his duties press in on him to such a degree that he has little time left for his family. His social life is restricted to associations with his colleagues in the diplomatic corps; he seldom has any contact with people on the outside except on official business.

Even critics concede that the Japanese Foreign Service officer is a hardworking, loyal, and dedicated public servant who is intelligent and well educated and trained for his diplomatic duties. But having made this concession, they paint a picture of an officer who is smug and self-centered, a man who wears the diplomatic mantle with arrogance and who feels superior to his fellow Japanese and disdain for service personnel of inferior rank. These rather harsh comments were delivered without malice; they were simply intended as statements of fact by a number of retired Foreign Service officers, newspapermen, and university professors.

Career officers on active duty with whom I talked could hardly conceal (nor did they seem to try to) their pride in themselves and the service, their elitism, or their superior attitude toward noncareer personnel.

There are considerable variations in attitudes toward the Foreign Service officer. One former ambassador to the United States described the FSO as lacking in spirit—too soft, and too privileged. He should work harder, be less concerned with assignments, and be more concerned with serving Japan. He must pay more attention to developing those qualities that make for a superior ambassador or director general.

Another former ambassador and former director general of a major bureau was equally sharp in his comments. "Today's diplomat has little or no imagination," he said. "He is too conservative, too conformist. Such qualities are the badge of the diplomat and the nature of diplomacy requires him to wear such a badge. But it is also time for more innovation and imagination in Japanese foreign policy. The career diplomat must lead the way."

A university professor who is well informed about the Japanese bureaucracy opined that the average career officer knows little about Japan's economic and social problems, and he apparently has no desire to study these problems. Career officers infrequently exchange assignments with other ministry personnel. This practice is a serious drawback to attempts to learn more about what is happening politically, culturally, economically, and socially in Japan.

A newspaperman who had long covered the foreign ministry had a somewhat different emphasis. He said that because a career officer considers himself an elitist, he feels uncomfortable when assigned to a less developed country (LDC). Because he is a rationalist in his thinking, he has little patience for what he perceives as the deficiencies in LDCs. He therefore tries to avoid such assignments whenever possible but will go if assigned. When posted to a Japanese Embassy in an LDC, he is not always an attractive representative of Japan in the eyes of the local population. This is dangerous for Japanese foreign policy, the newspaperman said. Japan must have good relations with LDCs, and this will require that career diplomats change their attitude and treat the people in LDCs with greater respect and consideration.

Friction is often created by the tendency on the part of some careerists abroad to show lack of respect and consideration for noncareer personnel, the newsman said. The leadership of the ambassador is important in avoiding such friction.

Discord among officers at a post sometimes involves their wives. A former ambassador told me that such situations are very unpleasant; the wives of career officers tend to share their husbands' attitudes toward noncareer personnel, to the detriment of personal relations among staff employees. He, too, believed that if the ambassador takes the initiative, much of the trouble can be avoided.

An example of the discrimination that frequently exists against the wives of noncareer officers was described to me by the president of an important research organization in Tokyo. This man had been assigned as a noncareer officer to the Japanese Embassy in a major country in 1960. He said that his wife had experienced many discourtesies from the wives of career officers, and as a result their assignment at the embassy was far from happy—they have never forgotten it. The experience has colored his image of the Foreign Service. Such discrimination, he asserted, is out of place in a Japanese Embassy and should be the object of stern measures by the ambassador.

One former career officer, recently resigned, claimed that the career officer lacks the will and capability to devote himself unselfishly to serving the national interest. It is a frame of mind that has been slowly developing since the end of World War II because peace, he thought, contributes to a lack of patriotism. He noted that the Japanese people have always tended not to trust their political leaders but have respected and had confidence in their bureaucrats. Now that political leaders are taking a more dominant role in the making of foreign policy, bureaucrats are perceived as only implementers of foreign policy, and this has caused morale problems. Officers will not talk about the morale issue in the presence of a group, he claimed, but individually they express their dissatisfaction with the long hours, the inadequate salary, and the decreased prestige of the foreign ministry. As a result, he said, only about one career officer in ten is truly devoted to serving the national interest. The other 90 percent are more concerned with getting ahead. The one principle that binds all Foreign Service officers together is their reputation for being dedicated to serving the national interest. When the sincerity of their dedication is challenged, they react bitterly, though they know in their hearts the challengers may be right.

I personally found little evidence to corroborate the views of this former career officer. In any bureaucracy there are dissatisfied officials, but in the Japanese Foreign Service, especially, the officers give few clues to their inner feelings. However, during my more than seven years as a U.S. Embassy officer dealing with foreign ministry personnel on a daily basis, I had no doubts about their loyalty, dedication, or patriotism.

Other critics of the career Foreign Service included disgruntled ex-noncareerists, journalists and scholars frustrated by the apparent lack of action and imagination shown by the foreign ministry, and businessmen and ministry bureaucrats who questioned the determination of the ministry to serve and protect Japan's political and economic interests. The more open criticism of the career service becomes, the greater the likelihood that the service will develop a "siege mentality." However, this does not yet appear to be happening.

The U.S. Diplomatic Establishment

The Department of State and the U.S. Foreign Service suffer from many of the same image difficulties that plague the Japanese foreign ministry and its career service. The State Department has no real public constituency. There are no powerful and/or vocal groups that will lobby for an increase in the department's budget or for more personnel. The Department of Agriculture has the farmers, the Treasury Department has the bankers, and the Commerce Department has the businessmen—groups that can influence the public and Congress to support the policies and programs of these departments. That the State Department lacks such support is a painful truth for those departmental officials responsible for the budget and for personnel. When an organization has no constituency, it usually has little power to influence events unless such power is derived from a forceful president who has strong public backing.

Most Americans probably know as little about the Foreign Service as about any group of public officials in the federal government. (Some, to the amusement of FSOs, have even confused the Foreign Service with the Forest Service.) For many years the work of the State Department had little direct effect on the personal lives of most Americans, and for this reason Americans were generally indifferent to what the State Department was doing. The long ordeal of the hostages in Iran, frightening as that experience was, probably did more to bring the Foreign Service to the public's attention than any other event.

The Foreign Service has been stereotyped for many years as an organization of effete diplomats in pinstripes who had little in common with the hard-working American. This perception has hurt service morale but apparently has had little effect on young Americans who, year after year, line up to take the Foreign Service Entrance Examination. The highly visible tribulations of FSOs serving abroad seem to have provided a counterweight to this image, at least for the time being.

The media exert a powerful influence on the public's perception of the State Department and the Foreign Service. Unfortunately, television and the press focus more on the foibles of the secretary of state and his senior assistants, rumors about the relative power position of the secretary and other Cabinet officers, and the significance of a particular appointment or firing on the secretary's relationship to the president than on the work and dedication of the State Department and the Foreign Service and their contribution to U.S. security.

Several decades ago when Congressman John Rooney was chairman of the House Subcommittee on State Appropriations, the State Department's officers constantly struggled with the Congressman to obtain reasonable increases in the department's representational allowance.[1] Rooney referred to this allowance as the "whiskey allowance" and emphasized his opposition to representational funds by characterizing FSOs as "cookie pushers." Rooney's image of Foreign Service personnel is indicative of the perception many Americans have of the U.S. Foreign Service.

However, some progress is being made by the State Department to improve its image. Greater efforts are being made to recruit officers from all segments of the population, especially minorities, thus making it easier to establish links with a number of citizen groups. Officers are also being assigned to state and local governments, to small and large corporations, and to universities and colleges as diplomats-in-residence. Another program that holds some promise is one in which well-known scientists and scholars are invited to work in the department for a certain period, contributing their knowledge to the foreign policy process and obtaining in return a better understanding of that process, the department, and the Foreign Service. Generally, these private citizens leave with good impressions of the department and its work.

Other individuals work at the State Department on a temporary basis, and they, too, come away with impressions about the Foreign Service that seem generally favorable, at least in the sense that they recognize that FSOs work hard and are dedicated to promoting U.S. interests. Nevertheless, the erroneous notion persists that every FSO has a splendid house and a fat entertainment allowance and is preoccupied with cocktail parties. The department is beginning to awaken to the fact that this image must be dispelled if it is to obtain public support for its work and for that of the Foreign Service. Efforts are being made in this direction, but more needs to be done.

CONCLUSION

I T IS CLEAR THAT THE CAREER FOREIGN SERVICE OFFICERS WHO REPRESENT Japan and the United States are professionals whose lives are dedicated to keeping the peace through diplomacy. This task requires a high degree of intelligence, common sense, tolerance, patience, understanding, and a deep sense of duty. It is not just a job but a way of life. Because of the nature of their responsibilities and because they must spend a good part of their careers working in foreign lands, their intricate role as practitioners of diplomacy is often misunderstood by the public they serve.

The fundamental premise of this study has been that an analysis of the distinctive roles of the members of the two diplomatic establishments in carrying out their respective responsibilities will contribute to better understanding between the two countries. It has been noted that differences in the value systems of the two societies have produced FSOs with contrasting behavioral patterns and attitudes toward diplomatic careers. Variations have been found in the organization of the two diplomatic services, in the operation of their personnel systems, and in the manner in which decisions are made. The diplomatic establishments of both Japan and the United States must face many problems, not the least of which is the lack of a favorable image.

An analysis of the role of the two bureaucracies in the societies they serve reveals one of the clearest distinctions between the two career services. In Japan the bureaucracy has been a powerful agency for building that nation into a world power. The bureaucracy is strong, independent, disciplined, career oriented, relatively free from undue political influence, and respected by the Japanese people. It has been able, through the years, to recruit the top graduates from the major universities.

The Japanese Foreign Service is bound by such age-old traditions as seniority, hierarchy, harmony in personal relations, class identification, and a strong feeling of elitism. To be a bureaucrat in the Ministry of Foreign Affairs means prestige, power, and job security.

By way of contrast, in the United States the federal bureaucracy has never had the cohesion or power that characterize the Japanese bureaucracy. Presidential prerogative has nurtured the spoils system, and as a result the State Department and the Foreign Service have found it difficult to remain free from undue political pressures from Congress and the executive branch.

Herein lies the fundamental difference between the two organizations: the foreign ministry is dominated by career officers; in the Department of State career officers must share authority with political appointees.

The U.S. Foreign Service has stressed egalitarianism and a dedication to competition and merit ("up or out"), but it has tolerated the pursuit of personal ambition to the point where rivalry has sometimes become graceless and lacking in good sense. Japanese FSOs are ambitious too, but their desire to achieve is tempered by rules of social conduct that discourage the overt display of ambition. Japanese diplomats are far more bound by the rules of protocol than are their U.S. counterparts.

The examination required for entry into the Japanese Foreign Service establishes from the beginning an unbridgeable gap between the career and noncareer corps that is the root cause of many personnel difficulties in the Japanese foreign ministry. The Department of State has one examination for career officers that covers a wide range of career options and one examination for civil servants (those employees not subject to overseas duty). There is no career division similar to that prevailing in the foreign ministry.

There is no grievance system in the Japanese Foreign Service and no union to represent career officers; both would be alien to the Japanese way of doing things. Grievance procedures and unionism in the U.S. Foreign Service are codified by law; the former are utilized without compunction by those FSOs who believe themselves to be unjustly treated.

Because of the relatively small size of the career corps, performance evaluation in the foreign ministry is informal. Position classification is nonexistent. The State Department, on the other hand, has an elaborate performance evaluation system and a position classification program to facilitate the assignment and promotion process.

The guarantee of lifetime employment gives a Japanese FSO a sense of security that his U.S. counterpart does not always share. The Japanese diplomat retires at an age not mandated by law but dictated by custom, whereas the U.S. Foreign Service officer must retire by law at age 65 if he was not separated earlier for unsatisfactory performance or allowed to continue in active service under conditions cited in Chapter 2.

Structurally both systems rely on geographic bureaus for policy direction and functional bureaus for policy support. The division (Japan) and the country directorate (United States) are responsible for initiating policy recommendations.

Within this broad organizational framework, the Japanese FSO performs his daily tasks—tasks that reflect the limited role Japan has chosen to play in international affairs. His U.S. counterpart works within a system geared to the United States' role as a superpower. His responsibilities are perhaps heavier and he has a greater choice of career opportunities.

In the vital area of decision-making, important differences exist regarding style and approach. For the Japanese, ringisei (the procedure of achieving consensus) is at the center of the decision-making process. Inordinate time is spent within a bureaucratic unit obtaining and sifting ideas and opinions, discussing alternatives, and reviewing the details of the subject under deliberation. Tradition is the arbiter of procedure, and each player in the process strives to conform to the rules. Ringisei allows each member of the unit to have his say and to contribute to the ultimate decision. Having participated in the process, each member is expected to support the final decision. Implementation then proceeds quickly and smoothly.

For the U.S. Foreign Service officer, the decision-making process usually means asserting a view and arguing forcefully in the hope of persuading superiors to accept it. There is respect for the individual's right to have his say, even though that right might not always be honored in the pragmatic world of decision-making; his position and the nature of the personal relationship existing between him and his supervisor often determine whether he will participate in the process.

The two diplomatic establishments face different challenges in the management of diplomacy. For Japan, the post–World War II period has been one of inordinate reliance on the United States with little concern shown for events outside Northeast Asia unless such events had implications for Japan's relations with the United States. The insular mentality of the Japanese has been largely responsible for such regionalism.

The global responsibilities of the United States have thrust the State Department and the Foreign Service into the center of worldwide concerns. This has impacted on U.S.-Japan relations. The United States expresses impatience and irritation with Japanese reluctance to do more to support common objectives; Japan reacts to such exasperation with puzzlement and dismay and wonders what role the Americans expect Japan to play in foreign affairs.

The world is pressing in on Japan, and that nation may soon be forced to shed its insularity, to face the economic and political realities of membership in a world society, and to become a full and participating partner in the quest for peace and a better life for all. Whether Japan will respond in a fashion befitting a world economic power will depend in the last analysis on the attitudes (and especially the resolve) of the Japanese people. The foreign ministry can help to develop these attitudes by skillfully conducting diplomacy abroad and by taking responsible actions at home to educate the Japanese public about Japan's emerging role in international affairs and the role of the FSO in diplomatic management.

The world of the United States is also changing. The Foreign Service officer is being forced to adjust to the new reality that U.S. power and influence are declining, in relative terms. He must learn to deal more effectively with other bureaucrats in Washington, as well as to master some of the new forces that are having an effect on international society (nuclear energy, new technologies) and to integrate this knowledge into the foreign policy process.

Like his Japanese counterpart, the U.S. Foreign Service officer will have to rethink his role and to discard some of the old career shibboleths. As the U.S. representative in the chancelleries of foreign countries, he will be the first to grasp the truism, however discreetly put, that the United States is being viewed in a new, less favorable light by some nations. He will feel frustrated in his work as he senses the public's reluctance to accept the decline in U.S. prestige. It will be a test of his patience, understanding, and powers of persuasion.

In this changing world, the FSOs of both countries have a new range of opportunities for the successful fulfillment of their respective mandates. Each must realize that the other is dedicated to serving the interests of his own country. Former Undersecretary of State Joseph Cotton reminded the members of the Foreign Service class of 1928 that they were the lawyers, their client was the U.S. public, and their sole duty was to protect and promote their client's interests.

I believe that the establishment of mutual respect by the diplomats of these two nations, including an appreciation of the limitations under which the other side must operate, may be a first and fundamental step toward adjustment of their diplomatic differences.

APPENDIXES

JAPANESE AND U.S. INTERVIEWEES,
AUGUST 1980–JANUARY 1982

Japanese Interviewee	*Title*
Asakai Koichiro	Former ambassador to the United States
Donowaki Mitsuro	Deputy director general, European and Oceanic Affairs Bureau, foreign ministry
Eto Yukihisa	Secretary general Foreign Service Training Institute
Fujii Hiroaki	Chief, Personnel Division, Minister's Secretariat
Hashimoto Jo	Assistant deputy vice-minister for administration, foreign ministry
Heima Izumi	Foreign Service Training Institute trainee
Hogen Shinsaku	Former vice-minister, foreign ministry
Hosoya Chihiro	Professor, Hitosubashi University
Hyoda Nagao	Chief, Russian Division, foreign ministry
Ikuta Toyoaki	President, Institute of Energy Economics
Ishikawa Tadao	President Keio, University
Ito Kenichi	Former Foreign Service officer
Kaji Misako	Foreign Service Training Institute trainee
Kamiya Fuji	Professor, Keio University
Kawamura Kinji	Managing director, Foreign Press Center
Kawamura Yasuhisa	Foreign Service Training Institute trainee

Kitamura Hiroshi	Consul general, San Francisco
Kotani Shunjiro	Administrative officer, Kanda Institute of Foreign Languages
Kubota Etsuo	Reporter, *Asahi Shimbun*
Kunihiro Michihiko	Chief, General Affairs Division, Minister's Secretariat
Kuriyama Takakazu	Deputy director general, Treaties Bureau
Kurokawa Tsuyoshi	Chief, First West European Division, foreign ministry
Maeda Toshikazu	Ambassador to South Korea
Matsuda Yoshifumi	Chief, Financial Affairs Division, Minister's Secretariat
Matsumura Takashi	First secretary, Japanese Embassy, Cairo
Matsuyama Yukio	Reporter, *Asahi Shimbun*
Mikanagi Kiyohisa	President, Foreign Service Training Institute
Miyajima Akio	Foreign Service Training Institute trainee
Muto Masatoshi	Member, Personnel Division, Minister's Secretariat
Muto Toshi	Director general, European and Oceanic Affairs Bureau, foreign ministry
Nagamura Toshio	Senior managing director, Bank of Tokyo
Nagano Nobutoshi	Editor, *Tokyo Shimbun*
Nakagawa Toru	Former ambassador to Italy
Nibe Kayoko	Foreign Service Training Institute trainee
Nikaido Yukihiro	Foreign Service Training Institute trainee
Ogata Sadako	Professor, Sophia University
Ohishi Shintaro	Ministry of International Trade and Industry
Okada Seiji	Foreign Service Training Institute trainee
Okazaki Hisahiko	Foreign Service officer assigned to the Defense Agency
Oki Hiroshi	Upper house Diet member; former Foreign Service officer
Oku Katsuhido	Foreign Service Training Institute trainee
Onda Takashi	Chief, Financial Affairs Division, Overseas Operations, Minister's Secretariat
Oshima Kenzo	Deputy chief, Personnel Division, Minister's Secretariat

Saito Shizuo	President, Foreign Press Center; former deputy vice-minister for administration, foreign ministry
Sakaguchi Satoru	Foreign Service Training Institute trainee
Samejima Keiji	Reporter, *Nihon Keizai Shimbun*
Sato Kuni	Foreign Service Training Institute trainee
Shimoda Takeso	Former vice-minister, foreign ministry
Shirayama Akiko	Foreign Service Training Institute trainee
Sobashima Hidenobu	Foreign Service Training Institute trainee
Takahashi Michitoshi	Former ambassador to Yugoslavia
Takaoka Masato	Foreign Service Training Institute trainee
Takenaka Shigeo	Director, Office of Administrative Improvement, foreign ministry
Takeyama Yasuo	Senior editor, *Nihon Keizai Shimbun*
Tamba Minoru	Chief, Security Division, North American Affairs Bureau, foreign ministry
Tanaka Kazunari	Foreign Service Training Institute trainee
Tomita Koji	Foreign Service Training Institute trainee
Toya Fumiaki	Foreign Service Training Institute trainee
Tsujimoto Yoshinori	North American Affairs Bureau, foreign ministry
Tsuruoka Koji	Southwest Asian Division, foreign ministry
Tsushima Teiji	Foreign Service Training Institute trainee
Tsutsumi Tomio	Ministry of International Trade and Industry
Uchida Fujio	Former ambassador to West Germany
Uchida Yoshio	Executive director, Japan External Trade Organization, San Francisco
Uchiyama Masakumi	Professor, Keio University
Ukita Hidetoshi	Foreign Service Training Institute trainee
Umezu Itaru	Deputy chief, First North American Affairs Division, foreign ministry
Ushiba Nobuhiko	Former ambassador to the United States
Watanabe Akio	Professor, University of Tokyo
Watanabe Koji	Deputy director general, Asian Affairs Bureau, foreign ministry
Watanabe Yasuo	Professor, International Christian University
Yamanaka Shinichi	Foreign Service Training Institute trainee

| Yanagiya Kensuke | Deputy vice-minister for administration, foreign ministry |

U.S. Interviewee	*Title*
Bacchus, William	Chief, Office of Program Coordination, Bureau of Personnel
Clark, Joan	Director general of the Foreign Service
Collins, John	Director of employee relations, Bureau of Personnel
Drexler, Robert	Director, Office of Recruitment, Examination and Employment
Gaither, Rowan	Director, Grievance Staff, Bureau of Personnel
Haynes, Alfred	Administrative Division, Department of State
Johnson, U. Alexis	Former undersecretary of state for political affairs
Junior, Don	Officer, Office of Career Development, Department of State
Lauderdale, Clint	Deputy assistant secretary of state for management
McBride, Joseph	Official of American Foreign Service Association, Department of State
Melton, Jack	Officer, Office of Position and Pay Management, Department of State
Ready, Francis X.	Deputy inspector general of the Foreign Service
Rouse, John	Director, Office of Performance Evaluation, Bureau of Personnel
Sampas, Dorothy	Officer, Office of Position and Pay Management, Department of State
Shoesmith, Tom	Deputy assistant secretary of state for East Asian and Pacific Affairs
Sprott, John	Deputy director, Foreign Service Institute
Steigman, Andrew	Deputy assistant secretary of state for personnel
Tienken, Arthur	Director, Office of Foreign Service Career Development, Department of State
Wieckoski, Gertrude	Chief, Retirement Division, Bureau of Personnel

THE FOREIGN SERVICE ACT OF 1980

Since the Foreign Service Acts of 1924 and 1946, the personnel system of the State Department has passed through a number of phases, the most prominent being a transition from a single system covering both Foreign Service and civil service personnel to a dual system for Foreign Service personnel and civil service employees, as specified in the Foreign Service Act of 1980. From 1946 to early 1950, the dual system prevailed. In 1955, the Wriston Committee recommendations underscored the need for a single system, and Secretary of State Dulles approved it. Almost from the day the single system was instituted in 1955, its opponents (generally those who wanted the benefits of the Foreign Service retirement system but did not want to work overseas) began to campaign for its elimination and for a return to the dual system. In addition, several important senators felt that the Foreign Service reserve (temporary) appointment procedure under the single (unitary) system was being abused by management to place noncareer senior officers in the career service—that is, to let them in "through the back door." There were also expressions of concern that the Foreign Service retirement system was being misused by Foreign Service reserve appointees, who were, in effect, domestic employees of the State Department. Finally, a growing problem of senior officer surplus was created by a change in the mandatory retirement age from 60 to 65 in the late 1970s; by a pay raise for Foreign Service officers in 1977, which persuaded a number of senior officers to stay in the service rather than retire; and by a concomitant policy of extending TIC for senior officers to 22 years, which made the TIC program literally unworkable. Many of the surplus senior officers had to go without assignments for months and a number of senior administrative positions went unfilled because few, if any, of the surplus officers had administrative skills or experience. The system was getting out of balance, and pressures increased for remedial action.

With the passage of the Civil Service Reform Act of 1978, pressure for a new Foreign Service act increased. The key issues debated prior to passage of the Foreign Service Act of 1980 were (1) whether there should be a single personnel system (Foreign Service) or a dual system (domestic and Foreign Service) and the related issue of rank-in-person versus rank-in-job (rank-in-person refers to a Foreign Service officer who carries his rank with him regardless of his assignment; rank-in-job refers to a civil service officer whose rank is determined by the position to which he is assigned); (2) the perennial problem of the generalist versus the specialist in assignment, training, promotion, and career development; (3) whether access to the Foreign Service should be open or closed (the former was strongly advocated by AFSA); and (4) salary level determined by level of position (also vigorously advocated by AFSA).

The Foreign Service Act, signed by President Carter on October 17, 1980, simplifies and consolidates legislation concerning the administration of the Foreign Service. It stresses career and merit principles as well as efficiency and economy. The functions of the Foreign Service are defined more fully than in the act of 1946, and authority and responsibility are fixed more clearly.

Specifically, the act of 1980 mandates the establishment of a Senior Foreign Service, comparable to the General and Flag Officer ranks of the armed forces and the Senior Executive Service of the civil service. It establishes a more rigorous process for selection into the senior ranks but preserves the existing independent Selection Board mechanism for promotion within (based on performance standards) and selection out. The career principle receives new and greater emphasis as a result of the requirements that noncareer appointments be limited to top levels in the service (a group that includes persons detailed from other agencies) and that all persons appointed to career status pass through a tenuring process, no matter what their grade. The act reduces the number of Foreign Service personnel categories and establishes a single pay schedule for all of them. A clear distinction is made between personnel obligated to serve abroad and those who serve only at home. Allowances and benefits, which are limited to those who serve abroad, are increased and improved. There are substantial increases in compensation, especially for those in the middle grades, and mandatory retirement age is changed from 60 to 65. Labor relations are placed on a statutory basis. The act improves interagency coordination in the interest of achieving maximum compatibility among agencies employing Foreign Service personnel and between the Foreign Service and the civil service. A number of organizational modifications are made; new units are created, existing ones are abolished, and the functions of continuing bodies are realigned. Some examples are described in the following paragraphs.

The act restores the statutory basis of the Board of the Foreign Service, which formerly was constituted under an executive order. The board has lost much of its authority under the 1980 act. Its functions in the area of separation appeals and labor-management impasse disputes have been transferred to other organizations; the former to the Foreign Service Grievance Board and the latter to the new Impasse Disputes Panel.

The act reconstitutes the Board of Examiners for the Foreign Service to develop and supervise the administration of the Foreign Service Examination for candidates wishing appointments as Foreign Service officers. The board consists of fifteen members, ten of whom represent five federal agencies using the Foreign Service personnel system and having responsibility for employment testing, and five of whom are public individuals who have knowledge, experience, or training in the fields of testing and/or equal employment opportunity.

The primary function of the Foreign Service Grievance Board continues to be adjudication of grievances, but several new responsibilities have been added by the act, including serving as a hearing forum in separation cases and acting as an appeal mechanism for resolution of labor-management disputes. Board membership has been increased from fifteen to seventeen.

The Foreign Service Labor Relations Board was established by the Foreign Service Act of 1980 as part of the Federal Labor Relations Authority. It performs some of the labor functions previously assigned to the Board of the Foreign Service.

The Foreign Service Impasse Disputes Panel was authorized by the 1980 act as a body to which labor and management can appeal when they are unable to settle an issue by collective bargaining. The chairman of the panel is also chairman of the Foreign Service Labor Relations Board.

Congressional hearings on the act shed important light on the State Department's personnel difficulties. Officials testifying at the hearings of the Subcommittee on International Operations of the House Foreign Affairs Committee and the Subcommittee on Civil Service of the House Post Office and Civil Service Committee on June 21, 1979, emphasized that the single or unitary personnel system was inefficient and inequitable and had been the subject of criticism by the Civil Service Commission in 1975 because of the lack of career opportunities for civil service employees. A senior officer admitted that the Foreign Service Act of 1946 could not serve as the instrument to manage the domestic service and that the unitary system had several disadvantages. For example, the rank-in-position concept in the civil service differed substantially from the rank-in-person policy of the Foreign Service. The net effect was that position classification in the civil service was more rigid and more tightly controlled than in the Foreign Service. If someone in the Foreign Service was not performing well on the job, that person could be transferred to another position either abroad or in the State Department. In the civil service elaborate, protective rules made it very difficult to move an employee from one position to another. Documentary proof of poor performance over an extended period was often required. It was also more difficult to employ a specialist in the civil service than in the Foreign Service. In the civil service, the job of an incumbent could be reclassified by his office to a higher grade and he could be promoted to the new position without competing with anyone, whereas in the Foreign Service, all officers were considered for promotion once a year on the basis of a written performance record.

It became increasingly cumbersome, the senior officer said, to administer the unitary personnel system with two such different methods of position classification, assignment, and promotion, so the 1980 act provided for a dual system. It also included a conversion plan that permitted Foreign Service domestic employees who were willing to accept worldwide assignments to remain in the Foreign Service. Other Foreign Service domestic employees would have three years in which to accept conversion to the civil service or leave the State Department. A total of 471 Foreign Service domestic employees were affected by this conversion plan. In the process of conversion there would be no loss in salary, and there would be unlimited protection against downgrading of the position occupied, as long as the incumbent did not voluntarily move to another position. The individual had the right to remain in the Foreign Service retirement system or, alternatively, to move to the civil service retirement system.

The second area that received considerable attention in the hearings of the two House subcommittees was the problem of senior officer surplus in the Foreign Service or, as described by a senior State Department official, the linking of tenure, advancement, compensation, and incentive pay, as well as retention in the Foreign Service, more closely to high levels of performance. The 1980 act establishes a Senior Foreign Service through career and limited appointments, hitherto covered by the following categories of personnel: Foreign Service officer, Foreign Service information officer, Foreign Service reserve officer, and Foreign Service reserve officer unlimited, classes 1 and 2; Foreign Service officers and Foreign Service information officers of career minister rank; and certain career Senior

Executive Service (civil service) members of the Department of Agriculture. The reformed Senior Foreign Service has three ranks of personnel: counselor, minister counselor, and career minister. (Under the old system, these were FSO-2, FSO-1, and career minister, respectively.) The restructuring of the remaining ranks in the career Foreign Service resulted in the old FSO-3 rank becomeing FSO-1, (FS-1), undoubtedly a major psychological boost to FSOs at that rank who were being forced to retire, and most likely an important consideration in the establishment of a new grade scale.

In testimony before the two House subcommittees, another senior State Department official explained that the senior officer surplus had caused serious problems at all levels of the Foreign Service and revealed important structural flaws in the system. For years, because many persons in the most senior positions had been exempt from annual performance evaluation and selection out for substandard performance, voluntary retirement and mandatory retirement were the primary means of reducing the senior officer surplus. The rate of reduction largely determined the limits on promotion in the junior and middle ranks. The executive pay raise of 1977 resulted in a 50 percent drop in voluntary retirement, because many members of the service who were considering voluntary retirement decided to remain for an additional three years to obtain the fullest pension benefits. In the same year, a lower court decreed that mandatory retirement at age 60 was unconstitutional, and until that order was reversed by the Supreme Court two years later, practically all mandatory retirement stopped. Furthermore, a 1976 administrative order had extended time in class for officers in classes 2 and 1 to 22 years. And lastly, selection out for substandard performance practically ceased. All these factors compelled the State Department to set the lowest promotion rates since World War II and to reduce intake accordingly. This had a crippling effect on morale, and some excellent younger officers left the service in disgust.

Officers can become members of the Senior Foreign Service in three ways: (1) conversion from senior officer status (a transition period of 120 days), (2) promotion from class FS-1 of the Foreign Service schedule, or (3) career appointment following a period of trial service as career candidates in the Senior Foreign Service. The 1980 act requires that the Senior Foreign Service comprise not less than 95 percent career Foreign Service officers; the remaining 5 percent is to consist of senior officials of other government agencies (specialists). Time in class regulations have been tightened. Officers whose maximum TIC period expires after they reach the highest class of their respective personnel categories may continue to serve under renewable limited extensions, the total not to exceed six years. Such extensions are to be granted only on the basis of Selection Board recommendations and the needs of the service.

A rigorous Senior Foreign Service threshold procedure is instituted under the act. Members of the Foreign Service in the threshold class (FS-1) established by the act must request consideration for promotion into the Senior Foreign Service and then can remain eligible for a period of six years. If not promoted into the service by the sixth Selection Board, the officer will be involuntarily retired. For example, an officer promoted to FSO-3 in October 1979 with ten years of TIC remaining (to October 1989) who requested Selection Board consideration for the Senior Foreign Service in May 1981, and was not recommended for promotion by any of the six succeeding Selection Boards, would be involuntarily retired in 1986–87 rather than in 1989.

Career officers promoted into the Senior Foreign service or appointed to the service following a trial period would be subject to the following TIC limits: career minister, four years; minister counselor, five years; counselor, seven years.

Beginning in 1984, limited career extensions (in blocks of three years) will be considered for senior FSOs not promoted in their last board review and facing TIC. Members recommended by the board for limited career extensions are ranked in order of merit and are granted such extensions in the rank order recommended by the board, provided limited career extensions are allowed in their occupational category and on the basis of the needs of the service.

There is some concern about how the limited career extension principle will be applied in practice—that is, whether management will strictly enforce the TIC regulation with regard to senior-level officers. A senior official in personnel opined that most senior officers eligible for limited career extensions in 1984 will probably receive them.

Some apprehension was expressed during the 1979 congressional hearings that limited career extensions could become a mechanism for removing senior officers from the service if their performance had not pleased the secretary of state. In his letter to Virginia Mona Schlundt, staff assistant of the Subcommittee on International Operations of the House Foreign Affairs Committee, Martin Herz, a retired ambassador who testified before the two House subcommittees, said: "But neither he [Dante Fascell, chairman of the Subcommittee on International Operations of the House Committee on Foreign Affairs] nor anyone else can guarantee that the witch-hunting that took place under Secretary of State John Foster Dulles and his Deputy Undersecretary Scott McLeod might not be repeated in some other form under some future administration whose political imperatives we cannot now foretell" (*Hearings* of the two House subcommittees on the proposed Foreign Service Act of 1980, September 14, 1979, p. 795).

Labor-management relations were the third area focused on during the hearings on the 1980 act. Through codification of labor-management regulations, the act has brought the Foreign Service into the mainstream of federal sector labor-management relations. Some of the more important changes are as follows.

1. Foreign Service inspectors (as well as employees who handle confidential information and management officials) are removed from the bargaining unit. They may not assist a union or be represented in collective bargaining. However, they may join or remain members of a union and can be represented in grievance proceedings.

2. Management's rights and obligations in providing information to exclusive representatives, or directly to employees, are specified in the act.

3. A mutual obligation is placed on management and the union to respond to a proposed change in working conditions with a written counterproposal within fifteen calendar days after the proposal is submitted.

4. Any party may bring a grievance concerning an alleged violation of a collective bargaining agreement before the Foreign Service Greivance Board.

5. The "ten-day rule," according to which management could implement a "final position" if the union representative did not appeal to the Foreign Service Grievance Board, is abolished.

6. The undersecretary for management will continue to approve or disapprove collective bargaining agreements. If the undersecretary fails to disapprove an agreement, it takes effect 30 days after execution by the parties. If he disapproves an agreement on legal grounds, the parties must return to the bargaining table within 30 days. The same requirement applies if the union fails to ratify an agreement in accordance with its charter and bylaws (*Foreign Service Manual*, vol. 3, June 17, 1981).

Management continues to have the right, without reference to the union, to (1) determine the mission, budget, organization, and internal security practices of the State Department; (2) hire, assign, direct, lay off, and retain individuals in the service of the department; (3) suspend, remove, or take other disciplinary action against such individuals; (4) determine the number of individuals to be promoted; (5) assign work, make determinations with respect to contracting out, and determine the personnel who will conduct the department's work; (6) fill positions from any appropriate source; and (7) take whatever actions may be necessary to carry out the mission of the department in an emergency.

The union continues to have the right to negotiate with management over conditions of employment in the State Department and to engage in collective bargaining with respect to these working conditions. Every employee has the right to form, join, or assist any labor organization or to refrain from such activity freely without fear of penalty.

With the passage of the Foreign Service Act of 1980, a new era began for the State Department and the career Foreign Service. How well the system will operate depends to a considerable degree on the success of negotiations between management and ASFA aimed at developing necessary implementing regulations. Attitudes within management differ as to the role the union should play. One group believes that a strong, mature union will exert a positive influence on the system, whereas another group is concerned that the pendulum might already have swung too far in favor of the union. There seems to be a general feeling, however, that AFSA has to gain more maturity in union affairs, and that this will come in the course of the debate over regulations to implement various parts of the new act. As one management official pointed out, as AFSA gains more experience, it will help management sort out the important problems, much as shop stewards do for large labor unions.

The 1980 act underscores the State Department's commitment to mitigate the hardships and strains on Foreign Service families and to promote equitable treatment for all without regard to race, color, religion, national origin, sex, handicaps, or age. Finally, the act is designed to improve the economy and efficiency of government by promoting maximum compatibility and interchange among the agencies authorized to use Foreign Service personnel and to foster greater compatibility between the Foreign Service and the civil service.

Whether the act of 1980 will set the tone and direction of the Foreign Service and the State Department will depend on the determination of management, and especially senior State Department officials, to faithfully and fairly carry out the mandate for change, on the willingness of Foreign Service officers to accept stricter rules concerning performance and promotion, on the readiness of AFSA and management to develop a mature working relationship free of undue adversarial posturing, and on the disposition of the administration to show an understanding of and confidence in the role of the Foreign Service and the State Department in the foreign policy process.

The phases through which the State Department and the Foreign Service have passed have all been in response to profound alterations in the conditions of public service, and especially to domestic and foreign pressures for change in the U.S. foreign policy establishment. The act of 1980 is certainly a result of such pressures. Yet there is skepticism and some cynicism on the part of Foreign Service officers that the act is but another attempt by management to alter the system to suit its own requirements, and thus they are wary of change. Time in class regulations, after all, have been tightened and loosened, the rates of promotion have risen and fallen, the personnel system has been changed from a unitary system to a dual system and back again, and management has used certain provisions of other Foreign Service acts to reward and to punish.

An analysis of the act of 1980, however, reveals that close attention has been given such matters as equity, due process, management accountabilty, and compassion for members of the service and their families. This is a new departure and bodes well for the future evolution of the service.

Just as pressures for change in the U.S. Foreign Service have resulted in passage of the 1980 act, the forces of tradition in the Japanese Foreign Service have come under increasing stress because of requirements for modifications in foreign ministry personnel policies and practices. Both services are in transition, for new personnel policies and organizational patterns are beginning to take shape. It is a period of new challenges and opportunities for diplomacy in both nations.

EXCHANGE OF DOCUMENTS ON VISIT OF NUCLEAR-POWERED SUBMARINE SEA DRAGON

Unclassified

No. 1195/AAS

Note Verbale

The Ministry of Foreign Affairs presents its compliments to the Embassy of the United States of America and, with reference to the visits to Japan of U.S. nuclear-powered submarines (SSNs), has the honour to acknowledge the receipt of the Embassy's Note dated August 24, 1964, together with a statement by the United States Government, on the operation of SSNs in Japanese ports and waters.

The Ministry, taking note that SSN visits will be made in accordance with what is set forth in the above mentioned Statement, and considering that the visits are based on the Treaty of Mutual Cooperation and Security between Japan and the United States of America, has no objection to the visits.

Tokyo, August 28, 1964

Unclassified

No. 202

The Embassy of the United States of America presents its compliments to the Ministry of Foreign Affairs, and has the honor to send herewith with reference to previous discussions concering the proposed visits to Japan of U.S. nuclear-powered submarines (SSNs), the statement of the United States Government covering the operation of its nuclear-powered warships while in any foreign ports and waters.

The Embassy has further the honor to assure the Ministry that, on the occasion of their visits to Japanese ports and waters, SSNs will be operated in accordance with what is set forth in the attached statement.

Tokyo, August 24, 1964

Embassy of the United States of America

During the past months, there has been an exchange of information between representatives of the Embassy and representatives of the Gaimushō relating to the visits to Japan of U.S. nuclear-powered submarines (SSNs). With the exception of the difference in propulsion systems, nuclear-powered submarines are not different from other units of the United States Navy presently calling at Japanese ports, and accordingly enjoy the same right of entry under U.S.-Japan security arrangements. While the entry of these submarines, therefore, is not subject to prior consultation under the Treaty of Mutual Cooperation and Security, the United States Government, aware of the concern of the Japanese people, has chosen to discuss this matter with the GOJ [Government of Japan] before exercising this right. *With respect to matters that do involve prior consultation, the United States Government, as stated in the Joint U.S.-Japan communiqué of January 19, 1960, has no intention of acting in a manner contrary to the wishes of the Japanese Government.*

Within the statutory and security limitations on the disclosure of information concerning nuclear-powered warships, the United States has made every possible effort to be fully cooperative and has given answers as set forth below to questions on SSN safety, compensation, and related matters.

1. Safety and Operational Aspects

There have been more than 100 visits of nuclear-powered warships to foreign ports without incident of any kind, and all of these visits have been accepted by the host countries solely on the basis of U.S. assurances as to the safety of the ships involved. Extensive precautions are taken in SSN construction, maintenance, operation and crew selection and training to insure safety of these ships. SSN reactors are so constructed as to be unable to explode like an atomic bomb. Safety features built into these reactors assure shutdown in event of emergency. All SSN crew members receive highly specialized training and carry out their tasks strictly in accordance with operating procedures which have been developed with rigid adherence to high safety standards. The history of the safe operation of naval nuclear propulsion plants indicates that these precautions have been successful. The stringent safety standards applicable to SSNs make the reliability of their operation at least equivalent to that of land-based reactors.

Throughout the history of operation of U.S. nuclear-powered warships, there have been no accidents that have resulted in damage to reactor plants or any radioactive hazards to the environment.

The same safety criteria are applied with regard to visits of U.S. SSNs to foreign ports as are applied in the case of their visits to U.S. ports. In this regard, it is understood that the Government of Japan will provide any information which it believes pertinent to safety consideration around ports in Japan to be visited by SSNs.

SSNs are required, in accordance with the United States Navy's radiological procedures and criteria reviewed by both the United States Public Health Service and the Atomic Energy Commission, to limit their radioactive discharges to safe concentration levels and quantities. SSN effluent discharges are wholly consistent with the Japanese laws and standards, as well as international standards. As a result of extensive tests made by U.S. Public Health Service officials at ports where large numbers of SSNs habitually operate, it has been shown that the SSNs have no effect on the general background radioactivity of the environment, including marine life. No contamination has occurred in any port visited by SSNs.

Demineralizer waste is never discharged in ports or near land areas and is therefore not of concern in connection with port visits. Furthermore, it is not discharged anywhere near known fishing areas. Solid wastes are transferred by SSNs to U.S. shore or tender facilities for subsequent packaging and burial in the U.S. in accordance with approved procedures.

The report on radioactive waste disposal from U.S. nuclear-powered ships prepared by the Nuclear Propulsion Division of the Bureau of Ships in January, 1959, a copy of which has been made available to the Japanese Government, constitutes an official and authoritative source of information regarding SSN waste disposal and the U.S. Navy's instructions pertaining thereto. In keeping with the principles stated in this report, the Navy's instructions have been revised to reflect new, more conservative recommendations of the ICRP [International Council on Radiation Prevention] and of National Bureau of Standards Handbook No. 69, rather than Handbook No. 52 as stated in the 1959 report.

It is not contemplated that SSN fuel would be changed or that power plant repairs would be undertaken in Japan or its territorial waters.

No material exposed to radioactivity is normally removed from SSNs while in foreign ports. If, under unusual circumstances, material so exposed were to be removed, this would be done in such a manner as not to cause a hazard and in accordance with procedures used in U.S. ports.

It is intended that SSNs call at Yokosuka and Sasebo. If the Government of Japan wishes to make background checks at these ports, the United States authorities would be glad to cooperate.

Entry and departure are accomplished by nuclear power. The use of auxiliary power does not provide sufficient maneuvering power to insure operational safety. Reactors are normally shut down shortly after mooring, and they are normally started up a few hours before departure.

It may be noted that without prejudice to the right of U.S. warships to innocent passage, and in accordance with usual practice, SSNs would normally transit Japan's territorial waters only when proceeding directly to and from port, utilizing normal channels and navigational aids. Port entry and departure are normally accomplished in daylight, although unusual operational requirements might necessitate night time movement. It is not necessary to stop normal sea traffic when SSNs enter and depart a port. SSN movements have no more effect on port traffic than other submarines, and they have less effect than larger warships.

The purpose of SSN visits is to provide (a) rest and recreation for crews and (b) logistic support and maintenance.

2. Liability and Compensation Aspects

Compensation in the event of an accident will be dealt with in accordance with provisions of the Status of Forces Agreement. To the extent that Japanese Law No. 147 of June 17, 1961 would apply to ships of the Japanese Self Defense Forces, it would be equally applicable under the provisions of Article 18, paragraph 5(a) of the Status of Forces Agreement, to the handling of claims for nuclear incidents involving SSNs where personal injury or death is involved, including sickness or disease caused by radiation contamination. Similarly, the exchange of Notes of August 22, 1960 and the Joint Committee Agreement of September 5, 1961 concerning small maritime claims also apply to SSNs.

Where the Status of Forces Agreement is not applicable, the United States Public Vessels Act, the United States Admiralty Claims Settlement Authority and the United States Foreign Claims Act are available under United States legislation for settling claims arising out of a nuclear accident involving a United States nuclear warship. Under the Public Vessels Act and the Admiralty Claims Settlement Authority, a showing of legal liability in maritime law is required. In this regard it may be noted that under the Public Vessels Act, the U.S. is liable for acts of its warships to the same extent as private owners are liable for the acts of their vessels. The U.S. may be sued in person, and the U.S. Executive Branch may settle or compromise suits under the Public Vessels Act for activities of its warships without further dollar limitation.

The Admiralty Claims Settlement Authority authorizes the Secretary of Navy to approve and pay a claim in an amount up to $1 million. Claims in excess of $1 million are to be reported to Congress for case by case appropriations. Under the Foreign Claims Act, settlement may be made by the Foreign Claims Commission without proof of legal liability, but there must be proof that the damage was caused by the United States. Under this legislation, claims up to $15,000 may be paid by the secretaries of the military departments. Large claims may be referred to Congress for necessary appropriations.

In any event, when the Status of Forces Agreement is not applicable, the United States Government assures its readiness to deal with claims arising out of a nuclear incident involving a visiting SSN through diplomatic channels.

August 17, 1964

D

BUREAUS AND DEPARTMENTS OF THE JAPANESE FOREIGN MINISTRY

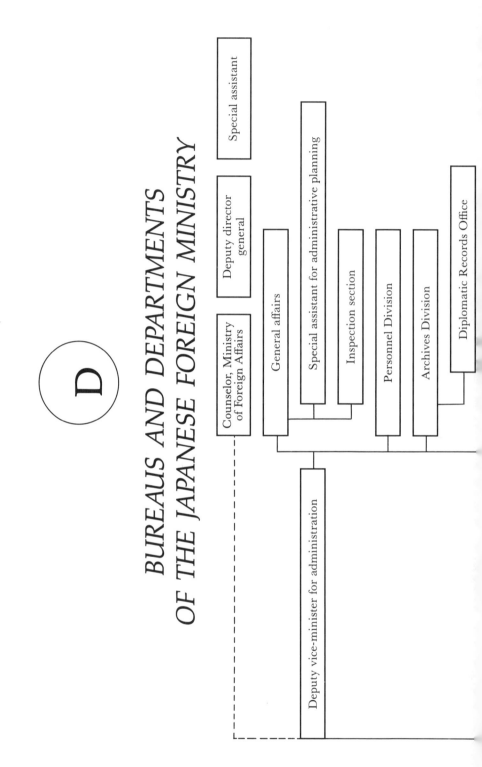

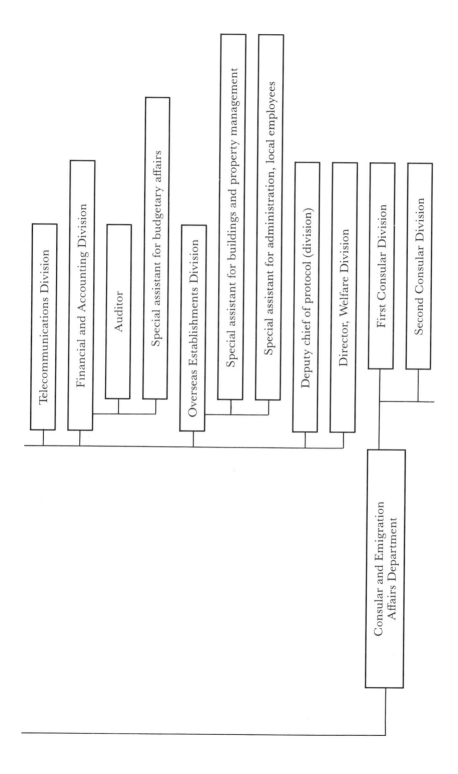

Telecommunications Division

Financial and Accounting Division

Auditor

Special assistant for budgetary affairs

Overseas Establishments Division

Special assistant for buildings and property management

Special assistant for administration, local employees

Deputy chief of protocol (division)

Director, Welfare Division

First Consular Division

Second Consular Division

Consular and Emigration Affairs Department

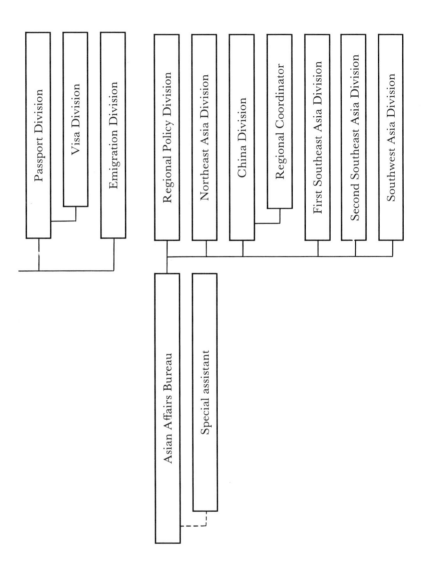

Asian Affairs Bureau

Special assistant

Passport Division

Visa Division

Emigration Division

Regional Policy Division

Northeast Asia Division

China Division

Regional Coordinator

First Southeast Asia Division

Second Southeast Asia Division

Southwest Asia Division

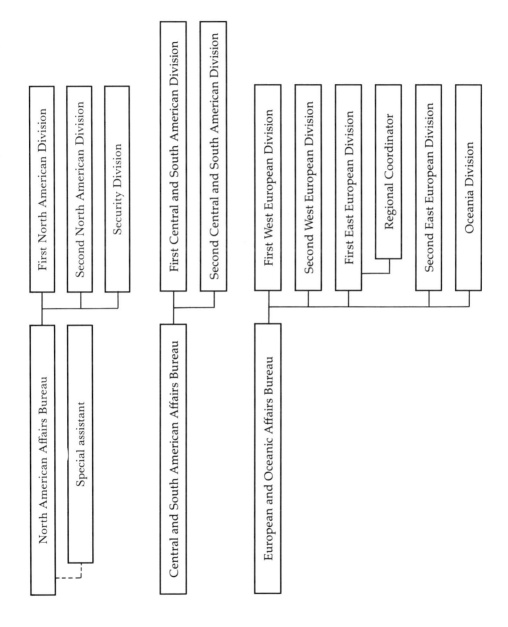

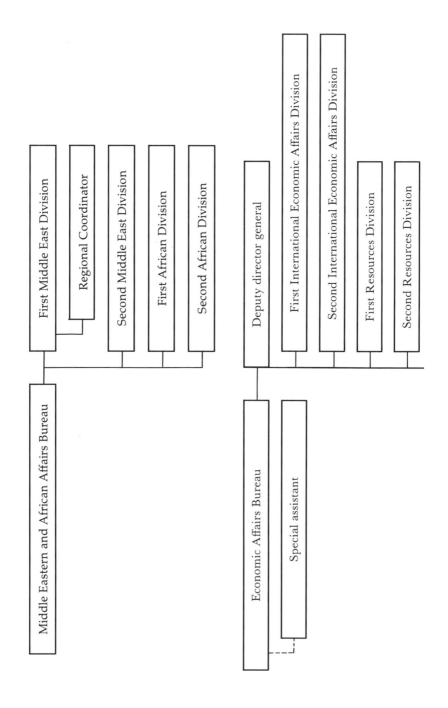

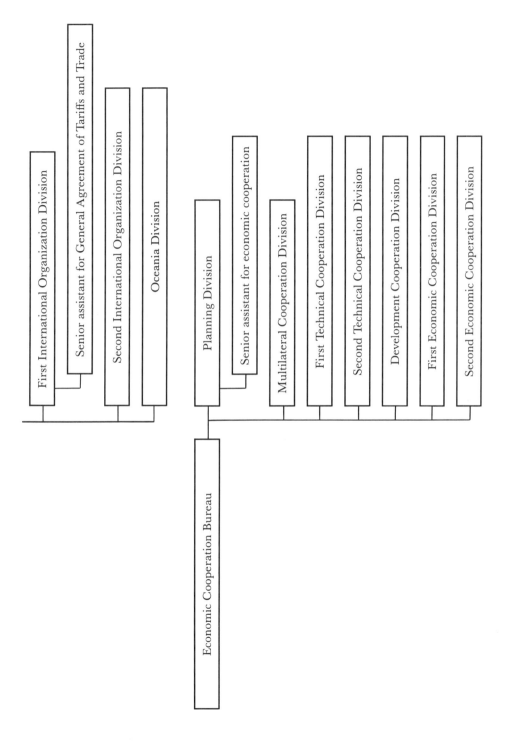

First International Organization Division

Senior assistant for General Agreement of Tariffs and Trade

Second International Organization Division

Oceania Division

Planning Division

Senior assistant for economic cooperation

Multilateral Cooperation Division

First Technical Cooperation Division

Second Technical Cooperation Division

Development Cooperation Division

First Economic Cooperation Division

Second Economic Cooperation Division

Economic Cooperation Bureau

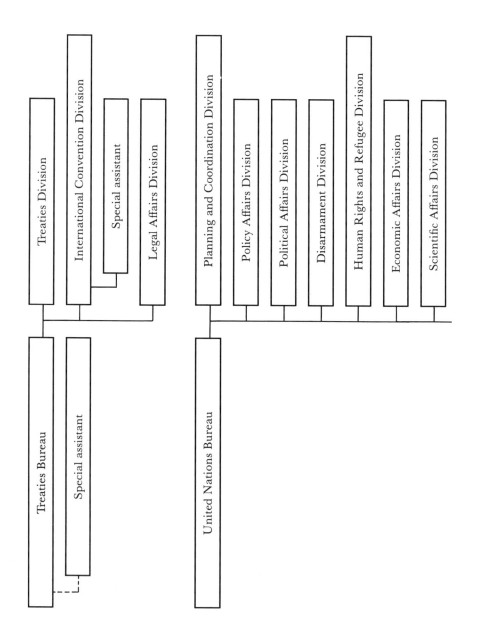

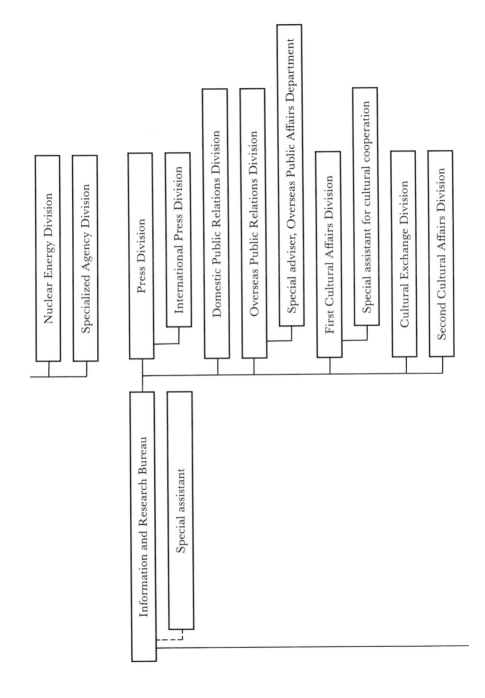

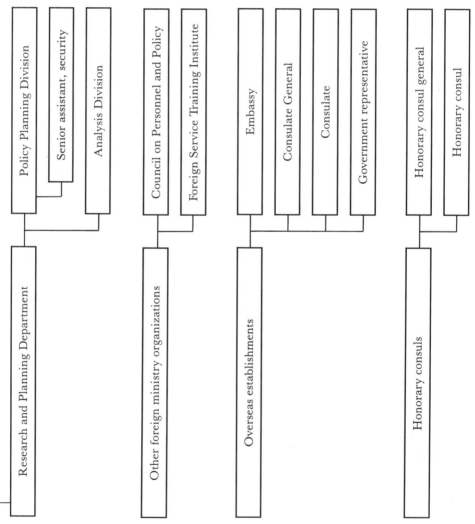

Research and Planning Department
Policy Planning Division
Senior assistant, security
Analysis Division

Other foreign ministry organizations
Council on Personnel and Policy
Foreign Service Training Institute

Overseas establishments
Embassy
Consulate General
Consulate
Government representative

Honorary consuls
Honorary consul general
Honorary consul

NOTES

Chapter 1

1. Uchiyama Masakuma, "The Foreign Office of Japan: Past and Present," *Keio University Journal of Politics*, no. 2 (1976), p. 18.

2. An example of the obligation hierarchy places on an official is the resignation of Foreign Minister Ito Masayoshi on May 16, 1981. After the Washington summit meeting earlier that year between Prime Minister Suzuki Zenko and President Ronald Reagan, the customary joint communiqué was issued. However, the prime minister was dissatisfied with the communiqué's contents and timing, and he criticized the foreign ministry when he returned to Japan. Ito reportedly asked him to temper his criticisms, which were not well received by ministry officials. When Suzuki persisted in leveling blame on the ministry, especially during a Cabinet meeting, Ito resigned, taking responsibility for the trouble. To complicate matters further, Vice-Minister Takashima Masao also tendered his resignation.

Considerable support and sympathy for Ito and Takashima were apparent in the career service, where their motivation for resigning was well understood. Career officers recognized the actions as fulfilling the requirements placed on them by their rank in the ministry. They felt a sense of pride that these ministry leaders should place respect and loyalty to tradition above personal considerations. They were also inspired, because they felt that the actions of Ito and Takashima had redeemed the reputation of the ministry in the eyes of the public after its censure by the prime minister.

All Japanese newspapers carried headlines and long commentaries on Ito's resignation. There was much speculation about the significance of his act for United

States–Japan relations. He was admired for his acceptance of the time-honored principle of taking responsibility for the actions of his ministry, and some reference was made to the requirements of hierarchy in handling such a situation. The media generally agreed that he had behaved as a responsible official whose actions reflected his respect for tradition.

The resignation of any nation's foreign minister or secretary of state is news-worthy, regardless of the circumstances. What differs in the Japanese case is the prominent reference by the media to the requirements of tradition in explaining the decision.

3. *Japan Echo* 5, no. 3 (1978): 51.

4. *Japan Times*, May 29, 1981.

5. Kurt Singer, *Mirror, Sword, and Jewel* (Tokyo: Kodansha International, 1973), p. 31.

6. Ibid., p. 34

7. Ibid., pp. 62–63.

8. Ibid.

9. Ibid.

10. Ishii entered the finance ministry as a clerical employee and, through hard work and dedication, succeeded in being appointed a director general. His appointment was front-page news mainly because his assignment represented a rather startling break with tradition. Finance ministry career officers were uncomfortable with the appointment but noncareer officers were jubilant. Reaction in the foreign ministry followed career/noncareer lines. My next-door neighbor in Kawasaki, who was a clothing salesman, thought the appointment highly unusual. His was not an uncommon opinion.

11. Uchiyama Masakuma, "The Foreign Office of Japan: Past and Present," p. 18.

12. *Japan Times*, May 26, 1981.

13. *Department of State Newsletter*, January 1981.

14. Ibid.

15. Ibid.

16. Interview, June 29, 1981, Tokyo.

17. Time in class refers to the maximum number of years in grade without promotion allowed an officer before he is subject to involuntary separation from the Foreign Service.

18. Remarks of Secretary of State Cyrus Vance before the House Committee on the proposed Foreign Service Act of 1980, June 21, 1979:

> The 1946 Act gave us a foreign service that answered the demands of that day. But today's circumstances are significantly changed. The number of indepen-dent governments has more than doubled during that period, and the range of multi-lateral institutions and efforts in which we are engaged have grown enormously.

Our international commerce has vastly expanded, and the international dimension of economic issues has become increasingly central. Major new areas of concern such as nuclear non-proliferation, narcotics control, environmental protection, and science and technology have emerged.

And a new emphasis has been given to traditional concerns of American foreign policy such as the advancement of human rights. Americans are travelling abroad in record numbers, with a commensurate increase in demand for consular services. The foreign service has had to respond to these increasing demands with roughly the same number of people as it had twenty years ago.

At the same time, personnel management is influenced now in ways that were hardly foreseen in 1946. Formal employee-management relationships only emerged in the State Department within the last ten years.

A change has also taken place in the perceived advantages of overseas service. The quality of life in many foreign capitals has deteriorated, while the threat to personal safety has increased. The declining value of the dollar and high inflation in many nations have made our task more difficult.

Moreover, with a growing number of families in which both spouses are pursuing professional careers, there is understandable increasing reluctance to leave the United States for foreign posts.

All these developments underscore the obvious fact that the foreign service is confronted by dramatically different circumstances that prevailed a third of a century ago. The service must adapt to these new conditions if it is to meet new responsibilities, now and in the years ahead.

Chapter 2

1. As of June 1, 1981, there were 10 women in the career service and 50 in the noncareer group, according to the deputy vice-minister for administration.

2. On September 27, 1979, Patrick Linehan, a senior research analyst in the Defense Intelligence Agency and author of the Linehan study of the Foreign Service, in his testimony before a congressional committee on the proposed Foreign Service Act of 1980, described some of the problems faced by career officers in the Foreign Service. He explained that when an officer, for example, is promoted to class 5 (junior), he is placed in a functional cone and is expected to remain in that cone for the bulk of his midcareer assignments. Many officers are not happy with this arrangement, in part because functional cones are not considered to have equal importance for career advancement. Political and economic assignments are believed to be in the mainstream of Foreign Service work and officers not in these cones often feel frustrated. Linehan also pointed out that the kinds of assignments an officer is given are indications of his potential for rapid advancement to the senior ranks. The political officer appears to have the inside track for a swift rise in the service. The staffs of geographic bureaus can often assist officers in their promotion plans, and officers thus seek identification with important bureaus through lan-

guage study and area specialization. Another indication of an officer's upward mobility is a relatively short period between promotions, especially in midcareer.

3. The Tenure Board meets every six months, and officers usually are given serious consideration after about one year. (It generally takes that long to develop enough information in the officer's official file to give the board some basis for judgment.) While in a probationary status, the officer can be considered for promotion by the regular Selection Boards, but he usually obtains only one promotion before being granted tenure. The two actions are separate.

4. Kurt Singer, *Mirror, Sword, and Jewel* (Tokyo: Kodansha International, 1973).

5. One theory held by Japanese FSOs is that the unsuccessful officer is sent abroad and kept there to spare him the embarrassment of facing his more successful colleagues and his family and friends in Japan.

6. Before the creation of the Senior Foreign Service under the Foreign Service Act of 1980, promotion to class 2 (the level of entry to the senior service under the old system) was automatic; officers were either promoted to class 2 or retired voluntarily or involuntarily for time in class (TIC). As a result of the senior officer threshold process established by the 1980 act, an FS-1 officer can choose to compete for promotion to the Senior Foreign Service, or he can elect to leave the service at the end of the prescribed period. Officers in the Bureau of Personnel are not sure how many midcareer officers will opt for entry into the Senior Foreign Service, but the private guess of several of them is that the majority will do so.

Chapter 3

1. Grade level structure in the ministry from senior to junior is as follows: Designated Class, classes 1 and 2, senior; classes 3, 4, and 5, midlevel; classes 6, 7, and 8, junior.

2. The seniority principle, *nenkō joretsu*, operates somewhat differently in other government ministries. In the Ministry of International Trade and Industry, for example, when the vice-minister resigns or retires, those officials on active duty and belonging to the same class as the vice-minister also resign. In the foreign ministry this does not happen, mainly because key ambassadorships would have to be vacated if the practice were followed. This bureaucratic custom (*nenkō joretsu*) creates a "brain drain," but it is also a revitalizing process that maintains upward movement in the system.

3. Kim Dae Jung, an important South Korean opposition leader, was kidnapped from Japan by alleged operatives of the South Korean government on August 8, 1973.

4. The division chief said that bureaus are not given money for their own disbursement. Moreover, each bureau has a travel allocation and when this amount is exhausted, additional funds must be approved by him. He also allocates about $300 per month to each division chief for representational (entertainment) expenses. Overtime pay cannot exceed 3 percent of the ministry's budget. This is a

relatively small amount, and consequently there is little compensation for officials who work overtime.

Chapter 4

1. The career examination is called the High Foreign Service Examination; the noncareer examination is the Middle Foreign Service Examination. All other ministries recruit career and noncareer personnel from applicants who take the governmentwide National Public Service Examination. Pay schedules for all personnel are established by the government and are uniform throughout the bureaucracy. An entering career officer would be appointed to salary schedule 7, grade 3, or ¥89,700 per month ($407 at ¥220 to $1). Salary increases follow at regular intervals.

2. In commenting on the relative qualifications of young career and noncareer officers entering the ministry, a senior official of the Minister's Secretariat opined that the qualifications of 10 of the 50 officers appointed to the noncareer group were equivalent to those of the average Tokyo University graduate entering the career ranks. He felt that these 10 young men should have taken the career examination but guessed that they were hesitant to do so because of lack of self-confidence—they had not graduated from one of the major public or private universities. He also pointed out that a few Tokyo University graduates from departments other than the faculty of law (the main source of appointments to career positions in the Japanese government bureaucracy) take and pass the specialist examination. Most successful candidates for the specialist corps are graduates of smaller universities and colleges.

3. Despite the increasing need for personnel, the system firmly prohibits lateral entry from outside the ministry. The examination route is the only acceptable route for appointment as a career or noncareer officer. The only exceptions I know of are two officers who had taken the high civil service examination and were graduates of Tokyo University. They were appointed as career officers and considered themselves lucky to have been so appointed.

4. *Asahi Shimbun*, July 29, 1981.

5. *Mainichi Shimbun*, August 19, 1981.

6. Ibid.

7. Ibid.

8. Ibid.

9. Excerpts from Ambassador Neumann's statement follow.

The glut [of personnel], especially in the upper ranges, did not occur overnight; it was clearly forseeable, evident for a long time. A more rigorous thinning out, not just on the top levels, but throughout the system, could have been accomplished by a greater supply of courage. What this would have meant was that the responsible officers throughout the system would have had the guts to look colleagues and co-workers in the eye and tell them frankly when their performance quality under review indicated that they were unlikely to rise above a certain level, or even that they would have been well-advised to seek a different career. This situation has worsened because the Freedom of Information system has compelled rating officers to show their findings to the rated personnel. Of course, it is also true that the previous system of secret rating lent itself to abuse. I should add that these shortcomings do not only affect the foreign service system, but the military and certainly the civil service system as well. Moreover, it is an international and not just an American phenomenon. It is perhaps a demonstration of human nature at its most appalling and least effective.

Another aspect of this lack of courage is the all-pervasive rating inflation. Few rating officers have the courage to tell their subordinates frankly where and when they have weaknesses. It is understandable; they are dealing with people, especially in the small missions abroad, with whom they work and mix socially every day. How much easier it is to give only a good rating and thus avoid trouble. . . . If, on the other hand, as I have seen on a few occasions, a conscientious rating officer does muster the courage to render an objective, hence not uncritical evaluation, he will inevitably inflict such destructive and possibly fatal damage upon the rated officer's career, as to be far out of proportion to the results intended. This is, of course, because in the ocean of inflated evaluations, the few honest ones stand out like acts of eternal damnation. A few courageous rating officers cannot change the system without doing incalculable harm. Only if a very large number of rating officers were to change their attitudes and take courage into their hands would there be a change.

This is even more the case when officers do not perform satisfactorily at a time when their age and years of service have not yet given them the right to an annuity. The temptation to take the easy way and not deprive a substandard but decent and honorable officer of his livelihood, becomes overwhelming, and he is likely to be allowed to coast along. This is humanly admirable, but destructive to the system. I have encountered a number of grade 3 officers whose performance was only mediocre and who should have been weeded out long ago, but neither had they deteriorated suddenly so as to justify expulsion at that late time. In this respect, the new proposed legislation offers a distinct advantage, provided the threshold requirements at present class 3 are vigorously enforced. (U.S., Congress, House, *Hearings, Subcommittee on International Operations of the Committee on Foreign Affairs and the Subcommittee on Civil Service of the Committee on the Post Office and Civil Service*, H.R. 4674, 96th Cong., 1st sess., July 17, 1979, pp. 228–29.)

10. The tour of duty of the president of the institute is about two years. He is generally a senior ambassador in the service.

Chapter 5

1. A similar situation has sometimes existed in the Department of State. There, the influence of the Policy Planning Staff vis-à-vis the geographic bureaus usually depends on the personality of the director of the staff and the nature of his relationship to the secretary of state.

2. The Japanese people have respect for the United States; in particular they admire its energetic and pragmatic pursuit of the modernization of life through constant technical and scientific innovation. They also deeply respect the United States for its sincere goodwill and contributions toward the peace and prosperity of the world, even if these efforts are not always successful... and they sometimes fear that by being allied with the United States, Japan might be dragged into an awkward situation which they would not approve or into a destiny which they might not wish to share.

Another important psychological aspect which stems from the Japanese sensitivity to hierarchy is that the United States is considered to have greater influence than it has in reality. This view creates in some Japanese a kind of *higaisha-ishiki*, that is, a feeling of having been wronged or injured....

At times Japan tends to put the United States on a pedestal of idealism. This is due partly to the over respect and sense of awe which the Japanese have toward Americans and partly to the overly idealistic and ideological manner in which the Americans until recently presented themselves. The psychological metamorphosis of the placing on a pedestal leads to a sense of disillusion or a sense of betrayal whenever the Japanese detect any sort of falsity in American action or inaction. This feeling of disillusionment tends to create resentment which would never have occurred had no pedestal been erected to start with....

The *amae* psychology also plays a very important role in formulating Japanese psychological attitudes in international relations, especially within a certain type of framework. The unbalanced relationship between Japan and the United States, for example, is highly conducive to initiating the *amae* [dependency] psychology. The Japanese people lost everything, including their national confidence, when they accepted unconditional surrender in 1945. The Occupation authorities treated them like 12-year-old children. Even after recovering independent status in international society in 1952, Japan had to depend heavily on American benevolence in almost all phases of national survival. It is therefore natural to see the *amae* psychology working, consciously or unconsciously, in the minds of many Japanese people....

When one becomes accustomed to having someone else meet a portion of his needs, he begins to underestimate the work involved in doing so. In this respect, the Japanese views of national and maritime security problems and of security and prosperity in Asia have been unrealistic. These views reflect a deep-seated notion that the United States will continue to provide for Japanese and Asian security....

When the desire to depend and presume upon another's benevolence is gratified, the desire for *amae* is satisfied, but when American actions do not satisfy the Japanese desire for *amae*, *amae* leads to frustration. And such frustration leads Japanese to feel that Americans lack understanding of their aspirations. Sometimes it even leads to a hostile attitude toward the United States. (p. 11)

3. *Japan Echo*, Winter 1978.

4. When the chief of the Security Division informed the embassy representative that the *aide-mémoire* was ready for presentation to the United States government by the Japanese government, he advised the embassy representative to enter by a side door because the press and opposition groups were waiting for him in the main entrance to the ministry. He did, and the five-minute ceremony was completed without incident.

5. James Reston, *New York Times*, October 25, 1981.

6. *Asian Security, 1980* (Tokyo: Research Institute for Peace and Security, 1980).

7. Testimony of Michael Nacht, professor of government, Harvard University, before the House of Representatives Committee on Foreign Affairs and its Subcommittees on International Economic Policy and Trade and on Asian and Pacific Affairs, *Hearings*, 97th Cong., 2d sess., March 17, 1982, p. 427.

8. *New York Times*, November 9, 1981.

9. Ibid.

10. Ibid.

Chapter 6

1. Statement by a former senior official in the Japanese delegation to the United Nations, January 22, 1981.

2. The assistant deputy vice-minister for administration said that Japanese Socialist Party support was a calculated move by the party to justify its vote against the defense budget by saying it was helping the foreign ministry achieve peace through diplomacy. Interview, November 11, 1980.

3. The chief of the Financial Affairs Division said that he did not take the career examination administered by the foreign ministry but rather one given by the government—the High National Public Service Examination. Sources in the ministry indicated that because of his outstanding ability and character and the not unimportant fact that he graduated from the University of Tokyo, he was integrated into the career service, one of only three officers who have entered by this route. Typical of the successful career officer, he has served in a number of different positions, among them the Japanese Embassy in Manila, where he was a protégé of the ambassador, and the North American Affairs Bureau. In 1981 he left the

Financial Affairs Division to return to the North American Affairs Bureau as deputy director general. His appointment to head the government's delegation to the 1982 United States–Japan negotiations on revision of the Civil Air Agreement indicated recognition of his versatility.

4. For an illuminating discussion of generational differences in the foreign ministry, see the article by Fukui Haruhiro, "Policy-Making in the Japanese Foreign Ministry," in *The Foreign Policy of Modern Japan* (Berkeley and Los Angeles: University of California Press, 1977), pp. 31–33.

5. The proposed merger via the joint examination bears some similarity to the Wriston Program in the Department of State in the early 1950s, in which noncareer officers (those who had not taken the career Foreign Service Entrance Examination) and career officers (those who had) were combined into one service. Complete assimilation required several years. "Wristonee" was a pejorative term for officers who had entered the career service without having taken the career examination, and many of them resented it. Unlike the foreign ministry proposal for a unified examination, the Wriston Program was not restricted by tradition. Although a certain elitist mystique surrounds the Foreign Service officer, it has had little effect on egalitarianism in the U.S. Foreign Service.

Chapter 7

1. Testimony of Dr. Patrick Linehan before the hearings of the Subcommittee on International Operations of the Committee on Foreign Affairs and the Subcommittee on Civil Service of the Committee on the Post Office and Civil Service of the House of Representatives on the proposed Foreign Service Act of 1980, September 27, 1979.

2. *Foreign Service Journal*, May 1982, pp. 27–32.

3. Interview, June 29, 1981, Tokyo.

4. See William Bacchus, "Foreign Affairs Officers: Professionals without Professions?" *Public Administration Review*, no. 37 (November–December 1977), pp. 641–50.

5. Ibid.

6. Charles Bray, deputy director of the USIA, in a speech made in San Francisco in 1980.

Chapter 8

1. The representational allowance is a shared sum of money used by ambassadors, consuls general, and members of their staffs to entertain local officials, business and professional persons, and outstanding and representative opinion-makers of the host country. It is important to the mission of the embassy or consulate

general (and an essential responsibility of every FSO) to have good local contacts in and out of government in order to obtain important information and to be able to evaluate it by checking it out with local sources. In some countries, especially in Asia and certainly in Japan, a good deal of time, effort, and expense must go into developing these contacts. The representational allowance was designed to partially offset the costs of this work. It has never been sufficient, however, and many FSOs have spent their own money to support their official duties. I understand from talks with officers in the State Department that the situation has improved, but because of the image of the extravagant FSO still held by many Americans, a penurious Congress continues to insist on trimming the representational allowance.

GLOSSARY OF
JAPANESE TERMS

amakudari	"Descent from heaven"—retirement from an official government position to a civilian position
chūkyū, or *senmon-shokū*	Noncareer language and area specialist
dōki ishiki	Class identification
Gaimushō	Japanese Foreign Office
jikan	Vice-minister
jō-ge kankei	Hierarchy
jōkyū	Career Foreign Service officer
jōkyū shiken	Career Foreign Service Officer Examination
kachō	Division chief
kambōchō	Deputy vice-minister for administration
kanrishoku	Management positions
katatataki	"Tap on the shoulder"—time for retirement
Kokusai Koryu Kyokai	International Cooperation Committee
koto nakare shugi	Excessive prudence or lack of initiative
kyokuchō	Director general of a bureau
my home shugi	Greater concern for family than for professional career
nenkō joretsu	Seniority

oyabun-kobun	Patron-client
ringisei	Procedure for reaching a consensus
sanjikan	Junior deputy director general of a bureau
shingikan	Senior deputy director general of a bureau
shokyū	Noncareer administrative and clerical personnel
somuhan	General affairs section (of a division)
taikoku ishiki	"Big-country consciousness"
tōyō seido	A program for the integration of noncareer officers into the career Foreign Service
wa	Harmony

SELECTED
BIBLIOGRAPHY

Allison, Graham, and Szanton, Peter. *Remaking Foreign Policy: The Organizational Connection*. New York: Basic Books, 1976.

Bacchus, William I. "Foreign Affairs Officers: Professionals without Professions?" *Public Administration Review*, no. 37 (November–December 1977).

———. *Foreign Policy and the Bureaucratic Process*. Princeton: Princeton University Press, 1974.

Blaker, Michael. *Japanese International Negotiating Style*. New York: Columbia University Press, 1977.

Committee for the Compilation of the 100-Year History of the Japanese Foreign Ministry. *A Century of the Foreign Office*. 2 vols. Tokyo: Hara Shobo, 1969.

Diplomacy for the 70s: A Program of Management Reform for the Department of State. Department of State Publication 8593. Washington, D.C.: Government Printing Office, 1970.

Hellman, Donald C. *Japanese Domestic Politics and Foreign Policy: The Peace Agreement with the Soviet Union*. Berkeley and Los Angeles: University of California Press, 1969.

Ilchman, Warren F. *Professional Diplomacy in the United States, 1779–1939: A Study in Administrative History*. Chicago: University of Chicago Press, 1961.

Japan Center for International Exchange. *The Silent Power*. Tokyo: Simul Press, 1976.

Kawamura, Ichiro. *Gaimushō*. Tokyo: Hobunsha, 1956.

Kawasaki, Ichiro. *Japan Unmasked*. Tokyo: Tuttle, 1969.

Kubota, Akira. *Higher Civil Servants in Post-War Japan.* Princeton: Princeton University Press, 1969.

Linehan, Patrick. *The Foreign Service Personnel System: An Organizational Analysis.* Washington, D.C.: American University School of International Service, College of Public Affairs, March 1975.

Morley, James W., ed. *Deterrent Diplomacy.* New York: Columbia University Press, 1976.

Nicolson, Harold. *Diplomacy.* London: Oxford University Press, 1963.

Pempel, T. J., ed. *Policymaking in Contemporary Japan.* Ithaca, N.Y.: Cornell University Press, 1977.

Scalapino, Robert A., ed. *The Foreign Policy of Modern Japan.* Berkeley and Los Angeles: University of California Press, 1977.

Shidehara, Kijuro. *My Fifty Years of Diplomacy.* Tokyo: Yomiuri Shimbunsha, 1961.

Shigemitsu, Mamoru. *My Reflections on Diplomacy.* Tokyo: Mainichi Shimbunsha, 1933.

Singer, Kurt. *Mirror, Sword, and Jewel.* Tokyo: Kodansha International, 1973.

U.S. Congress. House. *Report on the Foreign Service Act of 1980,* H.R. 4674. 96th Cong., 1st sess. Washington, D.C.: Government Printing Office, 1979.

———. Committee on Appropriations. *Hearings on Department of State Appropriations.* 95th Cong., 2d sess.; 96th Cong., 1st sess.; part 2, 1978; part 8, 1979. Washington D.C.: Government Printing Office, 1978, 1979.

U.S. Department of State. *Toward a Stronger Foreign Service* (Wriston Report). Washington, D.C.: Government Printing Office, 1954.

Ward, Robert E., ed. *Political Development in Modern Japan.* Princeton: Princeton University Press, 1970.

Yoshida, Shigeru. *Ten Years of Reflection.* 4 vols. Tokyo: Shincho-sha, 1957.

INDEX

Acheson, Dean, 13

Administrative Cone (U.S.), 182–84

Administrative Management Agency (Japan), 86, 138

Admiralty Claims Settlement Authority (U.S.), 220–21

Affirmative Action (U.S.), *see* Women and minorities in diplomatic corps

AFL-CIO, 47

Agency for International Development (AID; U.S.), 16, 57

Agriculture Department (U.S.), 52

Air Force attaché (U.S.), 53

Allison, John, 127

Ambassadors (Japan), 31, 109, 151; selection of, 31; retirement of, 109; career vs. non-career, 151

Ambassadors (U.S.): appointment of, 29, 89–91; career vs. non-career, 33, 89–91; authority of, 51–52

American Foreign Service Association (AFSA), 15, 17, 38, 100, 102–3, 177; influence on labor-management relations, 184–87

American Telephone and Telegraph Company, 76

Annual recruitment estimates (U.S.), 81 (Table 4)

Appointment as FSO: U.S., 77; Japan, 76

Arms Control and Disarmament Agency (U.S.), 16

Army attaché (U.S.), 53

Asian Affairs Bureau (Japan), 28, 42, 138

Assessment Center (U.S.), 76–77, 79

Assignment process (Japan), 3–5, 80–81, 83–84, 149–50, 161; tour of duty policy, 84, 157–58

Assignment process (U.S.): centralization vs. decentralization, 88; open assignments, 91–93, 184; stretch assignments, 93–96; tandem assignments, 93–94, 178; tour of duty policy, 94; language-designated positions, assignments to, 94; mechanics of assignment, 95

Assistant secretaries (U.S.), 47, 49, 91

Association of Southeast Asian Nations (ASEAN), 133

Atomic Bomb Casualty Commission, 52

Atomic Energy Commission (U.S.),
    219

Bacchus, William, 239
Benefits for FSOs (U.S.)., 77–78, 111
Bray, Charles, 239
Brown, Harold, 134
"Buddy-buddy" system (U.S.), 87–88
Budget, State Department, 12, 53–54
    (Fig. 5)
Budget, Ministry of Foreign Affairs,
    62–63, 138

Cabinet secretariat (Japan), 86
Career–non-career service (Japan), 3,
    8, 11, 20, 35–36, 39, 54–55,
    105–145, 147–52, 235
Career–non-career service (U.S.),
    45–46, 57
Carter, Jimmy, 134, 182
Central and South American Affairs
    Bureau (Japan), 42; establishment
    of, 138
Central Intelligence Agency (U.S.), 65
Centralization vs. decentralization
    (U.S.), 88
Chamber of Commerce in Japan
    (U.S.), 52
Civil Aviation Treaty, 115
Class identification (Japan), 6–7,
    33–35, 98
Commerce Department (U.S.), 15, 52
Conformity (Japan), 9–11
Congress (U.S.): State Department
    relations with, 11–12, 240
Consular cone (U.S.), 182–84
Consular Convention, U.S.–Japan,
    131–32
Consular Department (Japan), 84
Corridor reputation: U.S., 96, 174;
    Japan, 99
Cotton, Joseph, 200
Council on International Economic
    Policy (CIEP; U.S.), 65
Country Directorate for Japan (U.S.),
    see East Asian and Pacific Affairs,
    Bureau of

Country team (U.S.), 53
Crisis management (Japan), 115–16,
    159
Cultural Affairs Department (Japan):
    abolition of, 138

Date Muneoki, 85
Davies, A. Powell, 9
Defense Agency (Japan), 87, 117–18,
    129, 135; Self-Defense Forces, 53
Defense issue, U.S.–Japan, 132–35
Deputy secretary of state (U.S.),
    47, 64
Deputy vice ministers for adminis-
    trative, political, and economic af-
    fairs (Japan), 61
Designated Class (Japan), 31, 43,
    54, 84
Diet (Japan): ministry relations with,
    10, 63, 138, 144
Directorate for International Security
    Affairs (Pentagon), 121, 126
Directors general of bureaus (Japan),
    4
Division (Japan), 145–48
Dulles, John Foster, 13, 212

East Asian and Pacific Affairs, Bureau
    of (U.S.), 50–51, 126; organization
    of, 120 (Fig. 10); budget and per-
    sonnel of, 122–25 (Table 9)
Economic Affairs Bureau (Japan), 84,
    167
Economic Cooperation Bureau
    (Japan), 62, 167
Economic Planning Agency (Japan),
    86–87
Efficiency reports (U.S.), 100, 103,
    174
Elitism: Japan, 6, 8–9; U.S., 174
Embassy categories (U.S.), 57
Emmerson, John K., 130
European and Oceanic Affairs Bureau
    (Japan), 28, 42
Evaluation, *see* Performance evaluation
Examinations, entrance (Japan), 20,
    74–75, 150, 160–61, 235; High

Foreign Service Career examination, *aka* Foreign Service Career examination, 74–75, 235; High Civil Service examination, *aka* National Public Service examination, 74, 235; Unified examination, 165–67; Middle Foreign Service examination, 235

Examinations, entrance (U.S.), 21, 76–80, 82 (Table 5); assessment center, 76–77, 79; affirmative action, 77

Executive Secretariat (U.S.), 65, 96

Executive Seminar on National and International Affairs (U.S.), 107

Families in diplomatic corps (Japan), 27, 36–37, 72–73, 105–6, 152, 193

Families in diplomatic corps (U.S.), 15, 38, 78, 173, 178; tandem assignments, 93–94, 176, 178

Fascell, Dante, 212

First North American Division (Japan), 121; organization of, 146 (Fig. 15)

Fishermen's Association (Japan), 129

Five-year manpower expansion program, 55, 74, 76, 137–38, 144, 168

Foreign Agricultural Service (U.S.), 57

Foreign Claims Act (U.S.), 220–21

Foreign Commercial Service (U.S.), 57

Foreign policy: role of the Foreign Ministry, 1–3; of the State Department, 11–15

Foreign Ministry Establishment Law Revision bill (Japan), 42

Foreign Service Act of 1946 (U.S.), 13, 17

Foreign Service Act of 1980 (U.S.), 2, 13, 15, 30, 38, 42, 55, 57, 100, 102–3; generalist-specialist, 181, details of, 207–15; 56 (Fig. 6); 58 (Table 3); requirements for language proficiency, 108, supporters of, 177

Foreign Service Entrance examination, *see* Examination, entrance (U.S.)

Foreign Service Grievance Board, 65–66, 69, 186; elements of, 65; Grievance Staff, 68–69, 185–86

Foreign Service Institute (U.S.), 26, 65, 69–70, 105, 107; School of Professional Studies, 70; School of Language Studies, 70; School of Area Studies, 70, 107; language and area training, 107–8; language ability, 78, 94–95; training, 69–70

Foreign Service Training Institute (Japan), 24–25, 63, 75, 105–6, 162, language ability, 31; language training, 75–76, 105–6

Fukui Haruhiro, 239

Functional cones (skill categories; U.S.), 25–26, 68, 77, 92, 97, 100, 128, 182–84

Gakushuin University, 74

Generalist-specialist question: Japan, 144–45, 147, 153–56; U.S., 179–81

Generational differences: Japan, 160–62; U.S., 174–75

Greater East Asia Ministry (Japan), 145

Harmony (Japan), 7–8, 35, 98

Harvard University Center for International Relations, 118

Herz, Martin, 212

Hierarchy (Japan), 4–5

High Foreign Service Career examination, *see under* Examinations, entrance (Japan)

High National Public Service examination, *see under* Examinations, entrance (Japan)

Hitotsubashi University, 20, 72, 74

Hogen Shinsaku, 116

Honolulu Conference (June 1981), 134

House of Councillors (Japan), 86–87

House of Representatives (Japan), 86–87

Imai Takakichi, 60
Information Agency (USIA), 51, 53, 57, 107
Information and Research Bureau (Japan), 42
Interagency relations (Japan), 5, 6, 86–87, 129–30, 147–48, 153, 155, 163; within embassy, 87, 156–59
Interagency relations (U.S.), 13, 50–52; within embassy, 52
Integration program (Japan), 149–50, 164–65
Internal Revenue Service (U.S.), 52
International Cooperation Agency (Japan), 86
International Cooperation Committee (Japan), 157
International Council on Radiation Prevention (ICRP), 219
International Exchange Fund (Japan), 86
International Organization Affairs, Bureau of (U.S.), 51
Involuntary retirement (U.S.), 15, 23, 32–33, 38, 97, 101, 108, 186
Iran: U.S. hostages, 115–16
Ishii, S., 9, 232
Ito Masayoshi, 231

Japanese Constitution, Article 9, 1, 119
Japanese Imperial Navy, 145
Japanese language officers (U.S.), 126–27
Japan External Trade Organization (JETRO), 86
Japan Society, New York, 134
Johnson, U. Alexis, 127

Kasumigaseki, 189
Katori Yasue, 85, 160
Keio University, 20, 72, 74
Kennan, George, 13
Kennedy, John, 175
Kim Dae Jung, 60, 234
Kitamura, Hiroshi, 118

Kosaka Zentaro, 128
Kuriyama Takakazu, 85
Kyoto University, 20, 72, 74–75

Labor-management relations (U.S.), see American Foreign Service Association (AFSA); Grievance Board
Language and area training/ability (U.S.), 78, 94–95, 107–8; language-designated positions, 94
Lateral entry: Japan, 86, 235; U.S., 178–80
Law of the Sea Conference, 49, 65
Legal adviser's office (U.S.), 132
Liberal Democratic Party, 10, 61, 63, 135
Linehan, Patrick, 24, 233, 239

Management Center (U.S.), 49
Manpower problem (Japan), 39, 136–45, 142, (Fig. 13), 156, 158–60, 163, 168; solution of, 162–63
Manpower problem (U.S.), 45–46, 174–75, 179, 181; numbers of employees and posts, 45 (Table 1), 46 (Table 2)
Maritime Commission (U.S.), 52
Marshall Plan, 13
McCarthyism, 175
McLeod, Scott, 212
Media relations: Japan, 191; U.S., 195
Middle Eastern and African Affairs Bureau (Japan), 42, 115–16
Middle Foreign Service examination see under Examinations, entrance (Japan)
Minister's Secretariat (Japan), 27, 31, 61, 84; Personnel Division, 4, 61, 63–64, 71, 74, 83–84, 98–99, 106, 109; General Affairs Division, 61; Financial Affairs Division, 61–63
Ministry of Agriculture, Forestry and Fisheries (Japan), 87, 153
Ministry of Education (Japan), 87

Ministry of Finance (Japan), 6, 9, 63, 72–73, 87, 109, 135, 138, 153; role in international negotiations, 168
Ministry of Health and Welfare (Japan), 87
Ministry of International Trade and Industry (MITI; Japan), 6, 72–73, 87, 109, 135, 153; role in international negotiations, 168
Ministry of Justice (Japan), 87, 131
Ministry of Transportation (Japan), 155
Minority program (U.S.), *see* Women and minorities in diplomatic corps
Mitsubishi Trading Co., 159
Mitsui Trading Co., 159
Miyazawa Kiichi, 127
Morale, Foreign Service (U.S.), 175–76

Nacht, Michael, 238
National Bureau of Standards Handbook, No. 69 (U.S.), 219
National Commission on Foreign Language and International Studies (U.S.), 182
National Personnel Authority (Japan), 87
National Police Agency (Japan), 87
National Public Service examination, *see under* Examinations, entrance (Japan)
National Science Foundation (U.S.), 52
National Security Act, 1947 (U.S.), 13
National Security Council (Japan): non-establishment of, 116
National Security Council (NSC; U.S.), 13, 15, 50, 65, 121, 179; interdepartmental subgroup, 51
Naval attaché (U.S.), 53
Newmann, Robert, 103
North American Affairs Bureau (Japan), 11, 28, 42, 115–16; Security Division of, 117–18; First North American Division of, 121; organization of, 146 (Fig. 15)

North Atlantic Treaty Organization (NATO), 13
Northern Islands problem (Japan), 133
Nuclear-powered submarines (SSN; U.S.), 128, 130, 217–18; subroc, 129; exchange of documents on visits to Japan

Office of Foreign Service Career Development and Assignments (U.S.), 95
Office of Joint Chiefs of Staff (U.S.), 51
Office of the Foreign Vice Minister (Japan), 62 (Fig. 7)
Ohira Masayoshi, 134
Okawara Yoshio, 61, 160
Okita Saburo, 134
"Old boy" network (U.S.), 176
Open assignments (U.S.), 91–93
Operations Center (U.S.), 96, 159
Organization, Japanese Foreign Ministry, 40–42 (Fig. 1), 222–30; typical embassy, 44 (Fig. 3)
Organization, U.S. Department of State, 48 (Fig. 4)
Organization for Economic Cooperation and Development (OECD), 154
Osaka Liaison Office: abolition of, 138
Outside specialists for Foreign Ministry, 155, 167–68, 190; recruitment of, 169 (Table 11)
Overseas Economic Cooperation Fund, 86
Overseas posts (Japan), 44; manpower capacity, 140 (Fig. 11); staff complement, 142 (Fig. 13); less developed countries (LDCs), assignment to, 193
Overseas posts (U.S.), 51; organization of, 51–53; inspection of, 66; hardship posts, 172–73

Patron-client relationship (oyabun-kobun), 88

Pentagon, 15, 50, 65, 107, 179; Directorate for International Security Affairs, 121, 126
Performance evaluation (Japan), 98–99
Performance evaluation (U.S.), 104, 177; selection boards, 29–30, 33, 37, 66, 69, 100–101, 103, 108; efficiency reports, 103, 174
Performance Standards Board (U.S.), 102
Personnel, Bureau of (U.S.), 26, 68, 76, 88–89, 100; organization of, 67 (Fig. 8); Office of Career Development and Assignments, 68, 95; Office of Civil Service Career Development and Assignments, 68; Office of Employee Relations, 69; Office of Performance Evaluation, 69; Office of Position and Pay Management, 69; Office of Recruitment, Examination, and Employment, 69; Senior Officer Division, 96; Career Development Officer, 97–98
Pickup Program (Japan), *see* Integration program
Policy planning staff (U.S.), 51, 126, 237
Political influence on foreign service, Japan, 10; U.S., 173–74
Political-military Affairs, Bureau of (U.S.), 51, 126
Prime Ministers Office (Japan), 87
Promotions (Japan), 3–5, 25, 39, 55, 99, 150–51
Promotions (U.S.), 16, 22, 24, 30, 57, 100–104, 174; senior officer holdback, 93; projected promotions, 104 (Table 7)
Public Health Service (U.S.), 219
Public Vessels Act (U.S.), 220–21

Rayburn, Sam, 10
Reagan administration ambassadorial appointments, 33
Reagan, Ronald, 60, 231

Recruitment (Japan), 71–73, 76, 155; educational background of recruits, 20, 72, 155; motivation of recruits, 18–20, 73; age restriction, 74
Recruitment (U.S.), 76, 80, 180; educational background of recruits, 21–22, 78; motivation of recruits, 21–22; average age, 22; recruitment of minorities, 77
Reischauer, Edwin, 10, 127
Research and Policy Planning Staff (Japan), 117
Reston, James, 132
Retirement (Japan), 109–10
Retirement (U.S.), 23, 111; retirement projections, 110 (Table 8). *See* Involuntary retirement; Selection out; Time-in-class
Richardson, Elliot, 65
Ringisei, 148
Rogers Act of 1924, 13, 100
Rooney, John, 195
Roosevelt, New Deal, 73

Schlundt, Virginia Mona, 212
Science and Technology Agency (Japan), 129
Secretary of State (U.S.), 47, 64, 174
Security clearance (U.S.), 77
Security Division (Japan), 117–19
Security Policy Planning Committee (Japan), 118
Selection boards, *see* Performance evaluation
Selection out (U.S.), 30, 101–2
Self-Defense Forces (Japan), 53
Senior Executive Service (U.S.), 55, 58
Senior Foreign Service (U.S.), 23, 30, 32–33, 55, 57, 68–69, 100, 107
Seniority (Japan), 3–4, 144, 234
Senior officer holdback (U.S.), 93
Shidehara Kijuro, 192
Shimoda Takeso, 60, 116
Singer, Kurt, 27
Socialist Party (Japan), 138

Soka University (Japan), 73
Sonobe Ryozo, 85
Sophia University, 74
Soviet Union, 10; threat from, 132–33; invasion of Afghanistan, 134, 139; occupation of northern islands, 133
Special interest groups (Japan), 3, 129, 130
Special interest groups (U.S.), 47, 194
Special Review Board (U.S.), 102
Staff-line system (Japan), 113–14 (Fig. 9)
State-Defense Department Exchange Program, 50
Status of Forces Agreement, 52, 117
Stretch assignments, 93
Subroc, 129
Suzuki Zenko, 60, 231

Takahashi Nobuko, 60
Takashima Masao, 60, 116, 160, 231
Tandem assignments (U.S.), 93–94, 176, 178
Tenure, *aka* permanent status (U.S.), 23; tenure board, 234
Time-in-class (TIC; U.S.), 15, 23, 32–33, 38, 97, 101, 108, 186, 232, 234
Togo Fumihiko, 60
Tokyo University, 8, 20, 72–75
Tour of duty policy: Japan, 84, 157–58; U.S., 94
Toyo Seido, *see* Integration program (Japan)
Trade Center (U.S.), 52
Training (Japan), *see* Foreign Service Training Institute
Training (U.S.), *see* Foreign Service Institute

Trask, David, 14
Treasury Department (U.S.), 15, 52
Treaties Bureau (Japan), 11; Legal Division, 131–32
Truman, Harry, 13

Under secretaries (U.S.), 47, 64
United Nations Security Council, 44
Unions (U.S.), *see* American Foreign Service Association
U.S. Forces, Japan, 52, 118. *See also* U.S.–Japan Security Treaty
U.S.–Japan relations, 118, 126–28; consular convention, 131–32; defense, 132–35, *See also* Nuclear-powered submarines
U.S.–Japan Security Treaty, 52–53, 117; Status of Forces Agreement, 52, 117; U.S.–Japan Security Consultative Committee, 53, 117
Ushiba Nobuhiko, 60, 116, 127

Vance, Cyrus, 17, 232
Vice-minister (career), 59–61
Voice of America, 53

Waseda University, 20, 72, 74
Weinberger, Caspar, 134
White House, 65
Women and minorities in diplomatic corps (U.S.), 17, 22, 59, 68, 77, 100, 176, 195; women statistics on, 90 (Table 6)
Women in diplomatic corps (Japan), 19–20, 73
Wriston program, 175, 239

Yanagiya Kensuke, 85
Yasukawa Takeshi, 130

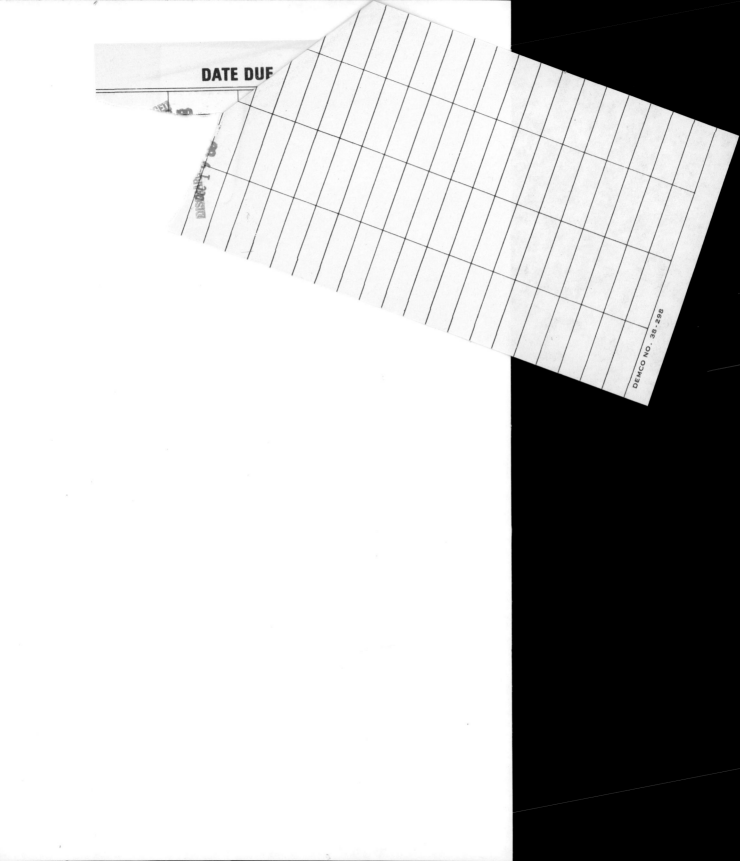

DEMCO NO. 38-298